Today's Military Wife

Meeting the Challenges of Service Life

3rd Edition

LYDIA SLOAN CLINE

STACKPOLE BOOKS

Copyright © 1995 by Stackpole Books

Published by
STACKPOLE BOOKS
5067 Ritter Rd.
Mechanicsburg, PA 17055

Printed in the United States of America

10 9 8 7 6 5 4 3 2 1

Third Edition

Cover design by Kathleen Peters

Library of Congress Cataloging-in-Publication Data

Cline, Lydia Sloan.
    Today's military wife : meeting the challenges of service life /
Lydia Sloan Cline. — 3rd ed.
        p.   cm.
    Includes bibliographical references and index.
    ISBN 0-8117-2580-4
    1. United States—Armed Forces—Military life.   2. Military spouses—
United States.   I. Title
U766.C48   1995
355.1'2'0973—dc20   95-13497
                                                                  CIP

*To Roger, the greatest
husband a wife could ask for*

*and to my parents,
Edward and Ann Sloan,
for their encouragement
in all my endeavors*

Recipe for a Military Wife

1½ cups patience
2 tablespoons elbow grease
1 pound courage
1 cup tolerance
dash of adventure

Marinate frequently with salty tears and pour off excess fat. Sprinkle ever so lightly with money, kneading dough well until payday. Season with international spices. Bake for twenty years or until done. Serve with pride!

—Author Unknown

≡ Contents

≡ Introduction

"I'm newly married and my husband's in the military. Since we're about to PCS, he asked if I want to live in quarters. He says we have to start a medical record on me and asked whether I'd like to take a hop anywhere for a honeymoon. He leaves tomorrow for two weeks and told me to check his LES to make sure his housing allowance was increased.

"Why is his boss ordering him away so soon, when he knows we just got married? Live in quarters? Take a hop? LES? Housing allowance? What is he talking about?"

If you can relate to what this woman's feeling, you're not alone. Most of us could, unless we grew up as service "brats" ourselves. The military can be a perplexing place at times! Strange customs, stranger acronyms, odd jobs, and odder duty hours . . . it takes a while to learn the ropes!

But know this: Servicewide, the past fifteen years have brought sweeping changes to the armed forces, changes that include a close attention to families. The powerful impact family happiness has on a military member's job performance is widely acknowledged, and philosophies of support have been developed on the premise that military members whose families are satisfied with the lifestyle will be more likely to make the personal sacrifices necessary for a strong defense.

> In 1993 the number of enlisted personnel who were married when they joined was 9.8 percent. After their first term, that number zoomed to 50.3 percent.

Military wives, no longer content to play the historic role of silent partner (really, were we ever?), communicate with officials as never before. Numerous studies and surveys have inventoried our wants and needs, culminating in programs such as Army Community Services, Navy Family Relocation Centers, child-care centers, civil service hiring preference, and spouse-employment assistance.

We are no longer expected to devote ourselves exclusively to promoting our husbands' careers. Today it is common for a wife to have her own career, and many military families cope with the same phenomena that have swept the rest of the country—the two-income family and the latchkey child.

So does this mean you're less important now than you were twenty years ago?

Not at all.

While the end of the Cold War, the fall of communism in Eastern Europe, and recession have led to the reshaping and redefining of America's military mission, the role of the wife has remained the same. Your direct influence on your husband's career is not as great as it used to be, but your influence on his *morale* is tremendous. That will never change. Your attitude toward his job may greatly influence his decision to stay in the service. In a volunteer force, with retention of quality people a number one priority, you can see how important that makes you to the Department of Defense. The role of military wife is multifaceted and as important as ever.

There are tremendous advantages to military life. We see more places in the course of a career than most people see in the course of a lifetime; we take our children skiing in Switzerland when we are stationed in Germany; we have an opportunity to make friends immediately at each new duty station through coffee groups and socials. Extraordinary benefits and low-cost recreation facilities stretch the paycheck.

Absence of job opportunities in an area may mean time to go to the local college and brush up on old skills or learn new ones or to develop a hobby at the base crafts center. It can mean time to do volunteer work at the local school and get a firsthand glimpse of the education your child is receiving. And although separations from relatives and temporary duty assignments are never fun, many women take pride in discovering how self-reliant they can be.

This book is written for the person who has married a member of the U.S. armed forces—the Army, Navy, Air Force, Marine Corps, or Coast Guard—and wants to learn the benefits and opportunities of military life. It is designed to help you make the most of your life with the military, whether your spouse is "career" or in for just a few years. For convenience, *she* will be used for family members and *he* for the servicemember, as that is chiefly the makeup of the armed forces. As for the word *dependent,* it's official—it no longer exists in the military! In February 1994 the Department of Defense tossed it from its jargon when referring to a military mate, acknowledging that it was perceived as derogatory by wives who see themselves as anything but. Terms such as *spouse* and *beneficiary* were offered instead. We'll refer to wives as *family members* in this book.

Issues unique to our lifestyle are covered, such as frequent moves, using the health-care system, maintaining our own careers, and coping with separations. The Reserves are discussed in detail, and when benefits and other services are discussed, their relevance to Reservists is noted.

Reasons behind customs and regulations are examined, on the premise that once they are understood, they are easier to work with. As with everything else in life, when you work with something, you can often obtain satisfactory results. The women who sincerely try to "bloom where they're planted" are the ones who are happiest in their environments. They are the ones who learn the most, see the most, know the most. They make "the system" work for them.

What does it take to make the system work for you? It takes some understanding of how the military operates. It also takes a sense of humor, a sense of adventure, and large amounts of flexibility and initiative. It is up to us to learn what is available and how to use it. We have a partnership with the Department of Defense. It implements programs and advertises them, but *we* must read the notices that come around, *we* must read the materials in our welcome packets, and *we* must be willing to participate.

The wife who refuses to go to any orientation briefings, information meetings, or socials; who is reluctant to participate in programs because she's "not in the military"; and who otherwise distances herself from the community does herself a disservice. She is cheating herself of potential friendships, knowledge, and new ideas. Life with the service is like anything else: What you get out reflects what you put in.

So let's get going!

1

≡ What Does Your Husband Do for a Living?

Everyone knows what doctors do; no one has trouble describing the duties of teachers, lawyers, or secretaries; and we have a general idea of what computer programmers do.

But what do airmen do? Do they all fly planes? Do all soldiers wear camouflage paint and crouch behind barbed wire? Do sailors swab decks? And the Marines and Coast Guard—what do they do?

If your first contact with the service was when you met your husband, your idea of what he did was probably pretty fuzzy—part Hollywood, part stereotype. Now that you're married (or about to be), is your idea any clearer?

If not, let's make it so. Understanding what your husband does for a living is the key to understanding why he may spend many days in the field or on a ship, why he may get called in for alerts, and why he may not get leave as often as you might wish.

Your husband is a member of the armed forces, the people that protect the United States and its allies, that guard the way of life of the free world. The accomplishments of Desert Storm help us to appreciate the full extent of this responsibility. Your husband is helping to ensure that our rights to vote, to say what we want, to assemble peaceably, and to worship as we please

> The *armed forces* are the Army, Navy, Air Force, Marine Corps, and Coast Guard. The *uniformed forces* include the National Oceanic and Atmospheric Administration and the United States Public Health Service.

are not taken away. He is helping to ensure that the flow of essential items to and from our allies is not impeded. Regardless of rank or job, every servicemember performs his or her duties with this mission in mind.

≡ A Few Facts and a Little Background

In 1789 our founding fathers determined that a civilian should head the military. Therefore, the president is the commander in chief of the armed forces. Under the president is the secretary of defense and under the secretary of defense are the secretaries of the Army, Navy, and Air Force—all civilians. At the top level in the military chain of command are the Joint Chiefs of Staff; they are the heads of the Army, Navy, and Air Force and report directly to the secretary of defense.

The Army is America's oldest military service, established in June 1775, when the Continental Congress first authorized men to serve in the Continental Army. The Navy came into existence in October 1775, and the Marine Corps was formed one month later. The Marine Corps is technically a part of the Navy, but it has its own commandant. The Coast Guard is the smallest service, with 38,832 members. Formed in 1915, it is part of the Department of Transportation in peacetime and part of the Navy in wartime. The Air Force was originally part of the Army, but in 1947 the Army Air Corps, the General Headquarters Air Force, the Army Air Force, and the aeronautical division and aviation sections of the Army Signal Corps were combined into a new and separate service. Because of the Army and Air Force's shared history, many of their customs and courtesies are identical.

The nickname "leatherneck" is a term applied to Marines (probably by sailors) from the days when Marines wore high leather collars to protect their necks from sword blows.

Q: How many people are on active duty? How many Guardsmen and Reservists are there? DOD civilian employees? Active-duty family members?

A: As of March 1993 there were 1,744,440 active-duty members, 1,879,583 Guardsmen and Reservists, 1,000,213 DOD civilian employees, and 2,589,852 active-duty family members.

There are more than 1,300 military installations and properties. About 890 are in the United States; the rest are scattered throughout twenty-three countries and twenty U.S.–owned territories. About 25 percent of all active-duty personnel are stationed overseas.

In 1993 the Department of Defense's proposed slice of the American pie was 4.3 percent of our gross domestic product and 12.1 percent of net public spending. In total, military spending was proposed at $275.5 billion.

☰ The Reserves

Those who want to combine military and civilian life can do so in the Reserves. Reservists are people who hold full-time civilian jobs but who can be called up to supplement the active-duty force.

☰ Purpose of Reservists

The purpose of Reservists and Guardsmen (both of whom will be referred to hence as *Reservists*) is to supplement and round out the strengths of the active-duty force.

Many Reserve units have skills and missions not found in the active-duty military, such as water purification. Others, such as medical personnel and pilots, supplement active-duty strengths. Reservists are called upon frequently, and for missions other than war, such as peacekeeping and humanitarian duties. They have become so indispensable that the military can no longer rely only on volunteers for missions. In recent years Reservists have rescued boats of Haitian refugees, fought floods in the Midwest, retrieved surplus Cold War equipment, and transported active-duty personnel from Somalia. They provide tactical air support and perform weather reconnaissance, aeromedical evacuation, and aerial spraying. In fact, 60 percent of all missions performed by the active component are supplemented by Reservists, and some military functions are carried out entirely by them.

The Active Guard and Reserve are Reservists whose jobs are full-time. Their benefits are identical to that of the active-duty force.

Q: Are there any requirements to being in the Individual Ready Reserve (IRR)? Any benefits?

A: Yes to both questions. An Individual Ready Reservist is required to report to a one-day annual "muster drill," where he is physically screened. He must inform his Reserve personnel unit of any changes in address or family member status and must obtain a physical examination once every four years. All other participation is voluntary.

One benefit is that IRRs receive fifteen free points toward retirement each year. Active Duty for Training and correspondence courses can be completed for additional retirement points. Also, IRRs with certain specialties receive monetary bonuses for reenlistment. Some IRRs have exchange and commissary privileges. Officers are eligible for promotion while in the IRR.

Reservists and active-duty members make up the "total force." The Reserves are actively marketed to young people as a part-time job that teaches a skill and provides money for college; thus, active-duty service is not required before joining. In fact, almost half of the people enlisting in the Reserves each year have no prior active-duty military experience.

Types of Reservists

There are three categories of Reservists: Ready, Standby, and Retired. Ready Reservists are immediately ready for activation. Standby Reservists are called only when there are not enough qualified members in the Ready Reserve to fulfill mobilization requirements. Retired Reservists have already attained military retirement but, like the Standby Reservists, can be called to duty if there is a need and there are not enough Ready Reservists.

The Standby Reserves category is broken down into Individual Ready Reservists (IRRs) and Selected Reservists. Most of the IRRs are not affiliated with a drilling Reserve unit. They are in a nondrilling status and are available only in times of national emergency; therefore, they generally do not collect checks or have access to military facilities. Selected Reservists are available for immediate mobilization. They are composed of the Army Reserve, the Naval Reserve, the Air Force Reserve, the Coast Guard Reserve, the Army National Guard, and the Air National Guard. Selected Reservists actively drill, are eligible for promotion, collect pay and benefits, and accumulate points toward retirement.

Each state, as well as the District of Columbia, Puerto Rico, Guam, and the Virgin Islands, has an Army National Guard unit and an Air National Guard unit. A Guard unit's purpose is twofold. As a state agency that swears allegiance to the governor, it can be activated to help with local emergencies, such as civil disorder or natural catastrophes. As a Reserve component of the U.S. Army and Air Force, it can be activated into federal service to help with national emergencies.

Standard Defense Department Acronyms for Reserve Components
AT—Annual Training
ADT—Active Duty Training
IDT—Inactive Duty Training
ATP—Additional Training Periods
IDTT—Inactive Duty Training Travel

Training Requirements

Selected Reservists are required each year to attend a minimum of forty-eight drills or assemblies (usually scheduled on evenings and weekends) and must devote two weeks each summer to their units. This ensures that their skills are kept up-to-date. They receive the same pay as active-duty personnel except for certain allowances and incentive pays that are based on an agreement to serve on active duty for a specified length of time. Pay is received in the month after the training occurs. Reservists with certain critical skills are eligible for enlistment and reenlistment bonuses.

Benefits

Selected Reservists and their families have unlimited access to the exchange. Commissary access is available during each day of active duty plus a maximum of twelve other visits per year; the exact number depends on the number of active training drills the Reservist attended the year before. Reservists joining directly from active duty are issued a number of commissary visits equal to the number of months spent on active duty that year. The visits may be made at any time, not just when the Reservist is actively training. During the two-week annual training and the weekend drills, Reservists and their families are allowed unlimited commissary visits; a copy of the orders and the military ID card is needed. For other visits, a commissary privilege card (DD 2529) and the ID card is needed.

Reservists and their families have access to most base morale, well-being, and recreation activities; military clothing sales stores; transient billets (if available); Servicemen's Group Life Insurance (SGLI); certain survivor benefits (discussed in chapter 2); and programs at Family Services centers.

Reservists are entitled to space-available travel in the United States and its territories. Reservists are also entitled to medical care for any injuries that occur while traveling to and from and during drills, but they are not entitled to medical or dental privileges at any other time. If a Reservist is activated for more than thirty consecutive days, his family is entitled to the base hospital facilities and CHAMPUS (discussed in chapter 2). Though his family members are entitled to dental care at military facilities that offer it, they are not eligible for the dental insurance plan.

Each state has a specific policy on benefits available to its Reservists. Local educational benefits vary, and some even provide additional pay for state active duty. Reserve units have a membership benefits booklet that describes their benefits in detail. Contact the unit's retention office.

Retirement

Probably the Reserves' main attraction is the opportunity to accumulate retirement points. Reserve retirement is discussed in chapter 2.

Employment Rights

Since 1960 federal law has required employers to permit Reservists unpaid, nonvacation time off to perform active training and other military duties. The law also gives a Reservist reemployment rights to his former position (or one of similar status, seniority, and pay) if the Reservist must leave his job temporarily for military duties. These reemployment rights apply whether the Reservist's service is voluntary or mandatory and during war or peace.

It is unlawful for a Reservist to be denied a promotion or other advantage of employment because of military duties. When the Reservist returns, the law mandates that he return to the same seniority, status, and pay rate that he would have reached without the interruption. If the Reservist was a probationary employee or in a training program, he is entitled to reinstatement in the probation period or training program.

The Reservist may continue to be covered by his employer's health plan, at his own expense, for eighteen months. The employer may end coverage if the Reservist begins coverage under another group health plan; however, military health benefits, including CHAMPUS, are not considered a group health plan (IRS Bulletin 1190–40). After mobilization, Reservists must be reinstated without penalty in their private health-insurance plans with no waiting period.

To exercise these rights, a Reservist must meet certain criteria:

- Have held an "other than temporary" civilian job (but not necessarily a permanent one). The job may be part-time or probationary. Temporary workers and independent contractors are not protected.
- Have left the civilian job to go on active duty.
- Have been released from active duty under honorable circumstances.
- Apply for reemployment within thirty-one days after release from active duty, or within ninety days if on active duty for at least ninety-one days. Reservists who are injured or disabled while on active duty have one year to apply for reinstatement in order to cover a period of hospitalization. If the Reservist can no longer perform his old job because of a service-related injury, he may request reemployment in the nearest comparable job that he is able to perform.

Employer Rights

The same law that protects Reservists gives the following rights to employers:

- The right to know the employee's military training schedule as far in advance as possible. The annual drill schedule published by Reserve centers fills this requirement. Some problems can be avoided by giving an employer the annual drill schedule and active-duty training and annual training dates as soon as they are known. It is also good practice to return to work the first working day after completing the training, or after a reasonable time of rest. Since it is sometimes impossible for a Reservist to say exactly when he will return, an employer may not demand it. Try to give an approximate date, however.
- The right to receive proof of a Reservist's military duty. This could be an unclassified set of orders or an official letter from the commanding officer.
- The right to deny pay or special work rescheduling for periods of military duty. Employers are not required to assist Reservists in making up pay or work lost because of military obligations.

Applying the law, however, is complicated, and there are special exemptions and situations that could have an effect. Problems should be taken to the local Veterans' Employment and Training Service (VETS). Check the government pages under the Labor Department in your phone book, or call the VETS national office at (800) 442-2838. Another source of help is the National Committee for Employer Support of the Guard and Reserve (a part of the Department of Defense), telephone (800) 336-4590.

Employer support does vary. Some states organize "boss lifts," where employers are invited to observe Reservists at work. They can be targeted to a specific place, such as a company where drill time is viewed negatively. "Boss lifts" can help dispel thoughts that Reservists are on vacation during their drill time. Some Reservists have reported that male bosses in particular often enjoy viewing the "gee whiz" training and holding the M-16s. Some employers don't pay Reservists during drill time. Other pay any difference between the Reserve and regular salary. Still others (like the government) generously pay an employee's entire salary.

═══ Other Rights

Renters cannot be evicted from their homes if they pay $1,200 monthly or less. Doctors, lawyers, and other professionals who have malpractice insurance to cover their private practices can stop paying premiums while on active duty and reinstate the insurance without penalty. While the insurance is suspended, court actions for damages are also suspended. Creditors cannot deny insurance or credit solely because of military service, and powers of attorney for those missing in action are automatically extended.

ENLISTED

ARMY	MARINES	NAVY	AIR FORCE	COAST GUARD
Sergeant Major of the Army (SMA)	Sergeant Major of the Marine Corps (SgtMajMC)	Master Chief Petty Officer of the Navy (MCPON)	Chief Master Sergeant of the Air Force (CMSAF)	Master Chief Petty Officer of the Coast Guard (MCPOCG)
Command Sergeant Major (CSM) Sergeant Major (SGM)	Sergeant Major (SgtMaj) Master Gunnery Sergeant (MGySgt)	Fleet/Command Master Chief Petty Officer Master Chief Petty Officer (MCPO)	Chief Master Sergeant, First Sergeant (E-9) E-9 (CMSgt)	Master Chief Petty Officer (MCPO)
First Sergeant (1SG) Master Sergeant (MSG)	First Sergeant (1stSgt) Master Sergeant (MSgt)	Senior Chief Petty Officer (SCPO)	Senior Master Sergeant, First Sergeant (E-8) E-8 (SMSgt)	Senior Chief Petty Officer (SCPO)
Platoon Sergeant (PSG) or Sergeant First Class (SFC)	Gunnery Sergeant (GySgt)	Chief Petty Officer (CPO)	Master Sergeant, First Sergeant (E-7) E-7 (MSgt)	Chief Petty Officer (CPO)
Staff Sergeant (SSG)	Staff Sergeant (SSgt)	Petty Officer First Class (PO1)	Technical Sergeant, E-6 (TSgt)	Petty Officer First Class (PO1)
Sergeant (SGT)	Sergeant (Sgt)	Petty Officer Second Class (PO2)	Staff Sergeant, E-5 (SSgt)	Petty Officer Second Class (PO2)
Corporal (CPL) Specialist 4 (SP4)	Corporal (Cpl)	Petty Officer Third Class (PO3)		Petty Officer Third Class (PO3)
Private First Class (PFC)	Lance Corporal (LCpl)	Seaman (Seaman)	Airman First Class, E-3 (A1C)	Seaman (Seaman)
Private E-2 (PV2)	Private First Class (PFC)	Seaman Apprentice (SA)	Airman, E-2 (Amn)	Seaman Apprentice (SA)
Private E-1 (PV1) (no insignia)	Private (Pvt) (no insignia)	Seaman Recruit (SR)	Airman Basic, E-1 (AB) (no insignia)	Seaman Recruit (SR)

ENLISTED INSIGNIA OF GRADE.

SERVICE			
Army	**Air Force**	**Navy**	**Marine Corps**
SILVER / BLACK — SILVER / BLACK W-1 — W-2 Warrant Officer — Chief Warrant Officer SILVER / BLACK — SILVER / BLACK W-3 — W-4 Chief Warrant Officer — Chief Warrant Officer	(None)	W-1 — W-2 Warrant Officer — Chief Warrant Officer W-3 — W-4 Chief Warrant Officer — Chief Warrant Officer	GOLD / SCARLET — GOLD / SCARLET W-1 — W-2 Warrant Officer — Chief Warrant Officer SILVER / SCARLET — SILVER / SCARLET W-3 — W-4 Chief Warrant Officer — Chief Warrant Officer
Second Lieutenant	Second Lieutenant	Ensign	Second Lieutenant
First Lieutenant	First Lieutenant	Lieutenant Junior Grade	First Lieutenant
Captain	Captain	Lieutenant	Captain
Major	Major	Lieutenant Commander	Major
Lieutenant Colonel	Lieutenant Colonel	Commander	Lieutenant Colonel

Officer's Grade Insignia.
Note: Grade insignia of 2nd lieutenant and major are gold; of other officer grades in Army, Air Force, and Marine Corps, silver. Naval insignia are gold color. The Navy pin-on (collar) insignia are the same as for the other services except that the devices are smaller and the enamel bands on the warrant officers' bars are navy blue.

SERVICE			
Army	**Air Force**	**Navy**	**Marine Corps**
Colonel	Colonel	Captain	Colonel
Brigadier General	Brigadier General	Rear Admiral (Lower Half)	Brigadier General
Major General	Major General	Rear Admiral (Upper Half)	Major General
Lieutenant General	Lieutenant General	Vice Admiral	Lieutenant General
General	General	Admiral	General
General of the Army	General of the Air Force	Fleet Admiral	(None)

Officer's Grade Insignia *(continued).*
Note: All insignia above are silver color except Navy, which is gold.

For more information on Reservists' rights when mobilized, see "The Soldiers' and Sailors' Civil Relief Act" in chapter 6.

≡ Military Jobs

Each service has its specific mission: The Army is to defend on land; the Navy, by sea; and the Air Force, by air. The Marine Corps is a readiness force ("soldiers of the sea"), and the Coast Guard protects our coastal borders and conducts search-and-rescue operations. All sorts of occupations are offered in the services' individual jobs and categories—not all airmen fly, and not all soldiers drive tanks. Furthermore, the dividing lines between services get quite blurred at times. Without the uniform, it's hard to tell a combat engineer in the Army from one in the Navy's construction battalion, or an Air Force control team member from an Army airborne trooper. A Coast Guard boatswain does the same work as a Navy boatswain, and both do the same job as a watercraft operator in the Army.

> Give a child a T-shirt with the ship's seal or the unit's crest on it. It will make it *his* ship or *his* unit and make him feel a part of it.

Enlisted personnel are assigned specific jobs, called *military occupational specialties* (MOS) in the Army and Marine Corps, *ratings* in the Navy and Coast Guard, and *Air Force Specialty Codes* (AFSC) in the Air Force. These jobs are grouped into functional categories. As a servicemember progresses through his career field, he goes from worker/apprentice to supervisor/technician to leader/manager.

Officers are assigned functional categories rather than specific jobs; their duties require more general administrative and supervisory skills than proficiency in one task. These categories are called *branches* in the Army, *groups*

> I've always heard, "Discuss your husband's job with him; it will help you better understand what he does." My husband is in intelligence and won't discuss a thing! For a long time I was resentful of this, but I gradually realized that he would be breaking federal law if he discussed such things with me. So my advice is this: What he can tell you, talk about. What he can't, don't push. His partnership to keep the military's confidence is as real and important as his partnership to keep your own confidences.

in the Navy and Coast Guard, *career fields* in the Marine Corps, and *career specialties* in the Air Force.

Warrant officers are people who enter the service as enlisted members and, after special training and testing, assume greater responsibility and supervisory power within a narrow, focused range.

All jobs fall into one of three categories: combat, combat support, and combat service support. Some involve spending large amounts of time away from the family; others are as nine-to-five as any civilian office job. Some are more highly technical than others. Many military jobs are identical to civilian ones (a big plus when leaving the service); others are unique to the military. Some jobs are highly dangerous. And all services have their share of them all.

Every enlisted servicemember has at least one job; he may be assigned it, or he may request it. Whether he gets the one he wants depends on many things:

- The needs of the branch of service he's in.
- The current and projected amount of people already in that job. Are there already too many?
- Physical limitations, such as color blindness or wearing eyeglasses.
- Administrative limitations, such as the level of education required or the ability to receive security clearances.
- Present requirements for that job. What experience from the civilian world is he bringing with him?
- Scores from the tests he took when he enlisted.

If he wants to change his job, all of the above plus a few more criteria are considered:

- Budgetary and travel restrictions. Is the job needed at his current duty station? If not, approval of the new one would require reassignment, something not usually done until he is eligible for reassignment.
- Commitments remaining on his current enlistment. For instance, if he received an enlistment bonus for his current job, a request for change probably wouldn't be approved until the commitment is satisfied.
- Time in service. If he wouldn't have enough time remaining in the service after training for the new job was completed, he probably won't be assigned it.

Despite all this, servicemember preference is definitely factored in. Retaining quality people is a high priority, and keeping the service-member happy aids in retention.

Officers can request a specific functional category, but whether they get it depends on the same factors as for enlisted servicemembers.

☰ Promotions

Promotion criteria vary from service to service. While all have minimum standards for job performance and a timetable based on time in service and grade, each service considers items appropriate to its own mission. Being the most combat oriented, the Marine Corps gives special consideration to combat time and conduct and relies more on meritorious promotions than the other services. (Such promotions have minimal time-in-service requirements.)

The Navy has a very formal promotion system with specific requirements in administrative and occupational ability and formal schooling. Candidates for promotion to grades E-4 through E-7 must perform satisfactorily on Navywide advancement exams.

The Air Force has the Weighted Airman Promotion System for personnel competing for promotion to grades E-5 through E-7. Factors such as time in service, time in grade, skill test scores, promotion test scores, performance reports, and awards and decorations are all considered, but each has a different weight.

The Army gives primary consideration to technical expertise in the MOS, but it also considers personality traits such as professionalism and pride in service. Soldiers up for promotion to grades E-5 through E-8 come before a board. Separate lists are kept for each MOS, and the cutoff score goes up or down according to the Army's needs.

Coast Guard promotions to grades E-4 through E-9 are determined through servicewide exams, proficiency in assigned duties, on-the-job performance, recommendation of the commanding officer, and performance on written exams.

Officers whose dates of rank (date they entered the service) are the same as, one year earlier than, or one year later than the date announced by the headquarters are considered for promotion at set intervals of time. During these intervals, called *zones of consideration,* a promotion board in Washington evaluates the officers' personnel records and compares them. Personal appearances before the board are not made.

There are three zones of consideration: below the zone, from which an exceptional few are promoted; the primary zone, from which most who are eligible are promoted; and above the zone, from which those who did not get promoted the first two times are given a third chance. The board members individually review each record, come to their own decisions, and vote. Performance appraisals, awards and decorations, schooling, and the exact nature of job duties are considered. Naturally, poor performance evaluations, judicial and nonjudicial punishments, and inadequate personal fitness levels (e.g., being overweight or failing physical training tests) are negatively considered by all services for both officers and enlisted personnel.

Congress determines the precise numerical strength of the services, and vacancies must occur in each rank and job before others can be let in. Zero promotions are often a direct result of a job's being over-strength. Some jobs have overages; others have shortages. When a job is overstrength, the service must implement measures to manage the excess, such as voluntarily or involuntarily reclassifying people or raising the cutoff for test scores. Conversely, low cutoff scores in a specific job and rank result from a shortage in that area. One way to deal with the frustration that comes with waiting to be promoted is to reclassify to a shortage task that offers more immediate promotion opportunities.

Jobs with shortages often offer bonuses for a renewed enlistment. That should not be the only consideration, though, when deciding to reenlist. Is the job truly interesting? After the bonus money runs out, there's still that years-long commitment. Is it a dead-end job, or does good promotion potential exist? Can experience gained from the job be applied to the civilian world? What bases use that particular job, and are they where you'd like to go?

≡ Education

Education is not only a plus in getting ahead; with the current drawdown, it is a necessity. Fortunately, the military offers many opportunities for it. In fact, many people join the service just for those opportunities. Classes are offered in everything from technical training in a servicemember's particular job to military subjects in general to leadership skills. Many of these classes are required for promotion. They're free, and the servicemember receives his full salary while taking them. If they're held on another base, his travel and per diem (daily) expenses are reimbursed up to a certain amount. Reservists are eligible for these classes, too.

Enlisted members who wish to become officers have several options. Since a college degree is necessary, all involve formal schooling.

≡ High School Equivalency

Although a high school diploma is not necessary to enter the service, it is needed for advancement. If a servicemember does not have a high school diploma, he can take the test that leads to a General Equivalency Development (GED) diploma or certificate. The GED covers math, reading, writing, social studies, and science. Before beginning a GED course of study, know if the goal achieved will be a certificate or a diploma; the requirements for each vary. The diploma is closer to a high school diploma; the certificate is not recognized by many colleges.

Many people enroll in classes before taking the GED test. All services have a basic functional skills or continuing education program that offers classes in the GED subject areas.

College

College courses and degrees are considered highly desirable and help make the servicemember more competitive for promotion. Recognizing that servicemembers' schedules do not always allow for traditional routes of study, services offer flexible, off-duty education programs to help them achieve their educational goals.

The Servicemembers Opportunities Colleges (SOC) is a servicewide network of 500 accredited colleges and universities that contract with the Department of Defense to offer programs right on base—including overseas bases—that lead to bachelor's and graduate degrees. A degree can be obtained without ever setting foot on the main campus. Curricula available on base are, of course, just a fraction of what is offered on the main campus, but many people find something of interest. The University of Maryland, Boston University, the University of Oklahoma, and the University of Southern California are just some of the schools that participate. Minimal residency requirements, the acceptance of large amounts of transfer credits, and the granting of credit for nontraditional means such as military classes and training are examples of how SOC accommodates servicemembers' special needs. SOC is also open to family members.

Service-Specific College Degree Programs

The Air Force offers the Community College of the Air Force (CCAF), which grants associate's (two-year) degrees to its enlisted active-duty, Air National Guard, and Air Force Reserve members. The Air Force also has a program called Bootstrap, which authorizes certain qualified people to take a temporary duty assignment at a college or university for up to one year to complete degree requirements.

The Navy operates the Navy campus, an umbrella activity encompassing several programs. These are PACE (Program for Afloat College Education), in which classes are taught aboard ship by college instructors; SOCNAV-2, which offers associate's degrees; SOCNAV-4, which offers bachelor's degrees; and the Apprenticeship Program, which allows enlisted members to apply training from their rating toward civilian journeyman certification. The Navy also operates the Enlisted

Education Advancement Program (EEAP), through which enlisted people can earn associate degrees.

The Army operates the Servicemembers Opportunity Colleges Associate Degree (SOCAD) program. Degrees are job related; most soldiers work on technical degrees that support their military jobs. This program is extremely flexible and is open to family members. Credits are transferable from duty station to duty station. There is also the Army Continuing Education System (ACES), which provides high school completion, college, and vocational-technical programs; independent-study classes; and testing services. ACES runs the Functional Academic Skills Training program, which helps soldiers improve math, reading, and writing skills, and the Bachelors Degree for Soldiers Program (BDFS), for soldiers overseas.

The Marine Corps operates the Staff Noncommissioned Officers Degree Completion Program, which enables certain NCOs to get bachelor's degrees that fulfill Marine Corps requirements.

The Coast Guard operates the Advanced Computer and Electronics Technology Program, open to enlisted personnel E-6 and above, chief warrant officers, and junior officers.

═══ DANTES

The Defense Activity for Non-Traditional Educational Support, or DANTES, is a servicewide umbrella activity under which many education-related programs operate. DANTES supports off-duty voluntary education efforts at both the high school and college levels.

Q: What is AARTS?
A: The Army/American Council on Education Registry Transcript System is a central database that translates a soldier's training, job experience, and educational testing into a transcript that can be used to tell a college or employer what education level he has obtained. The Army is the only service that offers this.

DANTES offers GED and college admissions tests, helps servicemembers apply to colleges, assists in obtaining civilian professional certifications, and gives tests to help people determine their career interests and abilities. It offers several programs through which servicemembers can take tests for college credit instead of attending classes. DANTES also operates an independent-study system whereby servicemembers can take correspondence courses offered by many accredited colleges. These are particularly useful for personnel who move a lot, are in remote locations, or have irregular work hours. Many servicemembers enrolled in DANTES-sponsored correspondence courses from the Middle East while engaged in Operation Desert Shield.

The Education Center

Every base has an Education Center, and it is the place to go for more information on the programs just described. Trained counselors are available to answer questions. You'll also find applications for graduate exams and detailed information on programs, curricula, degrees, and financial assistance.

Many wives take advantage of continuing education classes offered through the Education Center, such as Spanish, algebra, typing, quilting, English as a second language, aerobics, cooking, and calligraphy. The exact classes offered often depend on the wives living there, because they sometimes constitute the bulk of the teachers. So if you have a skill you think others would be interested in learning, the Education Center would like to meet you.

Obtaining a Commission

Enlisted members who wish to become officers have several options. Since a college degree is necessary, all involve formal schooling.

An option open to single servicemembers is an appointment to a service academy: the U.S. Military Academy at West Point, New York; the Naval Academy in Annapolis, Maryland; the Air Force Academy in Colorado Springs, Colorado; and the Coast Guard Academy in New London, Connecticut. Tuition is free, a monthly stipend is paid, and cadets are entitled to military privileges while attending; however, they may not be married or legally obligated to support children.

A far more common option is a Reserve Officer Training Corps (ROTC) program at a college. The military pays part or all of the servicemember's tuition while he attends as well as a monthly stipend, and upon graduation he returns as an ensign or second lieutenant. Participants must be younger than twenty-five when commissioned, get an honorable discharge from the military, and attend college full-time.

There are also Officer Candidate Schools (Army and Navy); Officer Training School (Air Force); Officer Candidate Class, Aviation Officer Candidate, and Platoon Leaders Class (Marine Corps); as well as warrant officer programs, medical scholarships, and enlisted commissions. These are open to college graduates and certain enlisted personnel. Check with the personnel office for details and other, service-specific, options.

Financial Aid

The old and new GI Bills, the Veterans Education Assistance Program (VEAP), and tuition assistance given directly by the services are some of the means available to help pay for schooling. There are also federal and state grants and loans, such as Pell Grants and Perkins, Stafford, and Guaranteed Student Loans, and scholarships offered by private groups such as veterans' associations, professional military organizations, relief societies, and local wives' clubs. They'll help pay whether the classes are taken at colleges, universities, or vocational-technical schools; through apprenticeship programs or correspondence schools; or even just to make up deficiencies in basic and functional skills.

Q: My husband has been contributing regularly to the Montgomery GI Bill. If he were to die before using it, what happens to the money?

A: In the event of a death, any built-up funds are returned to his family in the form of death benefits.

Check with the Education Center, the local Department of Veterans Affairs office, or the college of interest to learn more about the wide array of financial aid available.

VA assistance is available for Reservists who meet the following requirements:

- Have a high school diploma.
- Have completed initial active duty for training.
- Have a minimum of six years remaining on the Reserve obligation.
- Have not completed a bachelor's degree and are not using any other VA educational assistance programs.

Reservists may be also eligible for tuition assistance under the Reserve Montgomery GI Bill (RMGIB), which even offers assistance for graduate studies. Contact your Reserve unit's RMGIB coordinator.

≡ Learn What's Going On

Knowing what jobs are available, what education and experience it takes to get them, and how to get promoted while in them are just a few of the ways to take control of your destiny in the military. Learn about, familiarize yourself with, and seek to understand what's going on around you. Is your husband unhappy with his present job? Help him research a new one. Every installation has a library with pamphlets that describe each job, and they're available for your perusal.

Many installations have military museums. These are interesting places to visit, since their displays are directly related to the particular mission of the installation. You'll see photographs and equipment comparing how the mission was carried out 100 years ago with how it is done today.

There are many newspapers and magazines that center around each particular service, and reading them will give you a better idea of what the service is all about. A good place to start is the weekly newspaper published at most bases. There are the *Army Times,* the *Air Force Times,* and the *Navy Times,* weekly papers that cover issues affecting not only the servicemember, but also you, the family member. These papers keep readers abreast of everything from the latest schemes our elected representatives have for military pay and pensions to what's happening in global hot spots. Then there are *Off-Duty* and *Wifeline* (the latter for Navy and Marine Corps wives)—magazines that deal with issues of interest to military spouses—which are distributed free of charge at the commissary. *Military Lifestyle, Soldiers, All Hands, Leatherneck, Airman,* and *National Guard* are subscription magazines that cover items of importance to military personnel and spouses.

Military publications run the gamut. There are magazines for infantrymen, air reservists, retired naval personnel, Jewish veterans, and many more. Check your post library's periodical room to see which ones it subscribes to.

Army spouses should check out the AFTB program: Army Family Team Building. It's a three-part program that explains many things a soldier learns in basic training, such as acronyms and bugle calls. It also covers military customs, socials, agencies, benefits, stress and conflict management, the finance system, and other topics. Other services offer similar programs: Married to the Military, for Navy spouses, and Welcome to the Military, for Air Force spouses.

Who knows, once you start learning about all these career and education opportunities, touring the museums, and reading all the literature, you might get so interested you'll want to join the service yourself!

≡ Further Reading

Cox, Frank. *Enlisted Soldier's Guide, 3rd edition.* Mechanicsburg, PA: Stackpole Books, 1993.

———. *NCO Guide, 5th edition.* Mechanicsburg, PA: Stackpole Books, 1995.

Crocker, Lawrence P. *Army Officer's Guide, 46th edition.* Mechanicsburg, PA: Stackpole Books, 1993.

DANTES Independent Study Catalog and *External Degree Catalog,* found in base education centers.

Defense Almanac. Available from the Office of the Assistant Secretary of Defense (Public Affairs), Directorate for Public Communication, 1400 Defense Pentagon, Room 2E777, Washington, DC 20301-1400.

Estes, Kenneth W. *Marine Officer's Guide, 5th edition.* Annapolis, MD: Naval Institute Press, 1985.

Mack, William P., and Thomas K. Paulsen. *Naval Officer's Guide, 10th edition.* Annapolis, MD: Naval Institute Press, 1991.

Napier, John Hawkins III. *Air Force Officer's Guide, 30th edition.* Mechanicsburg, PA: Stackpole Books, 1995.

Ordered to Active Duty: What Now? A Guide for Reserve Component Families, available from the Office of the Assistant Secretary of Defense, (P&R) (PSF & E) (OFPS & S), Military Family Clearinghouse, Ballston Tower #3, Suite 903, 4015 Wilson Blvd., Arlington, VA 22203-5190, (703) 696-5806 or (800) 336-4592. This resource has a large array of books, pamphlets, and articles on more than forty topics of interest to the military family. It also publishes *Military Family Newsletter.*

Reserve Forces Almanac and *National Guard Almanac,* Uniformed Services Almanac Inc., P.O. Box 4144, Falls Church, VA 22044.

Times Handbook. Biennial supplements to *Army, Navy,* and *Air Force Times* newspapers.

Valey, Wayne A. *Airman's Guide, 3rd edition.* Mechanicsburg, PA: Stackpole Books, 1994.

Walker, Wilson L. *Up or Out: How to Get Promoted as the Army Draws Down.* Manassas, VA: Impact Publications, 1994.

Note: A phone line information system provides answers to questions about Navy programs, opportunities, and assistance twenty-four hours a day, seven days a week. Call (800) FOR-NAVY.

2

≡ Big Benefits

Here, from the Army's Family White Paper, is a chronology showing the evolution of the armed forces' commitment to their families.

1776–1847: Families considered a hindrance to military efficiency and operations.

1863: Conscription in Union Army; "exemptions" authorized for family or personal considerations.

1891: Congress reviews Army families' living and working conditions on the frontier. No record of action taken.

1896: Families of enlisted men recognized monetarily.

1913: Army regulations discourage marriage; marriage viewed in terms of its effect on efficiency to service.

1917: Congress enacts allotment system for families.

1942: Draftees could be married; enlistees could not. Public Law 490: Military family members' benefits granted.

1952: Study identifies lack of basic social services as a major problem.

1954: Family and soldier support programs enacted to improve retention. Results: expensive and ineffective.

1957: Serviceman's and Veteran's Survivor Act passed; family provided for when serviceman dies.

1960: Family members outnumber uniformed personnel.

1962: Family Service Program developed.

1965: Army Community Service Program established.

1972: Survivor Benefit Plan enacted.

1973: Supreme Court rule makes spouses of female servicemembers "dependents."

1975: Public Law 93-647: Garnishment of pay for child support/alimony.

1979: Quality of Life program established.

1980: First Family Symposium: DOD Directive 6400.1: Family Advocacy enacted.

1981: Second Family Symposium: Family Liaison Office established. Armed forces report majority (52.81 percent) of enlisted members married. Dependents Overseas Ceiling repealed.

1982: Third Family Symposium: Public Law 97-252: Retired pay may be treated as community property in divorce proceedings.

1986: Establishment of DOD Office of Family Policy.

1988: Military child-care package and outreach program policy for new servicemembers with families established.

1990: Permanent increase in family separation pay and the death gratuity.

1991: Youth divisions established at Family Member Employment Assistance Centers to help children find jobs.

Things sure have changed for us "camp followers"! A drive around your installation shows how much. The cornucopia of family supports and services is proof of today's philosophies that servicemembers are entitled to the same lifestyle and privileges as those of the civilians they are pledged to protect and that happy, healthy service families make for a happy, healthy service.

Big benefits add miles to the military paycheck. How grand to be able to leave the pharmacy with a bagful of bottles and pay for them with a smile! Or to breeze in for legal advice and breeze out just as easily! And who but military families can fly to Australia free! In civilian life, families would pay a lot of money for many of the programs we receive free.

In this chapter we'll take a look at the support system that exists for you. But first, a word about a very important item.

≡ The Identification Card

The ID card is needed to use all military benefits and services, and it's often needed just to get on base. If you forget your ID card, go home! "I forgot it" will never meet with sympathy. As soon as you're married (well, OK, after the honeymoon), go with your husband to the ID card facility; he'll need to sign your ID card authorization papers. Bring your marriage license and a photo identification.

The new ID card is credit-card size and has a digitized photo and bar codes with identification

---

Getting your ID card is the first order of business after marrying. Memorizing your husband's Social Security number is the second! You'll need it for everything from getting your medical records to consigning clothes at the thrift shop.

data. Active-duty personnel, retirees, Reservists, and family members are all eligible for one, as are spouses and children of servicemembers who died while on active duty or of Reservists who died while on active training. Family members of Reservists who die while not on active training and before receiving the "twenty-year letter" (see "The Pension Plan" below) are not entitled to ID cards.

Parents or parents-in-law who live with and are financially supported by the servicemember are eligible for ID cards. So are divorced spouses who were married to servicemembers for twenty years, of which twenty were on active duty, until they remarry. Widows and widowers lose their cards upon remarriage, but unlike divorcées, they can be reissued cards if that marriage ends. A divorcée or widow can obtain a card without the sponsor's signature after the issuing personnel verifies eligibility. A nonmilitary guardian of children with military benefits may obtain a "command authorization" letter to allow her to accompany the children to military facilities or services. Servicemembers who are legal guardians of children for at least twelve months may obtain military benefits for them. Children lose eligibility for the ID card at age twenty-one, or twenty-three if a full-time student. Disabled children are eligible indefinitely. Children also become ineligible when they marry. Direct all eligibility questions to the base pass and identification office or to a recruiting office.

The ID card is yours; as long as you are entitled to it, no one, including your husband, may take it away. The benefits derived from it flow directly to you from the Defense Department and cannot be taken away by your sponsor. It is government property and must be surrendered if asked; this sometimes happens when a holder presents an expired card to an ID checker. If you lend it to someone, even another cardholder, it can be permanently revoked. Keep it on your person at all times.

≡ The Exchange

Exchanges are military retail stores that range in size from giant shopping malls with dozens of specialty shops to tiny outposts aboard ship. They are called the PX (post exchange) in the Army, BX (base exchange) in the Air Force, NEX (naval exchange) in the Navy (ships store when afloat), MCX (Marine Corps exchange) in the Marine Corps, and CGX (Coast Guard exchange) in the Coast Guard.

The Army, Air Force, Navy, Marine Corps, and Coast Guard exchanges are administered separately and have separate headquarters. Their mission is twofold: to provide quality goods and services at reasonable prices and to generate profits to support the base morale, well-being, and recreation programs. When you shop at the exchange, you're helping to build bigger libraries and better child-care centers.

The exchange has all kinds of good stuff—clothing, jewelry, toys, video cameras, kitchen equipment, even exercise machines and major appliances. Not all exchanges stock the same things, however. Regional interest has its effect, as does the base population. If you're at a place where there are a lot of single men, you'll find lots of stereo equipment and flashy men's clothes. Places with many families stock a nice selection of baby items and children's clothes.

Congress dictates the type of merchandise that exchanges in the United States may sell, as well as their cost-price ratios, to ensure that they don't provide unfair competition to civilian businesses. Overseas there are no such limitations; exchanges can stock and special-order items stateside ones may not, such as cars, furs, and large diamonds. Overseas exchanges have rules to prevent goods from spreading into the black market; for instance, shoppers in Korea and the Philippines have limits on how much they may spend on certain items.

Surveys show the exchanges to be consistently lower in overall prices than civilian retail stores. Different items have different markups, necessities the lowest, and luxury goods the highest. No sales tax is charged. With careful shopping, you may find better deals elsewhere, but most exchanges offer price challenges: If you find the same item elsewhere, even if it's on sale, the exchange will charge the same price. Verification is typically done with a phone call. Exchanges have generous refund policies, accept major credit cards, and will cash personal checks, even if they're out of state or country.

If you can't find what you're looking for, ask customer service if the item can be ordered. If the exchange is running a sale but the sale items are gone when you show up, ask for a rain check. Exchanges will mail Reservists announcements of major sales events. To get on the mailing list,write AAFES, Attn.: MK-V/S, P.O. Box 660202, Dallas, TX. 75266-0202 or Navy Exchange, P.O. Box 5096, Clifton, NJ 07015-9771.

The exchanges operate mostly with nonappropriated funds—money generated by their own profits and profits from base recreational activities. Because Congress doesn't control the money (as it does with appropriated funds), the manager may run the store pretty much as he or she wants. As long as the volume of business justifies it, the manager can expand, hire more staff, and stay open longer. If you have suggestions for how the exchange could be better run, make them known. The manager meets regularly with an advisory board of representatives from different groups of customers.

For those who live too far from an exchange to shop there regularly, there is the thick, glossy, semiannual *All Services Exchange Mail Order Catalog,* which carries everything from clothing and home appliances to exotic finds from around the world. Supplements are also issued several times a year that feature specific types of products. The catalog costs $3 and comes with a certificate for $5 off the first order of $25. Call (800) 527-2345 or write Exchange Catalog Sales, P.O. Box 660211, Dallas, TX 75266-0211. Be aware that if you order an imported item, you'll have to pay a customs tax when it arrives.

Boots, shoes, shirts, insignia, patches, socks, towels, and accessories may be purchased through the *Military Clothing Mail Order Catalog* (AAFES MCSS Catalog). For a copy, write Hq AAFES/SD-U, P.O. Box 660202, Dallas, TX 75266-0202 or call (212) 312-3206.

DPP and NEXCARD

The Deferred Payment Plan is a variable interest-charging plan whereby payments may be stretched out for thirty-six months. Credit limits are based on the applicant's disposable income, not rank, and can go up to $5,000. Spousal income can be used in figuring the limits; in fact, family members with independent incomes may apply for their own DPP accounts. Credit checks are done on E-1 through E-4 applicants. DPP can be used for exchange catalog purchases. Apply at customer service or call (800) 835-2345.

NEXCARD has replaced the Home Layaway Plan at Navy exchanges. It is an interest-charging purchase plan that can be used at any Navy exchange. An application is filled out one time, and bills are mailed monthly. It is designed for major purchases; the minimum that may be charged is $200. The application requirements are less stringent than those for major credit cards, but applicants with bad payment histories are not eligible. Apply at customer service or call (800) NAV-EXCH.

Both DPP and NEXCARD are available to Reservists.

The Commissary

The commissary store is an appropriated-fund operation that provides brand-name groceries. It is run separately from the exchange. The two have entirely different missions and are not in competition. In 1992 the Defense Commissary Agency (DeCa) took over the operation of military commissaries, eliminating inequities between the different services' stores.

The commissary exists strictly as a nonpay benefit. DeCa makes no profit; it sells its wares for what it paid plus a 5 percent surcharge to cover operating costs (such as bags, utilities, and shopping carts). It is funded with tax dollars, thus Congress controls the purse strings. A set amount of money is provided commissaries, and they must operate within that budget. Thus, all decisions—operating hours, days of service, and so forth—are not motivated by profit. For instance, if a commissary that is open ten hours a day could ring up healthy sales twenty-four hours a day, it still could not stay open those hours if the money to pay salaries and other operating costs is not in its budget.

Because it is nonprofit, prices are typically 25 percent lower than in supermarkets. Although space constraints and federal law restrict what commissaries sell, if you want something not stocked, such as kosher meat, ask the manager if it can be special-ordered. Commissaries used to be no-frill, but that isn't the case anymore. Many have fresh seafood, candy, plants, delicatessens, and bakeries that offer theme birthday cakes and specialty breads. Commissaries occasionally hold tent sales, where items are sold by case lots at terrific savings. Ask if one is scheduled near you, and if so, stock up! The commissary and the exchange carry some of the same items; because of the different markup policies, however, these items will always be cheaper at the commissary.

Commissaries accept food stamps and manufacturers' coupons, and credit card acceptance is currently being tested at some bases. There is often a box at the entrance for coupon swaps.

If you live too far from a commissary to take advantage of its savings, ask your husband to stock up while he's there for a drill weekend. Refrigerated items can be brought back in a cooler.

Try to budget your money so that you don't have to bank or shop on payday. The lines are long! The best times to commissary shop are early in the morning the first day of the week it's open, because it's best stocked then, and late afternoon before it closes for the weekend, because meat and produce are reduced. Also, look for bargains on the damaged-goods shelf.

Q: I've heard that commissaries deliberately raise prices on paydays. Is this true?

A: No. What happens is that many of the vendors who supply the commissaries determine *their* prices monthly. They commonly make adjustments on the 1st and the 15th. Suppliers in many industries have this practice. That these dates happen to be military paydays is a coincidence.

Both the commissary and the exchange are for authorized personnel only. You may purchase bona fide gifts for nonmilitary friends at the exchange (but not at the commissary), but buying products for resale, even if no profit is made, can result in loss of your shopping privileges and in disciplinary action against your husband.

Don't brag about the commissary, the exchange, or any other military benefit to your civilian neighbors. There's no point, and it doesn't make for good neighbor relations.

≡ Medical Care

The primary mission of this much-cherished benefit is to serve active-duty personnel. Everyone else is treated on a space-available basis. Active-duty family members are second in priority, retirees third, and retiree family members fourth, assuming problem severity is similar. During mobilizations, such as Desert Storm, family members may be instructed to obtain civilian treatment so that more comprehensive care may be given to the servicemembers. Ordinarily, however, two thirds of the people treated at military hospitals are family members and retirees. So, obviously, it isn't hard to use these facilities on a space-available basis.

You need to enroll in the Defense Enrollment Eligibility Reporting System (DEERS), which is a registry system by which the military verifies that only authorized people are treated in its facilities. To enroll, fill out a form at the personnel office (your husband was automatically enrolled when he entered the service). You may verify your enrollment status with the hospital or with DEERS. Its Beneficiary Telephone Center number is (800) 538-9552; in California, (800) 334-4162; and in Alaska and Hawaii, (800) 527-5602. Next, go to the hospital to get a medical card and open a records file.

A Reservist not on active duty can "pre-enroll" his family; they will become eligible if the Reservist is activated for more than thirty days and the family has no other health insurance. Family members of Reservists who are activated for more than thirty days are automatically enrolled by their sponsor's command.

═ Primary Care at Military Facilities

Primary (routine) care is obtained at the base hospital. Some bases also operate walk-in clinics,

People wonder why I am a doctor in the military instead of private practice. I feel there's more to a profession than pay. I enjoy the camaraderie, field exercises, ministering to soldiers in need. I like wearing my uniform, and my wife and I enjoy the moving and friends we've made. What keeps the brigade commander or combat officer in the Army? Does anyone ask *them* whether they're in because "they can't do anything else"? I don't believe that. It's the intangibles of military life that keep careerists in, no matter what the field. As for the quality of military medicine, people who enjoy their jobs do them well, no matter what they're paid.

where appointments aren't needed; these are called NAVCARE in the Navy and PRIMUS in the Army and Air Force. Many military hospitals offer family practice clinics, where you're assigned a specific doctor. All hospitals and clinics are open to people from all branches of service.

Hospital staffing levels are set by Congress, which determines how many family-member-related practitioners (such as pediatricians) may be hired. Medical personnel also participate in field exercises, take leave, and make permanent-change-of-station moves like everyone else in the military. So there may be a wait for routine appointments.

Every hospital has a health benefits advisor (HBA), who will give you specifics on the care you may expect in a military facility, how to obtain civilian treatment under the government programs available to you, and how to file for reimbursement. The HBA will also discuss your specific situation and assist with any problems.

With both medical and dental facilities, it is critical that you arrive on time for your appointments. There are too few providers serving too many patients to allow them to wait for latecomers. Most clinics will cancel your appointment and fill your slot with an available patient if you're even ten minutes late. Two no-shows and you can lose your privilege of being treated at military facilities for an entire year. Also, the emergency room is just for that: emergencies. Routine complaints will often be met with an hours-long wait simply because there will always be someone more seriously ill and you'll have to wait until they've been treated first.

While most people have no complaints with the military health-care practitioners they see, *getting* to see them can be a problem. A phone with an automatic redial feature and a speaker option is helpful when making appointments.

If you plan to spend time asking lengthy questions during a medical appointment, mention that you'll need extra time when booking it.

If you're unhappy with care received at a military hospital, it is your right to complain to the NCOIC (noncommissioned officer in charge) of that department. Complaining to the receptionist is fruitless. You can also ask the patient representative to intervene.

In 1993 stepchildren and adopted children were authorized to receive treatment at military health-care facilities.

As a military health-care worker, I suggest you actively understand and take part in what is being done for and to you. It will make your care go smoother. Your most important possession—your health—is being dealt with. I often see delays because of things like patients not telling doctors that tests ordered for them have already been performed at another doctor's instructions, or going to a lab with incorrect instructions.

═══ **Medical Services Offered**

Services offered at military hospitals vary drastically, depending on the size of the hospital, the size of the community it serves, and where it is located. Some are huge, multimillion-dollar buildings that offer everything; others are tiny clinics that serve only basic needs. Generally, all of them offer the following:

- Treatment of medical and surgical conditions.
- Treatment of nervous, mental, and emotional disorders.
- Treatment of disease, including contagious diseases and chronic conditions.
- Routine physicals and immunizations.
- Prescription and nonprescription drugs.
- Maternity and well-baby care.
- Diagnostic services, lab tests, and X-rays.
- Emergency and routine dental care.
- Dental care as necessary to treat or prevent a medical problem.
- Eye exams.
- Ambulance service.
- Artificial limbs and eyes.
- Loan of wheelchairs and hospital beds.
- Family-planning services and supplies.
- Orthopedic braces, crutches, and other aids.

If you need something that isn't offered, either you'll be sent via military transportation—commonly called *medevac,* for medical evacuation—to another military facility or, more likely, you'll use CHAMPUS (discussed later in this chapter). In cases of catastrophic illness, you'll have access to world-renowned military hospitals, such as Walter Reed Army Medical Center in Washington, D.C.; Brook Army Medical Center in San Antonio, Texas; and the Naval Hospital in Bethesda, Maryland.

All services and medications you receive at military health-care facilities are free. If a hospital stay is required, family members are charged a small daily fee for meals. The law requires you to tell the military hospital if you have health insurance, such as that which might be provided by your own job. The hospital will then file with your insurer for the reasonable costs of the treatment. The insurance payment will be accepted as payment in full; no bill will be sent to you, even if your private policy requires a deductible and co-share of costs.

Medical Care for the Active Guard and Reserve

Active Guard and Reserve families not living near a military installation are entitled to equivalent medical care at specially designated civilian hospitals. Benefits in the plan include standard Health Maintenance Organization (HMO) features such as enrollment, capital payment, uniform benefits package, quality assurance, preventive care, and prescription drugs. Small fees for inpatient and outpatient services are required.

The Feres Doctrine

A 1950 Supreme Court ruling known as the Feres Doctrine claims that suits filed by subordinates against superiors would cause a breakdown in military discipline. Therefore, servicemembers cannot sue the government for damages that occur incidental to service. This includes suing for malpractice. Active-duty people can, however, receive compensation for malpractice in the form of a disability retirement or hospital care if they remain on active duty. If they're severely injured because of malpractice, they are also entitled to certain Social Security benefits and compensation from the Department of Veterans Affairs.

CHAMPUS

Q: How many CHAMPUS claims are processed every year?
A: About twenty million.

The Civilian Health and Medical Program of the Uniformed Services (CHAMPUS), instituted in 1967, is the mechanism for obtaining treatment unavailable at the base medical facility. CHAMPUS is a cost-share program, and not insurance. You don't pay premiums, but a portion of the medical bills incurred. There is no limit on the amount of medical bills CHAMPUS will share with you.

CHAMPUS is only for treatment unavailable at the base medical facility. If you live in the hospital's catchment area—certain zip-code zones around a military hospital or within a certain radius of one overseas— you must use it for all nonemergency care, including maternity care. If you're outside of this area or if the hospital cannot provide the treatment you need, your health benefits advisor will give you a statement of nonavailability. Getting this statement is the first step in obtaining CHAMPUS benefits. Unless you have it CHAMPUS won't pay. Nonavailability statements are good only for the area in which they're issued; they can't be transferred to another duty station. Naturally, if you're injured far away from a military hospital, or if you live a great distance from one, you won't need this statement—just hurry to the nearest civilian hospital, present your military ID card as proof of CHAMPUS eligibility, then file with CHAMPUS.

Claims must be filed no later than one year after the services are provided. They are processed by insurance companies that contract with the government. These companies are called fiscal intermediaries, or claims-processing contractors. Following are contractor addresses and their toll-free numbers:

Where to File CHAMPUS Claims

ALABAMA
WPS
P.O. Box 7889
Madison, WI 53707-7889
(800) 866-6337

ALASKA
BC/BSSC
P.O. Box 100502
Florence, SC 29501-0502
(800) 225-4816

ARIZONA
BC/BSSC
P.O. Box 100502
Florence, SC 29501-0502
(800) 225-4816

ARKANSAS
WPS
P.O. Box 8932
Madison, WI 53708-8932
(800) 388-6767

CALIFORNIA[1]
FHFS
Claims Department
P.O. Box 1810
Rancho Cordova, CA 95670
(800) 282-7105

CALIFORNIA[2]
Palmetto GBA
CHAMPUS Claims
P.O. Box 870001
Surfside Beach, SC 29587-8701
(800) 741-5048

COLORADO
BC/BSSC
P.O. Box 100502
Florence, SC 29501-0502
(800) 225-4816

[1] For care received prior to February 1, 1994 for any CHAMPUS beneficiary living in California or Hawaii.

[2] For care received after February 1, 1994 for California and Hawaii residents and all traveling beneficiaries.

Note: Send your claim(s) to the claims processor who handles claims for the state or country where care was received. (Residents of California and Hawaii and nonresidents traveling in California or Hawaii, see California and Hawaii listings.)

Key: ADSI—Adminastar Defense Services, Inc. (formerly USBPI); BC/BSSC—Blue Cross/Blue Shield of South Carolina; FHFS—Foundation Health Federal Services; OCHAMPUSEUR—Office of CHAMPUS, Europe; PALMETTO GBA—Palmetto Government Benefits Administrators; WPS—Wisconsin Physicians Service

CONNECTICUT
ADSI
P.O. Box 3066
Columbus, IN 47202-3066
(800) 842-4333

DELAWARE
ADSI
P.O. Box 3076
Columbus, IN 47202-3076
(800) 842-4333

FLORIDA
WPS
P.O. Box 7889
Madison, WI 53707-7889
(800) 866-6337

GEORGIA
WPS
P.O. Box 7889
Madison, WI 53707-7889
(800) 866-6337

HAWAII[1]
FHFS
Claims Department
P.O. Box 1810
Rancho Cordova, CA 95670
(800) 282-7105

HAWAII[2]
Palmetto GBA
Champus Claims
P.O. Box 870001
Surfside Beach, SC 29587-8701
(808) 592-2071
(800) 741-5048

IDAHO
BC/BSSC
P.O. Box 100502
Florence, SC 29501-0502
(800) 225-4816

ILLINOIS
ADSI
P.O. Box 3054
Columbus, IN 47202-3054
(800) 842-4333

INDIANA
ADSI
P.O. Box 3056
Columbus, IN 47202-3056
(800) 842-4333

IOWA
ADSI
P.O. Box 3058
Columbus, IN 47202-3058
(800) 842-4333

KANSAS
WPS
P.O. Box 8932
Madison, WI 53708-8932
(800) 388-6767

KENTUCKY
ADSI
P.O. Box 3061
Columbus, IN 47202-3061
(800) 842-4333

---

[1] For care received prior to February 1, 1994 for any CHAMPUS beneficiary living in California or Hawaii.

[2] For care received after February 1, 1994 for California and Hawaii residents and all traveling beneficiaries.

Note: Send your claim(s) to the claims processor who handles claims for the state or country where care was received. (Residents of California and Hawaii and nonresidents traveling in California or Hawaii, see California and Hawaii listings.)

Key: ADSI—Adminastar Defense Services, Inc. (formerly USBPI); BC/BSSC—Blue Cross/Blue Shield of South Carolina; FHFS—Foundation Health Federal Services; OCHAMPUSEUR—Office of CHAMPUS, Europe; PALMETTO GBA—Palmetto Government Benefits Administrators; WPS—Wisconsin Physicians Service

KENTUCKY (Fort Campbell Area)
WPS
P.O. Box 7889
Madison, WI 53707-7889
(800) 866-6337

LOUISIANA
(except CHAMPUS Reform areas)
WPS
P.O. Box 8932
Madison, WI 53708-8932
(800) 388-6767

LOUISIANA
(New Orleans area)
FHFS Claims Dept.
P.O. Box 1718
Rancho Cordova, CA 95670-1718
(800) 982-2882

LOUISIANA
(Alexandria/Fort Polk areas)
FHFS/Louisiana Claims
P.O. Box 2030
Rancho Cordova, CA 95670-2030
(800) 982-2882

MAINE
ADSI
P.O. Box 3064
Columbus, IN 47202-3064
(800) 842-4333

MARYLAND
BC/BSSC
P.O. Box 100502
Florence, SC 29501-0502
(800) 476-8500

MASSACHUSETTS
ADSI
P.O. Box 3063
Columbus, IN 47202-3063
(800) 842-4333

MICHIGAN
ADSI
P.O. Box 3053
Columbus, IN 47202-3053
(800) 842-4333

MINNESOTA
ADSI
P.O. Box 3057
Columbus, IN 47202-3057
(800) 842-4333

MISSISSIPPI
WPS
P.O. Box 7889
Madison, WI 53707-7889
(800) 866-6337

MISSOURI
WPS
P.O. Box 8932
Madison, WI 53708-8932
(800) 388-6767

MONTANA
BC/BSSC
P.O. Box 100502
Florence, SC 29501-0502
(800) 225-4816

NEBRASKA
BC/BSSC
P.O. Box 100502
Florence, SC 29501-0502
(800) 225-4816

Note: Send your claim(s) to the claims processor who handles claims for the state or country where care was received. (Residents of California and Hawaii and nonresidents traveling in California or Hawaii, see California and Hawaii listings.)

Key: ADSI—Adminastar Defense Services, Inc. (formerly USBPI); BC/BSSC—Blue Cross/Blue Shield of South Carolina; FHFS—Foundation Health Federal Services; OCHAMPUSEUR—Office of CHAMPUS, Europe; PALMETTO GBA—Palmetto Government Benefits Administrators; WPS—Wisconsin Physicians Service

NEVADA
BC/BSSC
P.O. Box 100502
Florence, SC 29501-0502
(800) 225-4816

NEW HAMPSHIRE
ADSI
P.O. Box 3067
Columbus, IN 47202-3067
(800) 842-4333

NEW JERSEY
ADSI
P.O. Box 3052
Columbus, IN 47202-3052
(800) 842-4333

NEW MEXICO
BC/BSSC
P.O. Box 100502
Florence, SC 29501-0502
(800) 225-4816

NEW YORK
ADSI
For zip codes 13000–14999: P.O. Box 3050
For zip codes 10000–12999: P.O. Box 3051
Columbus, IN 47202
(800) 842-4333

NORTH CAROLINA
BC/BSSC
P.O. Box 100502
Florence, SC 29501-0502
(800) 476-8500

NORTH DAKOTA
BC/BSSC
P.O. Box 100502
Florence, SC 29501-0502
(800) 225-4816

OHIO
ADSI
For zip codes 43700–44799:
P.O. Box 3060
Columbus, IN 47202-3060
All other zips:
P.O. Box 3059
Columbus, IN 47202-3059
(800) 842-4333

OKLAHOMA
WPS
P.O. Box 8932
Madison, WI 53708-8932
(800) 388-6767

OREGON
BC/BSSC
P.O. Box 100502
Florence, SC 29501-0502
(800) 225-4816

PENNSYLVANIA
ADSI
For zip codes 15001–15299 &
    19001–19199:
P.O. Box 3074
Columbus, IN 47202-3074
All other zips:
P.O. Box 3075
Columbus, IN 47202-3075
(800) 842-4333

RHODE ISLAND
ADSI
P.O. Box 3065
Columbus, IN 47202-3065
(800) 842-4333

Note: Send your claim(s) to the claims processor who handles claims for the state or country where care was received. (Residents of California and Hawaii and nonresidents traveling in California or Hawaii, see California and Hawaii listings.)

Key: ADSI—Adminastar Defense Services, Inc. (formerly USBPI); BC/BSSC—Blue Cross/Blue Shield of South Carolina; FHFS—Foundation Health Federal Services; OCHAMPUSEUR—Office of CHAMPUS, Europe; PALMETTO GBA—Palmetto Government Benefits Administrators; WPS—Wisconsin Physicians Service

SOUTH CAROLINA
BC/BSSC
P.O. Box 100502
Florence, SC 29501-0502
(800) 476-8500

SOUTH DAKOTA
BC/BSSC
P.O. Box 100502
Florence, SC 29501-0502
(800) 225-4816

TENNESSEE
WPS
P.O. Box 7889
Madison, WI 53707-7889
(800) 866-6337

TEXAS
(except Bergstrom/Carswell areas)
WPS
P.O. Box 8932
Madison, WI 53708-8932
(800) 388-6767

TEXAS
(Bergstrom/Carswell areas)
FHFS/Texas Claims
P.O. Box 1170
Rancho Cordova, CA 95670-1170
(800) 982-2882

UTAH
BC/BSSC
P.O. Box 100502
Florence, SC 29501-0502
(800) 225-4816

VERMONT
ADSI
P.O. Box 3068
Columbus, IN 47202-3068
(800) 842-4333

VIRGINIA
BC/BSSC
P.O. Box 100502
Florence, SC 29501-0502
(800) 476-8500

WASHINGTON
BC/BSSC
P.O. Box 100502
Florence, SC 29501-0502
(800) 225-4816

WASHINGTON, D.C.
BC/BSSC
P.O. Box 100502
Florence, SC 29501-0502
(800) 476-8500

WEST VIRGINIA
ADSI
P.O. Box 3062
Columbus, IN 47202-3062
(800) 842-4333

WISCONSIN
ADSI
P.O. Box 3055
Columbus, IN 47202-3055
(800) 842-4333

WYOMING
BC/BSSC
P.O. Box 100502
Florence, SC 29501-0502
(800) 225-4816

Note: Send your claim(s) to the claims processor who handles claims for the state or country where care was received. (Residents of California and Hawaii and nonresidents traveling in California or Hawaii, see California and Hawaii listings.)

Key: ADSI—Adminastar Defense Services, Inc. (formerly USBPI); BC/BSSC—Blue Cross/Blue Shield of South Carolina; FHFS—Foundation Health Federal Services; OCHAMPUSEUR—Office of CHAMPUS, Europe; PALMETTO GBA—Palmetto Government Benefits Administrators; WPS—Wisconsin Physicians Service

PUERTO RICO
WPS
P.O. Box 7985
Madison, WI, USA 53707-7985
(608) 259-4847

PACIFIC AREA
(China, Thailand, Korea, Australia,
   Japan, etc.)
WPS
P.O. Box 7985
Madison, WI, USA 53707-7985
(608) 259-4847

ADJUNCTIVE DENTAL
(Worldwide except OCHAMPUSEUR,
   CA & HI; TX & LA Brac sites)
BC/BSSC
P.O. Box 100599
Florence, SC 29501-0599
(803) 665-2320

EUROPE, AFRICA, MIDEAST
(Plus dental for those areas)
OCHAMPUSEUR
144 Karlsruhestrasse
6900 Heidelberg, FRG
or
OCHAMPUSEUR
Unit 29220
APO AE 09102
Heidelberg Military (2122) 575/633
FAX 06221-300063

CHRISTIAN SCIENCE
(except CA & HI; New Orleans;
   TX & LA Brac sites)
ADSI
ATTN: Christian Science
P.O. Box 3063
Columbus, IN 47202-3063
(800) 842-4333

CANADA, MEXICO, CENTRAL
   AMERICA, SOUTH AMERICA,
   BERMUDA, WEST INDIES
WPS
P.O. Box 7985
Madison, WI, USA 53707-7985
(608) 259-4847

Note: Send your claim(s) to the claims processor who handles claims for the state or country where care was received. (Residents of California and Hawaii and nonresidents traveling in California or Hawaii, see California and Hawaii listings.)

Key: ADSI—Adminastar Defense Services, Inc. (formerly USBPI); BC/BSSC—Blue Cross/Blue Shield of South Carolina; FHFS—Foundation Health Federal Services; OCHAMPUSEUR—Office of CHAMPUS, Europe; PALMETTO GBA—Palmetto Government Benefits Administrators; WPS—Wisconsin Physicians Service

Your CHAMPUS Costs

The following are your CHAMPUS costs:

- A yearly deductible for outpatient care. This is the initial amount you have to pay before CHAMPUS steps in. No deductible is charged for inpatient care.
- Your cost share. CHAMPUS pays 80 percent of the medical care costs for active-duty families (less for retirees and retiree family members). You must pay 20 percent even if the care is emergency care and

there is no military hospital available. (Note: CHAMPUS waived the co-payment on October 1, 1994, for families living in Europe, the Middle East, and Africa.)

■ Additional money if the provider you pick isn't a participating provider or one that accepts CHAMPUS assignment.

CHAMPUS has a table of fixed prices it will pay for services. If the provider agrees to charge those prices, he or she is a participating provider (accepts CHAMPUS assignment). Your costs then will be the 20 percent CHAMPUS doesn't pay plus the deductible. But if the provider doesn't agree to CHAMPUS prices, you must pay your 20 percent cost share, the deductible, and the difference between what is charged and what CHAMPUS pays. Recently, Congress made it illegal for participating providers to charge more than 115 percent of CHAMPUS's table of prices. While this may save some service families money, it has also had the unfortunate effect of making some providers shun CHAMPUS as a means of payment. Federal law requires that all hospitals that accept Medicare must also accept CHAMPUS, but individual providers that accept Medicare do not have to accept CHAMPUS.

Many providers accept CHAMPUS assignment, many don't, and many accept it on a case-by-case basis. There are even situations in which the hospital is a participating provider but the practitioner treating you in it is not. It's your responsibility to find out. Your share of the costs are your responsibility, and you'll need to make arrangements directly with your provider about how you're going to pay. Regardless of who files the claim, CHAMPUS will send you, the beneficiary, an Explanation of Benefits (EOB) describing the action taken on the claim. If you don't receive an EOB within six weeks of filing, check into it. Your claim may have been lost.

A common misconception is that CHAMPUS is for active-duty personnel. It isn't. CHAMPUS is only for family members and retirees. If an active-duty servicemember requires treatment at a civilian hospital, the government pays the bill (as long as the treatment was medically necessary and unavailable at a local installation). If, however, a commander or investigating officer decides that the treatment needed was due to the servicemember's own negligence or misconduct, the government will not pay. The servicemember may also be required to reimburse a military hospital for treatment costs in such a case.

What CHAMPUS Doesn't Cover

CHAMPUS doesn't cover every type of treatment, even if your doctor says you need it. For example, it *doesn't* cover the following: abortions, except in very limited circumstances; artificial insemination; birth control for which you don't need a prescription (it will pay for the Norplant birth control device); cosmetic, plastic, or reconstructive surgery, except in certain cases; dental care, except in limited circumstances; electrolysis; experimental procedures; eyeglasses and contact lenses, except in very limited circumstances; food, food substitutes or supplements, or vitamins outside a hospital; genetic tests not ordered by a doctor; preventive care such as school or annual physicals (except for well-baby care); private hospital rooms; or sexual inadequacy treatment. If you disagree with a decision made by CHAMPUS, however, you can appeal it.

CHAMPUS Supplemental Insurance Policies

If you receive care outside of the military system and you have no health insurance, your cost share could be very costly. Although Congress limits the catastrophic cap (out-of-pocket medical costs) of active-duty families to $1,000 annually (the cap for retiree families is $7,500), you might consider a supplemental insurance policy if you use CHAMPUS a lot. (Note that the catastrophic cap applies only to CHAMPUS's allowable charges. If you use a provider that does not accept CHAMPUS's fixed table of charges as payment in full, the extra you must pay does not apply to the cap.) Supplemental insurance policies are designed to reimburse you for the portion of your medical care that CHAMPUS or another coordinated-care system doesn't pay. Since federal law requires that CHAMPUS be used only when no other primary insurance (such as that through your own job, a school health plan, an automobile policy, workman's compensation, or Medicare) is available, make sure any supplemental policy you buy is a true CHAMPUS supplement, not merely a policy you have bought for that purpose. Otherwise, you might find CHAMPUS and the other insurer arguing over who will pay.

If you have other health insurance, such as that provided by your own employer, you must file for benefits with it first. CHAMPUS covers you only if you're not already covered by someone else. Also, CHAMPUS only covers care given by approved, authorized providers. Generally, that means the provider is licensed by the state, accredited by a national organization, or meets other standards set by the medical community.

If your husband is soon to leave the service, check into alternative insurance before he separates. CHAMPUS eligibility, like eligibility for the base medical facility, ends at midnight the day of separation.

For more information, read the CHAMPUS handbook. Pick one up at your base medical facility, or contact CHAMPUS, Aurora, CO, 80045-6900, telephone (303) 361-3907. It's best to know the rules beforehand.

The accompanying list gives addresses and phone numbers of military-organization-related CHAMPUS supplemental policies. Each policy has rules regarding eligibility, deductibles, mental health, long-term illness, well-baby care, handicapped care, Medicare conversion, widows' benefits, acceptance, overall benefit coverage, time limitations, waivers, and allowable charges versus excess charges, as well as information concerning noncovered charges. None are endorsed; it is up to you to carefully study each one and decide which, if any, best fits your needs. Also included is a list of questions to ask when choosing a policy.

CHAMPUS Supplemental Plans

AIR FORCE ASSOCIATION
1501 Lee Highway
Arlington, VA 22209-1198
(800) 727-3337 or (703) 247-5800

AIR FORCE SERGEANTS ASSOCIATION
AFSA Insurance Plan
400 Locust St., 8th Floor
Des Moines, IA 50398
(800) 247-7988

AMERICAN MILITARY ASSOCIATION
Fort Snelling Station
P.O. Box 76
Minneapolis, MN 55440-0076
(800) 562-4076

AMERICAN MILITARY RETIREES
    ASSOCIATION
AMRA Group Insurance Plan, Administrator
P.O. Box 2510
Rockville, MD 20852-0510
(800) 638-2610 or (301) 816-0045

AMERICAN MILITARY SOCIETY
P.O. Box 50282
Washington, DC 20004-0282
(800) 843-2043

ARMED FORCES BENEFIT
    ASSOCIATION
AFDBSI, 909 N. Washington St.
Alexandria, VA 22314
(800) 776-2264

ARMED FORCES BENEFIT SERVICES, INC.
AFBA Building,
909 N. Washington St.
Alexandria, VA 22314-1556
(703) 549-4455

ARMY AVIATION ASSOCIATION
    OF AMERICA
Membership Services, Inc.
1304 Vincent Place
McLean, VA 22101
(800) 394-4000

ASSOCIATION OF PERSONAL AFFAIRS
P.O. Box 3357
Austin, TX 78764
(800) 451-9143

ASSOCIATION OF THE U.S. ARMY
Kirke-Van Orsdel, Inc.
400 Locust St., 8th Floor
Des Moines, IA 50398
(800) 247-7988

ENLISTED ASSOCIATION OF THE
    NATIONAL GUARD OF THE U.S.
NGAUS Insurance Plans
P.O. Box 907
Minneapolis, MN 55440-0907
(800) 441-2590

FLEET RESERVE ASSOCIATION
Member Benefits—Milicare PLUS
Kirke-Van Orsdel, Inc.
400 Locust St., 8th Floor
Des Moines, IA 50398
(800) 322-8717, ext. 70108

MARINE CORPS ASSOCIATION
MCA Health Care Plan, Administrator
734 15th St., N.W., Suite 500
Washington, DC 20005
(800) 368-5682 or (202) 393-6600

MARINE CORPS LEAGUE
Membership Services, Inc.
1304 Vincent Place
McLean, VA 22101
(800) 394-4000

MILITARY BENEFIT ASSOCIATION
108 N. Center St.
P.O. Box 549
Vienna, VA 22183
(800) 336-0100

MILITARY ORDER OF THE PURPLE
    HEART
Membership Services, Inc.
1304 Vincent Place
McLean, VA 22101
(800) 394-4000

MILITARY ORDER OF THE
    WORLD WARS
Membership Services, Inc.
1304 Vincent Place
McLean, VA 22101
(800) 394-4000

MUTUAL OF OMAHA INSURANCE CO.
Mutual of Omaha Plaza
Omaha, NE 68175
(800) 228-7100

NATIONAL ASSOCIATION OF THE
    UNIFORMED SERVICES
NAUS Uniservices Insurance Plans
P.O. Box 92560
Washington, DC 20077-7505
(800) 843-2043

NATIONAL DEFENSE
    TRANSPORTATION ASSOCIATION
Membership Services, Inc.
1304 Vincent Place
McLean, VA 22101
(800) 394-4000

NATIONAL GUARD ASSOCIATION
    OF THE U.S.
NGAUS Insurance Plan, Administrator
P.O. Box 907
Minneapolis, MN 55440-9863
(800) 328-3323

NATIONAL OFFICERS ASSOCIATION
Membership Services, Inc.
1304 Vincent Place
McLean, VA 22101
(800) 394-4000

NAVAL ENLISTED RESERVE
    ASSOCIATION
Seabury & Smith, Administrator
Group Insurance Program
1255 23rd St., N.W., Suite 300
Washington, DC 20037
(800) 424-9883 or (202) 457-6820

NAVY LEAGUE
Murray Marketing Group
5959 S. Staples
Corpus Christi, TX 78413
(800) 628-9628

NAVAL RESERVE ASSOCIATION
Seabury & Smith, Administrator
Group Insurance Program
1255 23rd St., N.W., Suite 300
Washington, DC 20037
(800) 424-9883 or (202) 457-6820

NON-COMMISSIONED OFFICERS
    ASSOCIATION
NCOA Membership Services
P.O. Box 105636
Atlanta, GA 30348-5636
(800) 662-2620

RESERVE OFFICERS ASSOCIATION
Kirke-Van Orsdel, Inc.
400 Locust St., 8th Floor
Des Moines, IA 50125
(800) 247-7988

RETIRED ASSOCIATION FOR THE
    UNIFORMED SERVICES
RAUS Group Insurance, Administrator
P.O. Box 2510
Rockville, MD 20852-0510
(800) 638-2610 or (301) 816-0045

SOCIETY OF MILITARY WIDOWS
NAUS Uniservices Insurance Plans
P.O. Box 92560
Washington, DC 20077-7505
(800) 843-2043

THE RETIRED ENLISTED ASSOCIATION
P.O. Box 50584
Washington, DC 20004
(800) 441-6269

THE RETIRED OFFICERS ASSOCIATION
TROA Insurance Plans, Administrator
400 Locust St., 8th Floor
Des Moines, IA 50398
(800) 247-2192

THE UNIFORMED SERVICES
    ASSOCIATION
Membership Services, Inc.
1304 Vincent Place
McLean, VA 22101
(800) 394-4000

UNITED SERVICES AUTOMOBILE
    ASSOCIATION
USAA Life Insurance Co.
USAA Building
San Antonio, TX 78288
(800) 292-8556, ext. 86622 (policy service)
    or ext. 86945 (claims)

UNITED SERVICES LIFE INSURANCE CO.
4601 Fairfax Dr.
P.O. Box 3700
Arlington, VA 22203
(800) 424-2300

U.S. ARMY WARRANT OFFICERS
    ASSOCIATION
Seabury & Smith, Administrator
Group Insurance Program
1255 23rd St., N.W., Suite 300
Washington, DC 20037
(800) 424-9883 or (202) 457-6820

U.S. COAST GUARD CHIEF PETTY
    OFFICERS ASSOCIATION
Seabury & Smith, Administrator
Group Insurance Program
1255 23rd St., N.W., Suite 300
Washington, DC 20037
(800) 424-9883 or (202) 457-6820

U.S. COAST GUARD CHIEF WARRANT
    AND WARRANT OFFICERS
    ASSOCIATION
Seabury & Smith, Administrator
Group Insurance Program
1255 23rd St., N.W., Suite 300
Washington, DC 20037
(800) 424-9883 or (202) 457-6820

U.S. NAVAL INSTITUTE
HealthCOM
P.O. Box 5667
Madison, WI 53705-0667
(800) 388-1006

CREDIT UNIONS*
Credit Union Group Insurance,
    Administrator
P.O. Box 2510
Rockville, MD 20852-0510
(800) 638-2610 or (301) 816-0045

---

*Community Services Federal Credit Union; Davis-Monthan AFB Federal Credit Union; First Services Federal Credit Union; Global Federal Credit Union; Langley AFB Federal Credit Union; Luke AFB Federal Credit Union; Mather AFB Federal Credit Union; Maxwell AFB Federal Credit Union; Nevada Federal Credit Union; Pentagon Federal Credit Union; Sea West Federal Credit Union; Travis AFB Federal Credit Union; Virginia Beach Federal Credit Union; Western Horizons Federal Credit Union.

Ask the following questions when shopping for CHAMPUS supplements:

- Must you meet a deductible before the plan begins paying?
- Is there a maximum limit on benefits (lifetime, annual, or other)?
- Is there a preexisting-condition clause? Is there a waiting period before the policy will pay for preexisting conditions?
- Will the plan cover amounts beyond what CHAMPUS allows?
- Does the plan pay for services that aren't covered by CHAMPUS?
- Does the plan specifically *not* cover other conditions?
- Must certain kinds of care be approved *before* getting the care?
- Is inpatient care covered? Outpatient care? Long-term care?
- Will the plan pay the CHAMPUS outpatient deductible?
- Will the plan pay the patient's cost share under the CHAMPUS diagnosis-related group (DRG) payment system?
- Does the plan convert to a Medicare supplement? If so, must it be in force as a CHAMPUS supplement for any specified length of time before conversion?
- Will the plan cover you overseas? If you are overseas, you may not incur any disallowed charges under CHAMPUS, because CHAMPUS pays charges as billed overseas.
- How will the plan require premium payments? Monthly? Quarterly? Can you use a credit card to charge the premiums?
- Might premium payments be increased? Under what conditions?
- Does the plan offer rates based on military status (active or retired) or based on an age scale? What is the scale?
- What are the membership fees (annual, lifetime, or other), if any, when you join the organization that sponsors the plan?
- Does the plan cover the servicemember when he retires?
- Does coverage continue for surviving spouses at no charge?
- What are the time limitations, if any, for filing a claim?
- If applicable, does the plan have higher rates for smokers?
- If you're retired military and have a health-care plan (which pays *before* CHAMPUS) through a civilian job, do you still need a CHAMPUS supplement if, between them, your employer's plan and CHAMPUS will pay most or all of your civilian medical bills?

☰ TriCare

More than eight million people are currently eligible to use the military health-care system. When you add up all the illnesses treated, broken bones set, babies delivered, operations, and other procedures performed in military health-care facilities, the number of cases treated runs into the tens of millions. In response to escalating costs, the post–Cold War mission of military medicine, and the difficulties some recipients have accessing it, the entire military health-care system is undergoing a change. That change is called TriCare.

TriCare is the umbrella name for a system of health plans run by twelve military medical centers in the United States (a thirteenth may be developed for Europe). It is an attempt to take medical care out of the civilian sector and place it back under the control of the three uniformed services. It is currently being tested in California, Hawaii, Louisiana, and Texas and is expected to be implemented nationwide in 1998.

TriCare health plans include Standard, Extra, and Prime. Standard is identical to regular CHAMPUS, and TriCare Extra and Prime have replaced CHAMPUS Extra and Prime. Prime is a health maintenance organization, and Extra is a preferred provider organization. Prime requires the selection of a primary care manager (a family or general practitioner, internist, pediatrician, or obstetrician-gynecologist, who serves as a "gatekeeper" to specialists also in the Prime network. Extra allows some of the freedom of choice of Standard, plus cost savings when visiting a Prime provider.

There are fees and deductibles. Active-duty personnel, retirees, and the families of each are eligible for different benefits. They may or may not be able to get these benefits at their local installations.

≡ CHAMPVA

The Civilian Health and Medical Program of the Department of Veterans Affairs shares the medical bills of families and survivors of certain veterans, if they are not eligible for CHAMPUS or Medicare. Once the VA decides a person's eligibility, benefits are cost-shared the same way that CHAMPUS covers the families of retirees.

CHAMPVA is different from CHAMPUS in that you can get care in a VA hospital on a space-available basis, but you're not authorized care in a military hospital.

Q: Which veterans are eligible for VA health care?

A: Assuming an honorable discharge, veterans are eligible if they fall into one of the following categories:

- Single with income of $19,912 or less per year.

- Married or single with one dependent and an income of $23,896 or less per year (income is raised $1,330 for each dependent).

Veterans with service-connected disabilities are not subject to an income eligibility assessment. Read the *Federal Benefits for Veterans and Dependents* handbook, listed in the Further Reading section for this chapter, for more information.

Q: My husband is trying to get benefits for a medical condition that occurred while he was on active duty ten years ago. How do we get copies of his records?

A: Fill out Standard Form 180, available at any base personnel office, Guard armory, VA hospital, or veterans service office. Send it to the National Personnel Records Center (Military Personnel Records), 9700 Page Blvd., St. Louis, MO 63132.

Contact your local VA office for more information about CHAMPVA.

Fisher Houses

Fisher Houses are lodges for families visiting servicemembers hospitalized for serious injuries, operations, or treatment. There's one near every major military hospital. The cost is a small daily fee, and the surroundings are comfortable. All Fisher Houses are two-story, five-thousand-square-foot homes, each containing five single bedrooms, two suites, a living room, a laundry room, and a fully equipped kitchen. Each bedroom has a phone and TV. You can cook, wash, iron, and have all the comforts of home while being near the loved one hospitalized. A house manager oversees the house's daily operation. There are Fisher Houses at the following locations:

Brooke Army Medical Center, Fort Sam Houston, Texas.
David Grant USAF Medical Center, Travis AFB, California.
Dwight D. Eisenhower Army Medical Center, Fort Gordon, Georgia.
Fitzsimmons Army Medical Center, Aurora, Colorado.
Keesler Medical Center, Keesler AFB, Mississippi.
Madigan Army Medical Center, Fort Lewis, Washington.
Malcolm Grow Medical Center, Andrews AFB, Maryland.
National Naval Medical Center, Bethesda, Maryland.
Naval Medical Center, Portsmouth, Virginia.
Naval Medical Center, San Diego, California.
Walter Reed Army Medical Center, Washington, D.C.
Wilford Hall Medical Center, Lackland AFB, Texas
William Beaumont Army Medical Center, Fort Bliss, Texas
Womack Army Medical Center, Fort Bragg, North Carolina.

Other Fisher Houses are currently being planned or under construction at Tripler Army Medical Center, Honolulu, Hawaii; USAF Medical Center, Scott AFB, Illinois; USAF Medical Center, Wright-Patterson AFB, Ohio; U.S. Dept. of Veterans Affairs, Samuel Stratton Medical Center, Albany, New York.

☰ Dental Care

Dental care for family members is not as readily available at all duty stations as medical care is. Congress fixes the number of military dentists in proportion to the number of active-duty personnel; family members don't enter into the equation. If there's space available, we're treated. Some clinics that don't treat family members do, however, provide fluoride treatments, X-rays, and cleanings for children.

☰ The Delta Dental Plan

The Active Duty Dependents Dental Plan helps cover the cost of family members' dental care. It's a voluntary program through which family members living in the States, Puerto Rico, or the Virgin Islands may buy low-cost insurance for civilian dental care. Enrollment is automatic; if you don't want to be enrolled, you must ask to be disenrolled. To be eligible for the plan, the servicemember must have at least 24 months remaining in service. This is so that enough premiums can be collected to keep the plan viable. Overseas families aren't enrolled because dental care is still available to them. Upon returning to the United States, family members may enroll by completing DD 2494 at the personnel center (as long as the servicemember has twenty-four months in service remaining). Overseas-based servicemembers with family members in the United States may also enroll. So may personnel in the Active Guard and Reserve.

As with CHAMPUS, active-duty personnel are not eligible, nor are retirees and their family. Reservist families are not eligible unless the Reservist is on active duty for two consecutive years. If he is activated for more than thirty days, care is available for family members at military dental clinics. Be aware that waiting time is often long, and it takes careful planning for Reserve families to get an appointment.

The plan compares favorably to civilian dental plans. It is a cost-sharing program. About 40 percent of the premium is paid by the government, leaving you to pay between $9.65 and $19.30 monthly, depending on family size. There are no deductibles. As with CHAMPUS, there are co-payments and fixed prices for provider services. A participating provider will accept these charges as full payment, and his office will file the claim. You don't pay anything up front. You do not have to use a participating provider, but know that nonparticipants may require up-front payment. You would then be reimbursed by the plan. They may also not accept the insurance's allowable charges as full payment, in which case you would have to make up the difference (in addition to your cost share).

Covered services include diagnostic exams and X-rays, cleanings, fillings, sealants, endodontics, periodontics, oral surgery, prosthodontics and crowns, and orthodontics.

Ask the military dental clinic for a list of plan participants. Chances are great that you'll find one nearby, and if not, the plan will reimburse you in full for covered services.

Read the *Evidence of Coverage* book for more details. Ask your health benefits advisor for a copy, or contact DDP Customer Service, P.O. Box 269023, Sacramento, CA 95826-9023, telephone (916) 381-9368 (west of the Mississippi); or P.O. Box 9086, Farmington Hills, MI, 48333-9086, telephone (313) 489-2240 (east of the Mississippi).

≣ Legal Aid

Most installations have a legal office. Here you can get free legal advice and assistance. If your base doesn't have a legal office, go to the nearest office of another service. Any ID-card holder can obtain advice from any base's legal office. Many Reserve lawyers also work weekends to help people from all services. Appointment procedures vary; some offices will see you on a walk-in basis, while others require you to have an appointment. If you have a quick question, you can usually just phone in and talk to a lawyer or paralegal.

The following services are offered: the drawing up of wills, powers of attorney, and bills of sale; landlord-tenant problems and interpretation of leases; domestic relations (adoption, separation, nonsupport, and divorce); consumer problems (contract, product injury, and product failure); citizenship, immigration, and passports; change of name; notarization; civil rights; depositions; taxation; personal finances, debts, insurance; personal property; torts (civil wrongs for which you can receive monetary damages); contracts; and referrals to other agencies or civilian lawyers where appropriate. Many offices even provide arbitration services through which small-claims disputes between ID-card holders can be settled.

Military lawyers can't advise you on personal business ventures or disputes with your own employer. Nor can they represent you in court. The Army, Navy, and Marine Corps do have an Expanded Legal Assistance Program, however, wherein military lawyers will go to court with E-4s and below for personal cases (excluding criminal ones). The Staff Judge Advocate Office will provide a lawyer for servicemembers of all ranks who are being court-martialed, going before an administrative board, or facing a nonjudicial punishment.

Military lawyers must meet the same requirements as civilian lawyers and must be members of the bar of at least one state.

≡ Space-Available Travel

Most service families holding overseas permanent-change-of-station (PCS) orders travel to their new assignments via the Air Force's Air Mobility Command (AMC). When you're traveling on PCS orders, you reserve seats and your trip is a regular flight. When you don't have PCS orders but are riding AMC anyway, what you're doing is riding space-available (Space-A) or, as it is commonly called, "taking a hop." Space-available means just that: After all the scheduled passengers and cargo are aboard, any remaining seats are offered to people who would like to go where the plane is going. AMC flights are scheduled on both military planes and civilian airliners; on the latter, the government buys all the seats.

Hops are low-cost seats to the world. With Space-A travel, military families can take holidays many civilian families only dream about. Thanks to hops and low-cost lodging, you'll find military families enjoying some of the most expensive real estate in the world. Do you like sun? Hop to Hawaii and stay at the military's lovely Hale Koa Hotel, located on Waikiki Beach. Do you prefer snow? Hop to Germany, stay at the military lodge in Chiemsee, and ski the Alps. There's hardly a place on this planet you can't go using AMC as the principal means of transportation. To get anywhere from anywhere costs the same: nothing. Hops are absolutely free.

> Planes vary greatly in comfort. Some are cargo planes where you'll sit on a canvas bench the whole trip, possibly with a ship motor in your face! Dress warmly and bring a blanket on such planes, as they're cold. Also bring your own snacks. Other planes, such as KC-10s, are as comfortable as commercial flights. If you like to travel, the money saved is well worth the inconveniences of hopping. My whole family took a Bermuda vacation via AMC.

Space-A travelers can sign up for five places at a time. If the flight to Portugal is booked, how about Spain? Turkey? Germany? There's a lot of room for fun for the adventurous family.

Obviously, Space-A travelers need to be flexible. Plan things loosely. If you're on a tight schedule, hops are not for you. Depending on the season and the popularity of the place, hops can be very difficult to catch. Bring enough money for hotel rooms and meals. Know that the servicemember must return when he said he would, regardless of whether he and his family can get a hop back. Money or a credit card for a commercial flight must be available.

══ Restrictions

Because hops are so popular, Congress stepped in to prevent unfair competition with commercial airlines. Consequently, there are a lot of rules about using them. These are the most important:

Servicemembers no longer have to wear their uniforms while hopping.

Q: May students fly AMC unaccompanied to visit their parents?

A: Yes, when they meet the following criteria: The sponsor must be overseas and serving an accompanied tour, and the student must be single, under age twenty-three, and a full-time student of an accredited U.S. secondary or undergraduate school. The student may also fly to a place to meet the family for a vacation. Pets may not come along.

- Family members may take hops only to, within, and from overseas locations (including Hawaii). They may not hop within the continental United States unless the final destination is an overseas location. If, when returning from overseas, the plane lands anywhere in the continental United States, the spouse must disembark, even if not at her final destination.

- Sponsors must accompany family members while hopping unless the family members are on emergency leave orders, environmental morale leave, or have a personal medical emergency. Don't confuse this restriction with PCS orders; family members traveling on AMC with PCS orders may travel alone because they are not "hopping" but are taking a scheduled flight.

- Luggage is limited to seventy pounds per person.

- Servicemembers must be on leave before they may sign up for a hop. Leave orders are presented to AMC personnel as proof.

Who Has Priority

Even though Space-A accommodates people on a first-come, first-served basis, certain categories do have priority. In descending order they are as follows:

1. Emergency leave (leave taken because of sickness or death in the immediate family).
2. Environmental and morale leave (leave offered to people in remote, low-support locations); regular leave.
3. Permissive temporary duty (house hunting); unaccompanied family members on emergency leave; student family members of overseas-stationed sponsors; service academy cadets.

4. Retirees and Reservists. Family members may accompany Reservists outside the continental United States only after the Reservist starts drawing retirement pay.

Within each category, priority is set by the date and time travelers sign in. Sign-in must be done by the sponsor, either in person at the passenger terminal or by fax (the data header on the fax is the sign-in time). Family members don't need to come along if the sponsor is signing up in person, but the sponsor does need their ID cards, passports, immunization records, and visas if appropriate.

The easiest time to catch a hop to and from Europe is in September, after school starts.

Consider nondirect routes to get to your destination if the direct ones are full. For instance, if you wish to go to Mildenhall, England, from Crete, Greece, try going to Rhein-Main, Germany, first.

If hopping is impossible, ask commercial airlines about military discounts.

When faxing a Space-A request, include a copy of the service leave form. Also provide the first names of accompanying family members, a statement that border-clearance documents are current, and a list of five places you'd like to go. You can list the fifth place as "all" if you'll take an available seat on any flight. Reservists must fax a copy of their current DD 1853 (authentication of Reserve status for travel eligibility), a statement of border clearance documents, and the list of five places.

You may sign up for all portions of your trip at once. For instance, if you're traveling from Spain to the United States via Germany, you may sign up for the Spain–Germany portion and the Germany–United States portion at the same time. The date you signed up in Spain will be your priority for the Germany–United States trip. Thus you're not as apt to be beaten on the first-come, first-served list by those just starting their trips. But be aware that you can be bumped on that second portion to make room for scheduled passengers and cargo or for a higher-category passenger. Getting on at one place is no guarantee that you'll get on at another. As soon as you land, sign up for your return flight. Your priority for that flight will start from that date.

Where to Hop From

The following is a list of flight terminals in the continental United States and the destinations they serve.

Charleston Air Force Base, South Carolina: Germany, Panama, United Kingdom.

Dover Air Force Base, Delaware: Germany, Spain, United Kingdom.

McGuire Air Force Base, New Jersey: Azores, Iceland, Germany.

Norfolk Naval Air Station, Virginia: Guantanamo Bay, Iceland, Italy, Puerto Rico, Spain.

McChord Air Force Base, Washington: Alaska, Japan, Korea.

Norton Air Force Base, California: Korea, Hawaii, Japan.

Travis Air Force Base, California: Guam, Hawaii, Japan, Korea, Okinawa, the Philippines.

Charleston International Airport, South Carolina: Germany, Panama.

Los Angeles International Airport, California: Guam, Hawaii, Okinawa, the Philippines.

Oakland International Airport, California: Japan, Korea, Okinawa, the Philippines.

Philadelphia International Airport, Pennsylvania: Azores, Germany, Greece, Iceland, Italy, Spain, United Kingdom.

Lambert-St. Louis International Airport, Missouri: Germany, Japan, Korea, Okinawa, the Philippines.

Flights leave from the Dallas–Fort Worth, Atlanta, and Charleston, South Carolina, airports that will connect you to one of the above airports.

Call any of these bases and ask for flight information. It's typically given via a recorded message. If you live near a military airfield, ask if they offer hops. Most do. Hops are also available on Navy, Marine Corps, and Coast Guard flights and from Air National Guard and Air Force Reserve bases.

Know that AMC flight schedules change all the time. Scheduled flights get canceled; unexpected ones pop up. Call the terminal for the latest information the day before you leave. Sometimes, after everyone has boarded, more seats are suddenly released. So even though hanging around the lobby isn't fun, leaving can cause you to miss a flight. If your name is called while you're gone, you won't be removed from the list. You've simply missed the opportunity to take that particular flight.

Have fun! Socialize with your fellow Space-A travelers. One frequent "hopper" shares this story:

"It's a lot of fun when you meet and swap tips with fellow adventurers. In case of disappointments, help each other out. One time a flight was canceled and there were a bunch of unhappy Space-A people milling about. The military guest house was full, and only expensive hotel rooms were available. An Air Force couple offered to share a room with me. We ended up there for two days and split the hotel cost. Doing things like that makes disappointments with Space-A more bearable."

☰ The Pension Plan

A discussion of big benefits would hardly be complete without a discussion of the military pension plan. Among the most generous in the nation, it is a major reason careerists stay in.

═ Active Duty

A servicemember is eligible for retirement after twenty years of service; after thirty, retirement is mandatory. After eighteen years he has "sanctuary"—that is, he cannot be easily dismissed before completing twenty years.

There are three ways of calculating active-duty retirement pay, depending on the year the servicemember entered the military; all involve receiving up to half his base pay for the rest of his life. Cost-of-living adjustments are made periodically to the retirement paycheck. Know that if a retiree receives veterans' disability compensation, his retired paycheck is reduced dollar for dollar by that amount.

Retirees and their families retain all base privileges, unless they retire overseas where agreements between the U.S. government and the host country may call for them to be excluded from some benefits, such as exchange and commissary privileges. Dental care is not available to retirees anywhere, and since they're lowest in priority for medical care, they may find it difficult to be seen at the base clinic. CHAMPUS remains available to them until age sixty-five, at which time they must enroll in Medicare and use that instead. If they become 100 percent disabled before age sixty-five, however, they lose their CHAMPUS eligibility and become eligible for health benefits under Social Security. Since servicemembers contribute to Social Security, eligible retirees can receive Social Security retirement checks, as well as disability income and Medicare.

═ Reserves

Reservists are awarded points for each active training drill attended and each correspondence course completed. A minimum of 50 points per year are needed for a "creditable year"—a year that qualifies toward retirement. A Reservist's pension is calculated differently from that of an active-duty servicemember; it is based on the number of points accumulated, years of service, and rank. Any years spent on active duty are translated into 365 points for each year. A Reservist does not start collecting retirement checks until age sixty. Reservists with twenty years of service but who are not yet sixty receive a Notice of Eligibility (the "twenty-year letter") and are known as "gray area" retirees. They and their families retain their ID cards, which entitle them to unlimited exchange and recreational facilities and twelve commissary visits per year until age sixty, at which time their privileges are exactly the same as those of active-duty retirees: They and their families receive medical benefits, CHAMPUS, space-available travel, and unlimited commissary access.

Like active-duty personnel, Reservists have sanctuary after eighteen years (some after fifteen). For more information on this subject, see chapter 12.

If Reservists are combining active and reserve service to equal twenty years, at least six of those years must be in the Reserves. For example, someone with thirteen years of active duty who transferred to the Reserves would need a combined total of twenty-one years to qualify for retirement. Also, in order to be retirement eligible, both active and Reserve personnel must have twenty years of service before reaching age sixty. At age sixty a person must leave, retirement eligible or not. Some rare exceptions are made for certain medical personnel who are deemed "needed for a mission-based requirement."

The Survivor Benefits Plan

Unless your husband makes provisions for you to receive survivor's benefits by enrolling in the SBP after he retires, you will not receive retirement money if he dies before you do.

The SBP for Active-Duty Retirees

Upon retirement, a servicemember is automatically enrolled in the SBP. He can elect not to be enrolled, but this requires a signed agreement from you. It must be done before the first day he is entitled to retirement pay. A decision not to be enrolled can later be reversed, but at the cost of decreased benefits.

Participants set aside a certain amount from their retirement checks as a monthly income for their survivors. The most a survivor can collect from the SBP until age sixty-two is 55 percent of the monthly gross retired pay. After age sixty-two, the maximum is 35 percent of the pay. That can be lowered still if the retiree chooses. Cost-of-living adjustments are made periodically, and benefits increase proportionally. Beneficiaries don't have to be spouses; they can be children, relatives, or anyone else.

Also available through the SBP is spouse-and-child coverage, which provides you with a monthly income if your husband dies, and continues for your unmarried children if you die before they reach eighteen (twenty-two if full-time students). Child coverage continues for life if the child is unmarried and incapacitated from an illness or injury that occurred before he or she reached eighteen.

The SBP for Reservist Retirees

Reservists have three options available when they receive their Notice of Eligibility:

1. Decline the SBP.
2. Enroll. If the Reservist dies before age sixty, the spouse collects pension benefits immediately.
3. Enroll at lower premiums. If the Reservist dies before age sixty, the spouse must wait until he would have turned sixty to begin collecting.

With options 2 and 3, a Reservist doesn't start paying SBP premiums until he reaches age sixty. The premiums are taken out of his pension checks. With option 2, even though you receive pension checks immediately, premiums are still taken out of them. With both 2 and 3, you keep your limited ID card until the time when your husband would have reached age sixty; then you receive an unlimited privileges ID card.

If option 1 is chosen, the Reservist is not again given the chance to sign up for the SBP until age sixty. During his entire "gray area" time, he is ineligible to enroll. If he were to die before age sixty, you would keep your limited ID card (twelve commissary visits and unlimited access to exchange and recreational facilities, but nothing else) for the rest of your life. Nothing changes at the time when he would have reached age sixty.

Death Benefits

Active Duty

If a servicemember dies while on active duty, the government will pay funeral expenses up to the limit allowed by law. Military honors—an honor guard, taps, a flag for the casket, and a rifle salute—are provided, and the body may be interred in a base or national cemetery, including Arlington National in Washington, D.C. The widow receives a large Social Security death benefit, an allowance for travel to the funeral, a payment for any back pay and unused leave, and a monthly annuity from the Department of Veterans Affairs. She is also entitled to a plot near her husband when she dies. See chapter 3 for more information.

═ Retired

Upon death, the government will pay for a headstone and provide an honor guard if requested. If there's room, the body may be interred in a base or national cemetery, including Arlington National. The widow is entitled to a plot by her husband and a small Social Security death benefit. Retired reservists and their spouses may be buried in a national cemetery, too.

≡ Further Reading

Crawford, Roy, and Ann Crawford. *Space-A Air Basic Training.* Falls Church, VA: Military Living, 1992.

Budahn, P. J. *Veteran's Guide to Benefits.* Mechanicsburg, PA: Stackpole Books, 1994.

Federal Benefits for Veterans and Dependents, 1994 edition. U.S. Government Printing Office, Superintendent of Documents, Washington, DC 20402.

Sharff, Lee E., Eugene Borden, and Fred Stein. *Veteran's Benefits Handbook.* New York: Arco, 1994.

Space-A Travel, pamphlet available at Air Mobility Command terminals.

Tomes, Jonathan P. *Servicemember's Legal Guide, 2nd edition.* Mechanicsburg, PA: Stackpole Books, 1991.

3

≡ Other Benefits
and Services

In addition to the big benefits we've just discussed, military life has a lot of other things designed to enhance our quality of life.

≡ Child Care

Recognizing that over 60 percent of military spouses work, and that many servicemembers themselves are single parents or dual service, Congress appropriates tax dollars for base child-care centers. If you've used one, no doubt you've noticed that it is considerably less expensive than a comparable private center. Military child-care facilities, like other services, are government subsidized. Half of military child-care costs are paid with tax dollars, with parents supplying the remaining 50 percent.

Fees are based on both parents' adjusted gross incomes, including quarters and subsistence allowances (see chapter 6). Tax returns are required as proof as income. Fees vary from base to base because child-care costs vary in different parts of the country. Lower rates are in place for households earning less than $18,000 per year. Each center has a parent advisory board, with reduced fees offered to parents as an incentive to participate.

Although military child-care centers have standardized policies and procedures, there are some differences in matters such as drop-in care. In many places priority is given to working mothers over home-makers, so drop-ins are limited. In other places the distribution is more even, but appointments are difficult to make less than a week in advance. Still other bases operate centers solely for drop-ins. Most centers are open from 6 A.M. until 6 P.M. Bases with unique missions have centers that are open twenty-four hours.

Demand is strong for military day-care centers, resulting in long waiting lists. Single parent and dual-military couples are given priority over military-civilian couples on the waiting lists. They receive this priority because they must report for duty immediately after arriving at their new base. One reason Congress appropriates funds for child-care centers is to reduce servicemembers' potential lost duty time.

Q: If a base needs a bigger child-care facility, why can't one just be built?

A: To build or expand facilities, the military must prove a need to Congress. Though some funds are earmarked for certain projects, most must be prioritized. Barracks renovations, child-care centers, research and development, medical care, field operations and training, family housing, civilian employee salaries—everything competes with everything else.

Q: I've filled out surveys but have seen nothing come of them. What's the point?

A: One of the ways needs are determined is by circulating surveys, which ask your opinions on everything from dental care to child care. The results are analyzed, and if a need is indicated, it's presented to Congress. Results are not always immediately obvious, as surveys are used not only to present requests for immediate needs, but also to formulate long-range plans.

For parents low on a long waiting list or for those who prefer a less structured environment than that of a child-care center, all the military services offer a program that certifies people to provide child care in their homes. This program requires that any family member caring for an unrelated child more than ten hours a week within the boundaries of a military installation or in government-owned or leased housing be licensed under an extensive training program. Lists of such base-certified caregivers are kept at installation child-care centers.

Some working mothers have wondered why they can't leave their children with a quarters-based trusted neighbor even though the neighbor isn't certified. Whom you choose to care for your child is your prerogative, but when a person operates a child-care business from her government quarters, that business becomes a concern of the base commander, because he's liable for what happens on it. Thus there is a need to ensure that the child care provided meets minimum standards. There are DOD regulations, and each installation may add its own to them.

Caregivers must complete training in first aid, nutrition, health, special-needs awareness, parent relations, CPR, child growth and development, child-abuse identification, and safety and emergency procedures. Certificates are awarded, enabling the caregivers to legally provide child care. To keep the certificates, participation in continuing education is required. Child-care providers also undergo background checks and physical exams, are subject to unannounced inspections, and may only care for a limited amount of children at one time.

Many home-care providers charge as much as or more than the base day-care center. This is because private caregivers are not subsidized by the government as the base day-care center is. Many also work longer hours than the center workers and take special pains to accommodate shift workers and sudden alerts.

Here are some things you will want to settle at the outset with your caregiver, preferably in a written contract:

- Hours and days care is to be provided.

- Cost: How much, and what day is payment due? What about alerts, overnight duties, field exercises, unexpected overtime, early drop-off and late pickup?

- Supplies: Who provides toys and educational materials, napkins, toilet paper, crayons, coloring books, diapers, wipes, bottles, formula, and laundry detergent?

- Backup: When the provider is unavailable, who is the backup and who pays any difference in price?

Many installations have latchkey-child programs that give children a supervised place to go before and after school. Some have parent co-operative groups, where baby-sitting hours are exchanged instead of money. There are also youth programs. Ask at your child-development services office or at the local school.

≡ Defense Department Schools

Most military children stateside attend local schools, and the government compensates the towns for their economic impact. That is why you will be asked to fill out a lengthy questionnaire before you can enroll your child; the town uses it to obtain federal moneys. When the base is bigger than the town, and local facilities simply can't support all the kids, base schools are built. They're funded by the Defense Department but conform to state and local requirements for teacher certification, salaries, textbooks, and curricula. Therefore, the curriculum in a base school in one state might be quite different from that in another.

Overseas there is another system of educating military children, called the Department of Defense Dependents Schools (DODDS). DODDS is entirely different from stateside Defense Department schools. (See chapter 9.)

≡ Recreation

Whatever the name the recreation office goes by—Morale, Well-being and Recreation (MWR) or Special Services—its mission is to provide active-duty personnel, Reservists, and their families with low-cost leisure activities. In the past few years, however, activity managers have been under congressional pressure to make their activities profitable and self-supporting. That, coupled with a shrinking client base due to the drawdown, has resulted in increased user fees. Military recreational facilities do remain cheaper than civilian ones, though, and many charge according to rank. They are big business, generating more than $12 billion per year.

Probably the most popular recreation spot on an installation is the club. There are separate clubs for officers, NCOs, and junior enlisted personnel, as well as clubs for all ranks. Club sizes vary at each installation; at some places they're huge and elegant, while at others they're not so huge or so elegant but still keep their patrons happy.

I love the arts and crafts center. I've taken classes in stained glass, leather tooling, floral arrangements, woodworking, upholstery, and photography.

I consider the base laundry service a valuable benefit. The service cleans uniforms and most civilian clothes for very low prices.

Clubs cash checks and provide meeting and party rooms, catering, restaurants, lounges and bars, pools, and even serving equipment for loan, such as punch bowls and flatware. Some (mainly officers' clubs) offer MasterCard and VISA credit cards. Clubs are great places to hold social affairs too large to be held at home. On the club's monthly calendar you'll find happy hours, special dinners, costume parties, lunches, brunches, dancing, and more.

On most Navy bases everyone is considered a member of the club, and dues are not paid. In the Army and Air Force this is not the case; facilities are available to members only, and dues are collected. Reciprocity—one club allowing members of another to use its facilities—isn't always granted. Happily, though, all other military leisure facilities do allow reciprocity, not just from base to base, but from service to service. Marines are welcome to putt on Army greens, and Air Force wives can watch movies at Navy theaters. Just flash that ID card!

The military provides all sorts of activities to keep its families from being bored. Facilities vary, so stop in at the recreation office and inquire. You may find fitness centers; playing and track fields; boats, motors, and fishing gear for rent; swimming pools; riding stables; campers, trailers, tents, and camping gear for rent; bowling alleys; eighteen-hole, nine-hole, and miniature golf courses; tennis courts; theaters; skating rinks; libraries; arts and crafts centers; auto crafts shops; sports equipment for rent; photo labs; sports lodges; and theme restaurants. All bases have a library.

Information, Tour, and Travel (ITT) or Special Services often has reduced-priced tickets for local movie theaters, entertainment spots, and tourist attractions. If your base doesn't have a golf course, a reduced rate might be available at a local facility. ITT also sells tickets for concerts and cultural events and offers bus tours to local historical sites as well as shopping trips to cities for residents of remote bases.

And then there are clubs: skydiving, scuba diving, rod and gun, model ship, camera, square dancing, computer, riding, stamp, coin, and chess clubs, and more. Read your base newspaper to find out what's around. Of course, if you'd like to belong to a certain club but there's no local chapter, you can always start one!

Reservists have unlimited access to most recreational facilities. Some base commanders restrict this access due to space constraints, however, so call before you make the trip.

Children can participate in all the activities described or in ones of their own. Most bases have youth activities centers, places military kids can call their own. Supervised trips, tours, and activities are organized for children ages six through nineteen. Facilities and programs vary, but on your base you might find youth centers, arts and crafts and instructional classes, sports, cheerleading, teen dances, parties, summer camps, Scout troops, and latchkey-child programs.

≡ Rest and Relaxation Spots

The Department of Defense owns recreational properties all over the world, ranging from luxurious beachfront hotels to recreational vehicle campgrounds to mountain ski chalets. Active-duty, Reserve, retired, and Defense Department civilian personnel may enjoy them.

Check with the front desk at each regarding policies. Some are very busy and you need reservations practically a year in advance. Some accept reservations only for those traveling on official orders (e.g., temporary duty or change

The Special Military Active and Retired Travel Club (SMART), is a nationwide RV travel and social club for active-duty, Reservist, and retired personnel of all the uniformed services. Former prisoners of war, Medal of Honor awardees, and 100 percent disabled veterans are also eligible. It has twenty-six chapters throughout the country. SMART holds a national rally each spring, regional rallies each fall, and local chapter rallies several times a year. For membership application, write to SMART Inc., 600 University Office Blvd., Suite 1A, Pensacola, FL 32504.

Ask what amenities you must bring to a cabin. Some rooms are fully stocked; others require your own soap and towels.

To access a central reservation center that books rooms at any Army installation in the world and gives travelers information about the area, call (800) GO-ARMY1. In Germany, call 01-30-81-7065; in Korea, 00-78-11-893-0828; in Italy, 16-78-70555. To make reservations at Navy Lodges worldwide, call (800) NAVYINN or (301) 654-1795.

of station) and accommodate vacationers only as first-come, first-served or standby. Some give particular guests priority over others. Some operate only during certain seasons. All have different policies on payment, pets, motorcycles and minibikes, quiet hours, cooking in cabins, open fires, allowable check-in hours, limits on stays, and firearms. Some sites are near areas with full support and provide hookups for trailers; others are isolated with limited or no amenities. Fees at all are minimal or pegged to rank.

Here is a small sampling of military R & R spots:

- *Alaska:* Birch Lake Recreation Area, 130 miles northeast of Denali National Park. Mountain fishing, hunting, and spectacular scenery.
- *Arizona:* Fort Tuthill Recreation Area, 4 miles north of Flagstaff. Tall pines, mild summer weather, winter skiing.
- *California:* Admiral Baker Field Campground, 4 miles northeast of San Diego. Caters to avid golfers.
  Castle Fam-Camp, 7 miles north of Merced. Close to Yosemite National Park, San Francisco, Kings Canyon National Park, and the foothills of the Sierra Nevada.
- *Colorado:* Farish Recreation Area at the Air Force Academy in Colorado Springs. Smack in the Rocky Mountains, surrounded by Pike National Forest and 15 miles north of Pikes Peak. Spectacular scenery, wildlife, fishing.
- *Florida:* Shades of Green, at the Walt Disney World Resort. This is the former Disney Inn, located across from the Grand Floridian.
- *Hawaii:* Hale Koa Hotel, right on Waikiki Beach in Honolulu. Views of the Pacific Ocean and Koolau Mountains. Rooms are air conditioned with private lanais and color TVs. There are landscaped gardens, pools, and lots of sports activities.
  Kaneohe Bay Beach Cottages and Campsites. Overlooks the magnificent Kaneohe Bay.
- *Massachusetts:* Hanscom Fam-Camp, 20 miles northwest of Boston. In a wooded area near the Concord Bridge and other Revolutionary War historical sites.

- *New Mexico:* Kirtland Fam-Camp, in Albuquerque. Near the Sandia and Manzano mountains.
- *New York:* Lakeshore Travel Park, 55 miles southeast of Rochester. On the shore of Seneca Lake, center of New York's Finger Lakes region. Magnificent hunting and fishing; wineries.
- *Tennessee:* Arnold Fam-Camp, 60 miles southeast of Nashville. Lots of recreational and historical sites nearby, such as the Jack Daniels Distillery in Lynchburg.
- *Wyoming:* Grant's Village, 154 miles northeast of Idaho Falls. Located in the middle of Yellowstone National Park, close to the spectacular Yellowstone Lake, Old Faithful geyser, the Grand Canyon of Yellowstone, Mammoth Hot Springs, Teton National Park, and Jackson Hole.

Additionally, you'll find facilities in Alabama, Arkansas, Georgia, Idaho, Illinois, Indiana, Kentucky, Louisiana, Maine, Maryland, Michigan, Mississippi, Missouri, Montana, Nebraska, Nevada, New Hampshire, New Jersey, North Carolina, North Dakota, Ohio, Oklahoma, Pennsylvania, Rhode Island, South Carolina, South Dakota, Texas, Utah, Virginia, Washington, West Virginia, and Wisconsin. For a complete list and contact numbers, see *Military RV, Camping and Recreational Areas around the World,* listed in this chapter's Further Reading section.

The government also maintains vacation spots in foreign countries. You'll find places to stay in Guam, Puerto Rico, Canada, Germany, Greece, Italy, Japan, and Korea. The following are particularly noteworthy:

- The Armed Forces Recreation Centers in Berchtesgaden, Chiemsee, and Garmisch, all located in the Alps.
- The Iraklion campground on the Greek island of Crete.
- The Admiral Carney Park in the port city of Naples.
- The Okuma Beach Resort in Okinawa, on the East China Sea.
- The Dragon Hill Lodge in Seoul.

Take a hop and enjoy!

≡ SATO Travel

Scheduled Airlines Travel Offices (SATO) were created in 1953 by the major U.S. airlines as a system for distributing airline tickets to DOD personnel traveling on official business. In 1970 it began handling the travel needs of other government agencies. It provides business and leisure travel services that include plane tickets, hotel and car rental reservations, cruises, tours, and custom-made vacation packages. There are more than

900 SATO offices and automated ticketing locations around the world. Because its business is to serve only Department of Defense military and civilian employees (including Reservists), it specializes in knowing all the government and military discounts that hotels, car-rental companies, and resorts offer. SATO also negotiates big savings with specific hotels and resorts that are available only to its customers.

Its biggest advantages to you are its enormous buying power and the noncompetitive nature of its organization. It is owned by eleven major airlines and represents them all equally, so unlike other travel agencies, SATO doesn't accept incentives from individual airlines; thus its agents have no reason to favor one airline over another or to hide a lower fare.

A Vacation Plus card is offered, which allows you to make monthly payments for tickets via payroll deduction.

≡ Property Disposal Sales

Do you like bargains? Then property disposal sales are for you. These sales, conducted as auctions, are open to the public and advertised in the base and local newspapers. They offer the chance to buy everything from electric typewriters, programmable calculators, furniture, and complete sets of the *Encyclopedia Britannica* to oddities like contaminated petri lab dishes and scrap metal by the ton. It's all government surplus. Items that are broken or obsolete, or that a unit has no further use for, are turned in to the property disposal office (PDO) and auctioned off. You are allowed to inspect the items a week before the auction, and you should always do so. You will occasionally find something that will appeal to you. Not everything is broken; some items are in perfect working order or just need minor

> When examining items offered at PDO sales, always inspect them the last day before the actual sale. Lots of people look at these items and poke and prod them. An appliance you tested and found working on Monday may not work on Friday, or parts may be missing.

repair. Auction is by closed bid; the highest bidder gets the item. Since PDO sales aren't restricted to ID-card holders, local merchants often buy items to repair and resell.

Similar to PDO sales are Defense Reutilization and Marketing Office (DRMO) sales. These offer an opportunity to buy quartermaster furniture (furniture the government provides for base housing), much of it in excellent condition, for next to nothing. Resale is not authorized here; the intent of these sales is to enable junior enlisted families to purchase good furniture at low prices for personal use. The DRMO also occasionally sponsors open-bid and spot-bid auctions of anything from copy machines to golf carts.

☰ Survivor Assistance Program

If an active-duty servicemember or a Reservist on active duty dies, both primary and secondary family members (or whomever the servicemember has listed on his emergency contact sheet) are notified. The family is assigned a survival assistance officer (SAO) or a casualty assistance calls officer (CACO) to help with funeral arrangements, transportation, child care, claims filing, and anything else you need. He'll handle as many of the burial arrangements as you wish. The Department of Defense will pay for burial expenses up to the limit allowed by law, and the servicemember may be buried with military honors in a national cemetery.

You'll receive the following benefits:

- A death gratuity of six months' base pay, up to the maximum allowed by law. This is an immediate payment to help survivors pay living expenses until they start receiving long-term benefits under the SBP and SGLI.
- All outstanding pay and allowances, including accrued leave, up to the maximum allowed by law.
- Servicemen's Group Life Insurance.
- Permission from the installation commander to remain in quarters, if you're currently living there, for 180 days.
- One-time transportation of you, your children, and your household goods to anywhere in the continental United States (this is not available to Reservist families). Overseas survivors of servicemembers who die on active duty are entitled to two government-paid moves. One is an interim move, to allow them time to decide where they wish to settle permanently. On an interim move the government will ship household goods but not unpack them. Property will be stored for up to one year.
- A wide range of college programs and other educational benefits for you and your children under the War Widows and Orphans Educational Assistance Act.
- Dependency and Indemnity Compensation, paid monthly to you and your unmarried children by the Department of Veterans Affairs until you remarry or they reach age eighteen (twenty-three if still in school). This is also paid to families of veterans who die of service-related causes.
- A Social Security lump sum payment and benefits.

Be aware that before the DVA and Social Security dispense their benefits, they examine each case to ascertain whether the servicemember died while actually performing military duties. This makes a difference in the money received.

If a Reservist dies while on inactive duty, his unit may furnish a ceremonial escort at his funeral.

≡ Family Services

As the numbers of married servicemembers rose, certain situations detrimental to military readiness occurred. Personal and family problems became more prevalent and affected servicemember job performance. Unit commanders were spending more and more time assisting with those problems. Many servicemembers who had considered the military a career left when the services couldn't help resolve the difficulties inherent in military life.

In response to this situation, organizations were set up to aid military families. Whatever name this organization takes where you are—Army Community Services, Navy Family Services, Air Force Family Support Center, Marine Family Services, or Coast Guard Mutual Assistance—the mission is to give help in both everyday living and crisis situations. They are typically open to Reservist families on a space-available basis. Reserve units have family support programs too. Contact the unit or the State Family Program Coordinator for information.

Military chaplains are a good source for counseling. They are accredited ministers who are serving on active duty, and they perform the same spiritual services as civilian ministers. They are insulated from the chain of command and will protect your confidences.

One of the best things I did as a new mother was enroll in a Family Services parenting class. Just a little knowledge of the child-development process gave me confidence and made parenting more fun than I ever imagined. And the tip swapping among the new mothers was tremendous—we were all there to learn and to share.

Family Services is provided by the military to make your life less stressful. The people who work in Family Services offices are trained civilians, military personnel, and volunteers. This section describes the core of programs provided at most duty stations. You'll be given a referral to a local civilian resource for anything Family Services can't help you with, and they'll later follow up to ensure that your needs have been met.

Special Needs

Any family member who has a physical, developmental, educational, or intellectual disorder that requires special treatment, therapy, education, counseling, or medical care is eligible for the Special Needs Program. Called the Exceptional Family Member Program in the Army, Air Force, and Marine Corps and Special Needs Families in the Navy, it is a liaison between the family and the systems that exist for support. Special Needs assists with respite care, transportation, and receiving treatment at medical facilities (medical and civilian), and provides recreational and cultural activities, family support groups, and individual support. The program also educates the servicemember on the family member's problems and discusses the rights and responsibilities entailed by being in this program.

Enrollment information is not given to promotion or school selection boards. A family member's enrollment in Special Needs is not grounds for a servicemember's deferment or consideration for special duties. It doesn't guarantee that a servicemember won't serve a tour unaccompanied by his family, nor does it guarantee he will always be able to travel with them during permanent-change-of-station moves. Special Needs personnel are primarily interested in making sure that handicapped family members aren't sent to places with inadequate facilities.

Additionally, the special education office of every State Department of Education has an advocate for children with special education needs. It can assist parents in finding services their children need. Write this office in care of the state capitol building.

Family Advocacy

The Family Advocacy Program is geared toward prevention and short-term treatment of physically abused or neglected family members. It provides individual and group counseling, crisis intervention, and grief counseling. A preventive education program, usually for servicemembers only, teaches how to identify and report suspected cases of abuse or neglect. Personal and family counseling are also offered. All these responsibilities are shared by chaplains, mental health personnel, and the hospital. Social workers work closely with commanders, and installation police and are on call twenty-four hours a day.

There is usually a separate office for child advocacy. If you feel in need, don't hesitate to use these offices. The staff is trained and can offer insights and solutions you may not have thought about.

Foster Care

The Foster Care Program works closely with the family advocacy office. Trained, supervised caregivers provide a temporary safe haven for physically abused or neglected children. They maintain their own lending closet to provide foster parents with extra clothes, bedding, toys, and food for the children.

Community Food Locker

The Community Food Locker will provide a free three-day supply of staples for emergency situations, such as money mismanagement, pay problems, or unplanned expenses. Typical staples are canned goods, dry milk, bread, meat, margarine, baby food, diapers, and formula. A referral from a social worker, commander, chaplain, financial counselor, or Family Services or Emergency Relief counselor is required before receiving food. Sometimes families will be referred to other agencies, such as Financial Planning, Emergency Relief, or local food stamp programs, to help correct the problem that led to the food shortage. The purpose is not to augment a family's pantry, but to help out in emergencies.

Consumer Affairs

At the consumer affairs office, you'll find one-on-one assistance with balancing your checkbook, developing a budget, and other financial matters. You don't have to be command-referred to take advantage of this excellent service. A consumer advocacy office that mediates problems between you and local businesses is usually operated, too.

Crisis Line

A crisis line is manned by trained volunteers supervised by a social worker. You decide what kinds of problems to take to the crisis line. A crisis is simply something you have no experience dealing with.

Relocation Office

People at the relocation office assist new and departing members of the community. If you're incoming, show them a copy of your husband's orders and they'll loan you household items to tide you over until your own things arrive. If you're leaving, you can borrow from the loan closet again and get a checklist of things to take care of and an information packet on the installation you're moving to. You can also get references to Realtors. The relocation office conducts sponsorship training seminars, provides sponsors with welcome packets to send to incoming personnel, and conducts newcomer and predeployment briefings.

Thrift Shop

Go to the thrift shop for low-cost items. Bookcases, sofa beds, vacuum cleaners, irons, plants, and baby items are just a sample of what you're likely to find. The thrift shop is a real hit-or-miss place; sometimes you'll find just trash, and sometimes there are great bargains. One wife loves to talk about the mink coat she bought for $100. If you go once and are unimpressed, try again another day. Someone about to make a permanent-change-of-station move might have brought in a load that contains just what you're looking for. Overseas, the thrift shop is the first place to check for transformers and 220V appliances from people who moved back to the States.

> Check the thrift shop regularly for baby items. They are an especially good buy because babies outgrow their clothing before they wear it out.

Bringing unwanted items to the thrift shop is an easy way to turn them into money. Low-priced, useful items sell very quickly. The thrift shop accepts items on consignment only and keeps a small percentage of the selling price, typically 20 percent of the purchase price. This compares favorably to private consignment shops, which generally keep 40 percent to 60 percent. You must reclaim any unsold items after the specified time on your contract, or they become the property of the thrift shop. Clothes with rips, stains, broken zippers, or frayed collars are not accepted, and toys and appliances must be in working order. Because of space constraints, there's a limit to how many items you may consign at one time, but these limits are greatly expanded if you're making a permanent-change-of-station move. Just bring your orders in as proof, along with a stamped, self-addressed envelope, and the shop will forward the proceeds to you.

Family Member Employment Assistance

At the family member employment assistance office, you'll find people who will help match your skills with advertised openings and assist in writing a résumé, cover letter, or Standard Form 171, the application for federal employment. They have advice for the prospective employee entering or reentering the job market, and because they're in constant contact with the installation civilian personnel office, the exchange, and civilian employers, they can pass on some good tips.

Volunteer Services

If you're interested in volunteering but aren't sure where, someone at Volunteer Services will show you descriptions of positions open at Family Services, the USO, Red Cross, and other worthy places and discuss which would fit your strengths, interests, and goals.

══ Emergency Aid

Army Emergency Relief, Air Force Aid, the Navy Relief Society, and Coast Guard Mutual Assistance are private organizations closely connected with the services but not officially part of them. The services give office space and pay salaries for one or two employees, but the money used for aid comes strictly from donations. Their mission is to provide financial assistance to servicemembers and families in special times of need.

Navy Relief provides even more for sailors and marines: It has nursing services for new mothers and homebound retirees; budget counseling; assistance with transportation and housing; and information on benefits, allowances, pensions, and government insurance. It assists in locating and communicating with Navy personnel and advises on local community resources. It also sponsors thrift shops, distributes infant layettes to needy families, and has waiting rooms where you can leave your children while at a doctor's appointment.

Aid offices also help family members directly as long as the family member has a general power of attorney given by the sponsor. (The Navy Relief Society does not require this to help family members.)

When you visit a relief office, bring all supporting evidence of need—for example, leave papers, Leave and Earnings Statements, payment books, auto repair estimates, and dental or medical bills. Each case is considered on its own merits, without publicity. When a need is proven, interest-free loans, loan and grant combinations, or outright grants are given.

Family members of prisoners and deserters are also eligible for assistance, but in these cases, aid is limited strictly to what is needed to avoid immediate privation, and it is available only until the servicemember is either given a discharge sentence or dropped from the rolls.

Emergency aid can be given in the following situations:

- Personal needs in case of nonreceipt or loss of pay.
- Emergency medical expenses.
- Travel expenses when emergency leave has been authorized.
- Expenses in meeting authorized port calls.
- Initial rent payments or payments to prevent eviction.
- Purchase of food if you have none and payday is a long way off.
- Utility deposits or payments to prevent service from being cut off.

- The expenses for a parent's funeral that the servicemember is required to pay or to help pay.
- Repairs to a servicemember's private vehicle, or transportation costs when the vehicle is essential for the unit mission.
- Essential medical or dental bills.
- Sudden expenses of an unexpected move.

As you can see, these are true emergencies. Money is not provided for ordinary leave, liberty, or vacations. It is not provided for divorce or marriage fees, civilian court fees, fines, bail, legal fees, bad-check fees, income taxes, or any other outstanding debts. Nor does car insurance or auto licensing count as an emergency. Finally, assistance will not be given on a continuing basis.

If you're in need after hours, try the Red Cross. If there's no relief office from your branch of service nearby, apply with the relief office of another's; they have reciprocal agreements. Don't be embarrassed to use these or any other Family Services offices. These organizations exist simply because there's a need for them.

The relief office system also has a very underused secondary program that provides scholarships between $500 and $1,500 to undergraduate college students who can prove need.

Other Resources

What else might you find at Family Services? Outreach programs, information on voting registration and food stamp eligibility, programs for foreign-born spouses and bicultural families, and lists of quarters-cleaning teams. There are classes on stress management, suicide prevention, family communication skills, budgeting, and parenting. Air Force families will find the Airman's Attic, which gives donated clothes, kitchen utensils, furniture, and other items to married E-4s and below. Visit the Family Services center; chances are you'll find something you can take advantage of. And it's always smart to learn what is available before you actually need it.

The Red Cross

In the 1860s a Swiss businessman walked the battlefields of Solferino, Italy, and surveyed the French and Austrian soldiers lying there. Believing that all wounded soldiers should receive aid no matter what their allegiance, he founded what was to become the Red Cross.

Today the Red Cross is a giant humanitarian organization that ministers to victims of natural calamity, poor health, and war. More than

I work for the Red Cross in Germany. We make a special effort to reach out to non-command-sponsored spouses, because they're often isolated. Once we got a call from a young wife with a sick baby. Her husband was away, and she couldn't get to the hospital. One of our volunteers drove her to the emergency room, waited while she got a prescription filled, and took her back home. She was grateful for the service, and we were grateful for the opportunity to show that we care.

100 countries belong to the League of Red Cross Societies. The International Red Cross remains an autonomous organization run by Swiss businessmen. It has two missions: to be the initiating relief agency for victims of natural disaster and to act as a liaison between the civilian and military populations. The American Red Cross, founded in 1881, staffs 277 stateside and overseas military installations and is linked to every Navy ship at sea.

The Red Cross offers classes in first aid, CPR, lifesaving, swimming, boating, baby care, and many other areas, similar to those Family Services offers. There are situations in which both Family Services and the Red Cross can help, and situations in which one can help but not the other. The following Red Cross services are particularly relevant to military families:

- Individual, personal, and family counseling and guidance.
- Answers to legal, medical, family, and child welfare questions.
- Communication between a servicemember and family for emergencies and birth announcements.
- Verification of emergency leave to military authorities.
- Help in gathering documents necessary for compassionate reassignments, deferments, and hardship discharges.
- Emergency financial assistance (interest-free loans or grants).
- Services to patients in military hospitals.
- Overseas recreation.
- Services to veterans.
- Quick communication home for family emergencies.
- Assistance in applying for governmental benefits.
- Training volunteers for work at military hospitals and dental clinics.

The United Services Organization (USO)

The USO was formed in 1941 when President Franklin D. Roosevelt asked private organizations to provide leisure activities for the troops who were preparing for World War II. Six nonprofit agencies—the Salvation Army, the YMCA, the National Catholic Community Services, the National Traveler's Aid Association, and the National Jewish Welfare Board—pooled their resources and formed the USO. In 1979 it became an independent organization.

The USO is not just for servicemembers, but is a resource for family members, too. The USO is a private, nonprofit organization that provides a vehicle for civilian volunteers to serve the spiritual, social, welfare, and educational needs of the armed forces and enhance the quality of military life. The USO operates stations all over the world and has about 500 paid staff members and 20,000 volunteers.

USOs provide information about the base and the local civilian community. They sponsor job fairs, scholarships, trips, tours, and community-involvement programs and will make reservations at local hotels for servicemembers and their families. You will also often find mailing services, laundry facilities, game rooms, recreation programs, telephones, temporary sleep areas, refreshment stands, and gift shops. Classes, family assistance groups, and self-help forums provide you with opportunities to learn and to make new friends. Some even maintain lists of baby-sitters. The New Mothers Program sends, on request, a trained outreach worker to visit a new mother, bring gifts, and answer questions.

There is also an outreach program for newly arrived spouses in foreign countries. The USO often offers orientation tours (with baby-sitting and lunch usually provided), information on train and bus schedules, currency exchanges, translation services, intercultural understanding programs, and programs to help people with the foreign economy. And, of course, there are the famous celebrity tours for servicemembers in remote locations and VA hospitals.

The USO operates lounges exclusively for service families at major airports where they can relax, while away the time, even sleep between flights. They are located in these commercial airports: Saint Louis; Charleston, South Carolina; Philadelphia; Seattle-Tacoma; Baltimore; Kennedy, in New York; San Diego; Los Angeles; Oakland; and San Francisco. Typical amenities are refreshments, TVs, videotapes, a library, a sleeping area, a nursery, a play area, and a worldwide military phone service.

≡ The Armed Forces YMCA

The Armed Forces YMCA is a social service agency that focuses heavily on junior enlisted families. It offers outreach programs in which trained volunteers visit families in civilian apartments, trailer parks, and other hard-to-reach areas and offer counseling on parenting and money management, and help with other difficulties they may be experiencing. The YMCA supplements military services, so what it offers varies from base to base. Typical programs include shuttle buses to the commissary and exchange, English as a second language classes, and recreational activities for young, first-time servicemembers. Most programs are free.

☰ Volunteers

A chapter on organizations and services would not be complete without some words about the people responsible for making them work: the volunteers. It is the willingness of people to give of themselves—not for money, but simply to help make the world a better place—that makes social programs work. Government alone does not and cannot do it all. Through volunteering you can make another person's life happier and more meaningful. You can make it a little more bearable or comfortable, maybe less desperate or hopeless. Charitable and social service agencies could not function without volunteers. Even organizations that use volunteer help strictly as a supplement can't function as well as they'd like to without it. Volunteers provide the "extras" for which there will never be enough paid staff, and without volunteers, programs like the crisis line, instructional classes, and many youth activities would simply not exist.

Volunteers have helped the previously unemployable, such as former prison inmates and inner-city youth, get jobs by teaching them skills, tutoring them for General Equivalency Diplomas, accompanying them to interviews, and giving them pep talks along the way. Some have even stood by their sides at the job for the first few weeks. Most political workers are volunteers, grass-roots campaigners that pass out information and offer rides to the polls. A great many YMCA and YWCA programs are staffed with volunteer labor. Scout troops? Entirely volunteer. The thrift shop? Entirely volunteer. The USO and Red Cross? Almost all volunteer, operating with donated money. Churches, the Humane Society, senior citizens' centers, Little League, the United Way, and Big Brother and Big Sister programs are just a few of the many important organizations that rely on volunteers.

Many people with full-time jobs and kids still find time to volunteer. Here are some of their comments:

"I have two small babies, so an outside job is out. My husband went away to school once for nine whole months. I don't have many friends here, and I'd spend all day in our apartment with the children. After three months I couldn't stand it anymore. Working at the thrift shop turned out to be just the

thing. They provided free baby-sitting; I met people and had things to write to my husband about. And there was a terrific fringe benefit: Since I saw consignments as they came in, I got first pick! Got some great baby things that way!"

—Army Wife, eighteen

"I tried for a year to get a job and couldn't. So I decided to volunteer at my son's elementary school. I wasn't there for more than two months when they offered me a job as a teacher's aide. Naturally, I took it. What a break! I don't know why I didn't do it sooner."

—Air Force wife, twenty-four

"My husband is always attending schools. He loves them and talks about what he learns all the time. I don't work and never went to college. I use volunteering to learn new things myself and sort of keep up with him."

—Marine wife, twenty-two

"Everyone at the senior citizens' center says I do such good work for them. I love to hear them say this, but actually my motives are selfish. Visiting elderly people, helping them write letters, knowing I'm needed gives me the emotional rewards I don't get from my paying job."

—Coast Guard wife, thirty

"I took two months of maternity leave before I had my baby, and I used the time to volunteer at the base child-care center. That way, I was able to check out its quality firsthand. This made me feel a lot better about leaving my child there when I returned to work."

—Army wife, twenty-six

"Volunteering helped keep my energy up in a positive environment when I was job hunting and the hunt wasn't going well."

—Army husband, twenty-nine

"Before I started volunteering at the hospital, I used to wonder why it sometimes took so long to get appointments or get prescriptions filled or why inpatients often had to get their food from carts in the hall instead of having it brought to them. I came to realize it's because military hospitals never really have the amount of staff they need. Doctors must run down lab reports and do their own typing. Nurses have to answer phones, type notes, escort patients, chaperone during exams, and follow up lab studies. Volunteering sure helped out in areas like those."

—Air Force wife, twenty-eight

"My church group does a lot of volunteer stuff for handicapped people. One day I went out with them to a home. I read a book to a blind man there. You know, blind people don't care if you're white, black, ugly, or good-looking. They're just so happy to have you read. They ask you when you're coming back."

—ARMY COLONEL'S SON, TWELVE

"When military people take an active interest and involvement in the civilian community, we're perceived as a valuable part of it. Involvement with civilian groups provides stabilized friendships and opportunities not available on base. Besides, by keeping contact with civilian society, you're better prepared when you rejoin it."

—NAVY WIFE, THIRTY-SIX

A person who gives even two hours a week makes herself part of the solution instead of part of the problem. You'll find volunteers teaching crafts to kids and comparison shopping to adults. You'll find them serving as directors of the Red Cross, as newspaper publishers, and as public relations personnel. Can you answer a telephone? Can you listen to problems? Can you type, translate, file, phone the homebound, take kids to a ball game? Can you fix toys, play games, take photographs? Then you can volunteer. Can you sew, knit, crochet, arrange flowers, talk, shop for groceries or operate a ham radio? Then you can volunteer. Volunteer duties range from the routine to the professional. Some volunteer slots have job descriptions and accompanying qualification requirements. Programs exist to recruit, train, and supervise volunteers and to recognize good work. Volunteers are limited only by their imagination and that of the organization using them. During Operation Desert Storm, volunteers served in the Army Family Liaison Office in the Pentagon as telephone operators, information specialists, case workers, data collectors, and resource developers.

Volunteering can help people who have lots of education but little experience. Many volunteers have successfully used their experience to land a paying job; places that give credit on job applications for volunteer work include the federal government, TRW, United Airlines, Atlantic Richfield, AT&T, Coca-Cola, Levi Strauss, Avon, Sterling Drug, Union Carbide, Bell & Howell, American Can, and Transamerica.

Some payments are made for jobs that are officially recognized as liaisons between families and commands, such as Navy ombudsmen and Army mayors. They're also made for volunteers at Family Service centers and museums. And Congress has authorized base commanders to reimburse volunteers for related expenses out of taxpayer funds. Certain unreimbursed expenses may be tax-deductible. Write for the *Volunteer Expense Fact Sheet* from the Army Family Liaison Office, HDQA (DAPE-ZAF), Attn.: Volunteer Coordinator, Washington, DC 20310-0300.

Military installations are self-contained societies that operate virtually independent of their nearby civilian communities. They're towns in themselves! Take a walk around your "town" and see what's there. Use the facilities; take advantage of their low costs. Voice any suggestions you have for improving them. They are your facilities; they are here for you.

≡ Further Reading

Crawford, Ann, and Roy Crawford. *Military RV, Camping and Recreational Areas around the World.* Falls Church, VA: Military Living Publications, 1994.
———— *Temporary Military Lodging around the World.* Falls Church, VA: Military Living Publications, 1994.

4

≣ Socials and Protocol

You have just been invited to your first coffee. What should you wear and what should you take? What should you say to the people there? Why should you even go?

Every military wife has asked herself these questions when she received that first invitation, whether it was for a coffee, a welcome luncheon for the sergeant major's wife, or a formal dinner for the out-going general. And there is the question of *protocol:* What is it and how much do you need to know of it for the event you'll be attending?

≣ What Is Protocol?

The State Department defines *protocol* as the "rule book by which international relations are conducted, which aims to create an atmosphere of friendliness in which the business of diplomacy may be transacted." It is the practice of customs that define who does what first, where, and when.

Simply put, protocol is military etiquette. But what it really means is just *good manners.* Before you agonize over whom you should introduce to whom first, what to serve at a coffee, when to stand up and face the flag, or how many calling cards to leave

> I like to think that protocol courtesy is extended to the spouses because spousal support is part of service strength. A man's success is to no small degree a result of his wife's support.

in the host's tray, know that it is far better to do the wrong thing graciously than the right thing rudely or poorly. Protocol is more common sense and a pleasant attitude than anything else.

In today's military, affairs are not as formal as they once were. Nevertheless, the protocol and customs that remain have the same purpose they've always had, which is to create order. As a certain diplomat once observed, "We all can't go through the door at the same time." Protocol is not intended to promote snobbery; it is a courtesy designed to recognize official status and give respect to those who, by their achievements, time in service, and experience, deserve it. And the exercise of that most certainly extends to spouses.

> When overseas, learn the customs and protocol of the host citizens. For instance, women in Saudi Arabia cover their arms when outside, and everyone removes his or her shoes before entering a house in Japan.

Back to the woman who has received her first invitation to a coffee. Does she *have* to attend? Certainly not. But there are many reasons she might *want* to.

≡ Importance of Social Functions

We in the military are a transient people. We spend a great portion of our lives separated from our parents, siblings, and other relatives. Moving to a new town is stressful. Sometimes the permanent residents stick together and are disinclined to be welcoming.

Through social gatherings, we are offered the chance to make new friends, people who are in the same situation and who know our unique needs and stresses. They can help ease the isolated feelings many wives get when arriving at a new duty station. Social gatherings are an easy way to make friends because the people attending are often there for that reason, too. They can offer tips on where to shop, tell which employers are hiring, give pointers on day-care centers and baby-sitters, and inform you

> If you want to entertain, entertain! It makes no difference whether you live in a palace with Louis XVI furniture or government quarters with secondhand furniture. Your hospitality is more important than your table service.

about church activities and youth groups. And when you have gotten to know them, you will feel easier about asking them for help when you need it. This is particularly important when your husband is away.

Now what about "command performances"—affairs our husbands are *told* to attend?

Social affairs in the service have their roots in tradition. They are intended to promote camaraderie and esprit de corps. They enable servicemembers to get to know one another outside the workplace. Social affairs promote unity. If a commander sees that people in his unit know nothing about one another and are uninterested in socializing with one another, he sees a need for unity. If his unit is ever called upon to fight, that sense of unity will be critical. Although your attendance is not mandatory, it does make the affair more fun and it shows your support for the unit and its mission. Affairs are as lively and interesting as the people who attend them.

Some wives choose not to participate in military social affairs for personal reasons. Your involvement is your choice. But don't let a lack of self-confidence be the reason keeping you away. How are you ever going to develop that confidence if you never go? Don't worry about making mistakes; the only people who never make mistakes are people who never do anything.

≡ General Guidelines
═ Some Tips

- Don't call an older woman by her first name unless she invites you to do so. When speaking directly to her husband, always use his title, no matter how informal the occasion.
- Don't discuss your medical problems with doctors, your legal problems with lawyers, or your quarters problems with the head of the housing office at social affairs. They want some time off, too. Discuss these things in the proper places and during office hours.
- Don't refer to yourself and your husband collectively as "we're sergeants" or "we're lieutenants" unless, of course, you both really are sergeants or lieutenants.
- Avoid discussing controversial or sensitive subjects at socials.

═ Invitations

When an invitation includes RSVP, which stands for the French phrase *Répondez s'il vous plaît* (Please respond), do answer the invitation. The hostess needs to know how much food to buy and how many chairs to borrow. No person is so busy she can't find three minutes for a phone call. Furthermore, when the RSVP reads "regrets only" and you don't plan to go, not calling shows an especial contempt for the invitation.

When writing invitations to your own affairs, the preprinted kind, with the information handwritten, is the most correct. The photocopied version has made its way into invitation protocol, however, and

Please Join Col. and Mrs. O'Brien in a reception to celebrate the New Year.

Where: Drake House, Ft. Campbell

When: Jan. 5

Time: 4 p.m.

RSVP: 555-8500

Dress: Semiformal

Join Us For Our
Halloween Coffee!

Linda Johnson's Place
Quarters 101
Altus Air Base
Oct. 9, 7:00 p.m.

RSVP 555-4192

*It's our Christmas coffee!
Bring a gift to swap! Dec. 12, 6:30, at Tara
Holbrook's house, 1820 Magnolia Lane,
Jacksonville. Regrets only, 555-7821*

Invitations prepared using a personal computer.

looks as though it is here to stay. Many women have personal computers and do clever layouts on them. Even if you don't own a computer, you can produce attractive invitations with calligraphy or some rub-on letters, and a little imagination.

Thank-You Notes

Always send a written thank-you, addressed to the hostess, after attending an affair in a supervisor's or commander's home, in addition to the thanks you give them as you leave. You can do this on a preprinted thank-you card or on personal stationery. You should also send written thank-yous to people who give you baby shower presents, invite you to dinner, or do something special for you.

Introductions

At any affair you attend, make a point of introducing yourself to the senior people there. It is a wonderful courtesy—protocol at its finest. So often luncheons and welcome coffees are great successes in terms of attendees, food, and gaiety but absolute failures in that most guests never meet the people the event was for. Introduce yourself to the senior woman and to her husband, if he is there; both will be delighted.

You're going to be introducing people to each other for the rest of your life. Here is the correct way to do it:

- A man is presented to a woman (but junior female servicemembers are presented to senior male servicemembers).
- The honored or higher-ranking person's name is stated first, then the name of the person being presented.
- Young people are presented to older people of the same sex.
- A single person is introduced to a group.
- A man rises if seated. A woman doesn't, unless she's being presented to an older woman or the wife of a senior official. She should remain standing until the other is seated. She doesn't rise if being presented to another woman about her own age.
- A woman should extend her hand to a man.

Here are some examples:

"Major Seymour, this is my sister Norma."

"Mrs. Awana, may I present Tae-Won."

"Everyone . . . I'd like you to meet Cindy Barba. Why don't you all go around and introduce yourselves?"

"First Sergeant, this is Specialist Nelson. Specialist Nelson, First Sergeant Lunn."

If you feel uneasy about military etiquette, read some of the books listed at the end of this chapter. Also, study people around you. Whose mannerisms do you admire? Who seems especially poised? Just use common sense, and eventually your own style will develop as your familiarity with social affairs grows.

☰ The Main Social Functions

How to Address Military Personnel

Army, Air Force, Marine Corps

Title	In Person	In Writing
General	General	Gen.
Lieutenant General	General	Lt. Gen.
Major General	General	Maj. Gen.
Brigadier General	General	Brig. Gen.
Colonel	Colonel	Col.
Lieutenant Colonel	Colonel	Lt. Col.
Major	Major	Maj.
Captain	Captain	Cpt.
First Lieutenant	Lieutenant	1 Lt.
Second Lieutenant	Lieutenant	2 Lt.
Chief Warrant Officer	Chief, Mr., or Ms.	CWO2, CWO3, CWO4
Warrant Officer	Mr. or Ms.	WO1
Cadet	Cadet	Mr. or Ms.
Chaplain	Chaplain	Rank (Ch.)
Doctor	Doctor	Rank (Dr.)
Sergeant Major	Sergeant Major	Sgt. Maj.
Chief Master Sergeant	Chief	Chief MSgt.
First Sergeant	First Sergeant	1 Sgt.
Master Sergeant	Master Sergeant	MSgt.
Gunnery Sergeant	Gunnery Sergeant	GySgt.
Staff Sergeant	Sergeant	SSgt.
Technical Sergeant	Sergeant	TSgt.
Sergeant	Sergeant	Sgt.
Specialist	Specialist	Spec.
Corporal	Corporal	Cpl.
Private First Class	Private	Pfc.
Private	Private	Pvt.
Airman First Class	Airman	A1C
Airman	Airman	Airman

Note: Officers are addressed by their titles and last names.
Doctors and chaplains are "doctor" and "chaplain" unless a lieutenant colonel or above; then use the military rank.

═══ **Coffees**

Coffees, or meetings, are the most traditional of military wives' socials. They are monthly forums in which spouses get together to socialize, coordinate activities, and discuss community information.

A well-run coffee starts no later than half an hour after the stated time on the invitation. The

As a battery commander's wife, I organize coffees for the unit spouses. Getting a good group started can be hard. Some tips: Find out what the unit spouses need and want in a group. Read the Navy Wifeline ← Association's booklet on support groups, available by calling (202) 433-6565. Also read Army pamphlet 608-47, *A Guide to Establishing Family Support Groups,* available from Army Community Services.

Navy and Coast Guard

Title	In Person	In Writing
Fleet Admiral (Navy only)	Admiral	FADM
Admiral	Admiral	ADM
Vice Admiral	Admiral	VADM
Rear Admiral	Admiral	RADM
Commodore	Commodore	COMO
Captain	Captain	Cpt.
Commander	Commander	Cmdr.
Lieutenant Commander	Mr. or Ms.	LtCmdr.
Lieutenant	Mr. or Ms.	Lt.
Lieutenant Junior Grade	Mr. or Ms.	LtJG
Ensign	Mr. or Ms.	Ens.
Chief Warrant Officer	Mr. or Ms.	CWO2, CWO3, CWO4
Warrant Officer	Mr. or Ms.	WO1
Doctor	Doctor	Rank (Dr.)
Chaplain	Chaplain	Rank (Ch.)
Cadet	Cadet	Mr. or Ms.
Midshipman	Mr. or Ms.	Mr. or Ms.
Master Chief Petty Officer	Master Chief	MCPO
Senior Chief Petty Officer	Senior Chief	SCPO
Chief Petty Officer	Chief	CPO
Petty Officer First Class	Petty Officer	PO-1
Petty Officer Second Class	Petty Officer	PO-2
Petty Officer Third Class	Petty Officer	PO-3
General Apprentice	Seaman	____
Recruit	Seaman	____

Note: Officers and petty officers are addressed by their titles and last names. Doctors and chaplains are addressed "doctor" and "chaplain" unless a captain or above, then their military rank is used.
A general apprentice is addressed "seaman," "fireman," "airman," "stewardsman," and so on as appropriate.

Most of the people I know who disparage coffees as "hen parties" have never even been to one. And, sadly, they are usually the same ones with the greatest need for the social interaction and information the coffees provide.

If you can't find the perfect outfit to wear to an affair, put on something less than perfect and go anyway. You'll be in good company—no one else has the perfect outfit either. Your hosts would rather you show up in your less-than-perfect outfit than not at all.

Q: We just moved to a new base and I'd like to attend the socials, but I don't know any baby-sitters. Where can I find some?

A: You can get referrals from friends and neighbors; other wives in the unit; day-care centers; the Family Services office; newspaper ads; senior citizens' groups; the Red Cross and USO; job placement centers of high schools and colleges; churches; and Boy and Girl Scout leaders.

A great dish to serve at a coffee is fruit salad made of fresh watermelon, pineapple, apples, and pears, served in the scooped-out watermelon shell. Also good are raw vegetables and dip. If you are short on preparation time, you can buy a platter of cold cuts and cheese from your commissary or supermarket deli. Serve it with pickles and chips. Take-out pizza or big bowls of popcorn are always a hit. Iced tea and soft drinks are nice; in fact, they usually go over better than the coffee.

---

senior officer's or NCO's spouse will have information on things particular to that base, such as commissary hours and hospital regulations. She often has new information to impart, such as changes in those hours or regulations, upcoming activities and events, which organizations are seeking volunteers, and so on. Many groups even have the delightful practice of inviting a person from the local community to give a talk or demonstration. Fund-raising ideas are discussed; the money is used to sponsor activities such as children's egg hunts at Easter, Santa at Christmas, and parties and picnics. If you get a phone call from an active member of a wives' group asking to donate baked goods or other items for a fund-raising effort, know that they're trying to get all the support they can so their fund-raiser—*your* fund-raiser—will be a success.

A hostess often gives the invitations to her husband to distribute to his coworkers, who in turn bring them home to their spouses. Or should! While this works most of the time, some women never seem to get theirs. If you never receive invitations to anything, check with your husband. If you feel the present method of disseminating information is poor, bring it up with the other wives. Suggest a telephone tree where the hostess telephones the information to four or five women, and they in turn telephone the rest of the wives. Then volunteer to be one of the four or five women.

Unless the coffee is a potluck, don't bring anything; it is the hostess's responsibility to provide food for her guests. And unless you have a very good reason, arriving late is not polite. Neither is arriving early; the hostess may not be ready for you.

Here are tips for when it's your turn to host a coffee:

- Many hostesses serve the traditional sweet desserts as refreshment, but such treats often go uneaten. Low-calorie choices are usually a lot more popular. As a general rule, hors d'oeuvres are most appropriate.
- Always extend invitations to the women servicemembers in the unit. Many of them enjoy coffees and do attend. Don't forget the male spouses, either. Many of them want to be included but are self-conscious and need a little encouragement.
- Some groups raffle off a door prize each month. A prize between $5 and $10 is standard, and tickets are usually 50¢ to $1 each. Small plants or flowers make great gifts, and it is a special surprise

When hosting a coffee, don't spend hours cleaning your bathroom and removing fingerprints from the windows. It's neither necessary nor important. Put your energies into seeing that your coffee is well planned and well run. No one cares whether your toilet sparkles!

Try setting a theme for coffee, such as a "margarita night," where drinks and Mexican food are served. (You can double up with another wife to share expenses.) Or have a potluck, a cookie exchange, a "recipe night," a "build-your-own-potato night," or a "hero-sandwich night." Try a "mystery gift night," where everyone brings an inexpensive wrapped gift and auctions it off. The money goes into the wives' fund. Try a "wok night," where each wife brings a prechopped ingredient, like celery, green peppers, onions, water chestnuts, carrots, tomatoes, sausage, beef, or chicken, to be cooked at the table in a wok or electric frying pan. Or how about meeting at a local restaurant for dinner? (Everyone pays their own way, of course!)

Invite speakers to your coffee, for example, the unit doctor or chaplain, someone from the commercial solicitation office to discuss ways to protect yourselves against unscrupulous vendors, a cosmetician or hairdresser from a local salon, a commissary officer, or a home decorator. Local businesses are often willing to send someone to speak.

when the plant or flower has been on the coffee table all evening and the hostess invites the winner to take it. Stationery, knickknack boxes, humorous coffee mugs, and recipe boxes are also well received.

Proper Dress for Spouses

Event	Dress
Coffees	Casual or informal
Teas	Semiformal
Hails and farewells	Informal
Receptions	Semiformal
Banquets	Formal
Cocktail parties	Semiformal
Barbecues and other casual outdoor affairs	Casual
Open houses (before 6 P.M.)	Semiformal
Parades and change-of-command ceremonies	Informal
Graduations	Informal or semiformal

Type of Occasion	Dress	
	Women	Men
Casual	Something like khaki slacks and a polo shirt, a blouse and skirt, or leggings and a sweater. Not cutoffs and a tube top!	Sport coat, no tie.
Informal	Something you'd wear to a nice restaurant. If you wouldn't wear it there because it's too dressy or not dressy enough, it's probably not appropriate here.	Conservative slacks and sports jacket or sweater. Tie optional.
Semiformal	Fancier than informal. Could be a nice suit or cocktail dress.	Conservative slacks and sports jacket or sweater. Tie.
Formal	Long gown or tea-length dress, super-dressy cocktail suit, a luxury coat if you have one.	Dark, conservative suit and tie, dinner jacket, or tuxedo.

- Don't spend all your time with your best buddy, even if you haven't seen her in three months. It's your responsibility to see that everyone is mingling and having a good time and that the newcomers are introduced around and drawn into a group. If the first coffee a newcomer attends turns out to be a bad experience for her, she might not attend any more.

- Don't have your coffee in conjunction with a baby shower. Both events are time-consuming, and the combination makes for a very long evening indeed. It also pressures women who just want to attend a coffee to bring a present.

Teas

Teas are late-afternoon affairs, usually held to honor an incoming or outgoing wife of a high-ranking commander. But sometimes they're held just so the wives of different units in the same command can meet one another. Teas are elegant, dressy affairs, usually held at the base club or in a local hotel that has a large social room. Finger foods are served, and seating is not pre-arranged. Often there is a piano or harp player.

> Don't be afraid to call the hostess to ask what to wear or to bring, or about protocols for the event. You're not displaying ignorance, you're displaying a desire to do right. Besides, protocol is flexible. What is popular for D.C. may not be for the Deep South.

A tea usually lasts about two hours. If it's being held in honor of an outgoing woman, a gift is presented and a small speech made. If it's in honor of an incoming woman, be sure to introduce yourself to her; she'll appreciate it.

Hails and Farewells

Before World War II, when the services were much smaller, it was the custom for a new officer or NCO and his wife to pay a social call at the home of his superior. The superior and his wife then later returned the call. When the couple left, a social was held for them.

In today's service, with more than 2 million members, you can see how that could be impractical. So this charming custom has been replaced with the hail and farewell, the modern equivalent of all calls made and received. It is held about every two months or at whatever interval is necessary to accommodate the turnover of people.

> A function you should never miss is your husband's own promotion ceremony!

A hail and farewell usually takes the form of a dinner at a restaurant. Dress is informal (depending on the restaurant). After dinner, speeches are made. People leaving receive a going-away gift, usually an inscribed plaque, mug, or article special to the unit. These are paid for out of a fund to which everyone contributes. Newcomers are then welcomed.

Attendance at such an affair shows respect for the people leaving and gives a warm welcome to those coming in. For this reason, the service-member's attendance is usually required. These socials are good opportunities to see your friends and make a few new ones.

Receptions

In the "old days" it was the custom for an officer or NCO new to a post to pay a social call to his superior on holidays, a call that was later returned. Like the hail and farewell, receptions now serve as the equivalent of all holiday calls made and received. They are held for holidays, in honor of someone, such as for a promotion or a retirement, or for a special occasion, such as the christening or commissioning of a ship.

Receptions can be held in the afternoon or evening and may be formal or informal. Those that start after 6:00 P.M. are always formal.

At the beginning of the reception you will have to go through a receiving line. This is the official "calls made and received" portion of the event, and probably the only aspect of military life that never gets easier with practice! The receiving line consists of the host, hostess, various important guests, visitors, and the guest of honor, if there is one. The spouse goes first in the Army, Navy, and Marine Corps; in the Air Force, the servicemember goes first.

Receiving lines are not the place for conversation. When your turn comes, smile, extend your hand, greet the first person by name, introduce yourself, and say, "How do you do? Lovely afternoon/evening/dress," then move on to the next. Don't rack your brain trying to think up some clever small talk that the folks in the line haven't already heard—they've heard it all.

Sometimes there will be an aide at the beginning of the line to introduce you to the host. You don't shake hands with the aide. If you're wearing gloves, it's not necessary to remove them when you go through the line, but leave your cigarette or drink behind.

By the way, if you prefer to have a soft drink during the cocktail hour, that's perfectly all right. Don't feel obliged to drink alcohol at any affair. It's neither required nor even particularly encouraged.

Receptions for individual units are held in the commander's home. The invitation to an affair of this nature will often state a specific time frame. Punctuality is critical, since all units under that commander will arrive at and remain until their designated times. The reception line here consists of the commander and his wife, who stand at the doorway and greet everyone when the appointed time for that unit arrives.

Banquets

Banquets, or formal dinners, are held for special holidays like Christmas or special occasions like the field artillery's St. Barbara's Day Ball. They are often held in conjunction with receptions and present an opportunity to dress up in your finest, enjoy an elaborate meal, and dance afterward. The Posting of the Colors ceremony is usually performed, and toasts are made. Seating is prearranged, with name cards to indicate locations. Look to the people at the head table for guidance about when you should toast and when you should stand, sit, eat, and anything else you might be wondering about. Etiquette and table manners are no different here than they are anywhere else. Talk to people around you. Do your part to make the evening a success.

After the meal, a waiter will probably come by to light the candle on your table. This is a remnant from the old tradition of lighting the after-dinner smoking lantern that indicated it was now permissible to smoke. Here's a contemporary word about smoking at the table, however: Don't. If you must have a cigarette, go to the lobby.

Flags that are carried on foot are called *colors*. Flags mounted on vehicles are *standards,* and flags on ships are *ensigns.* Flags are half *mast* in the Navy, half *staff* in the other services. During the Posting of the Colors ceremony, stand when they are six paces before you and remain standing until they pass six paces behind you.

Q: What are reveille and retreat, and what do I do during them?

A: Reveille (REH-vuh-lee), or morning colors, is the name of the bugle call that accompanies the daily ritual of raising the American flag, signaling the start of the day. Retreat, or evening colors, is the evening lowering and folding of the flag into a star-topped triangle, signaling the end of the day. It is accompanied by the bugle call "To the Colors." Both are played over the amplifier system that has replaced the lone bugler of old.

If you're outdoors on a military base during retreat, stand quietly in the direction of the music, hold your right hand over your heart (military members hold a salute), and wait for the call to be finished. If you're driving, get out and stand the same way. If on a ship, stand facing the flag.

Change-of-Command Ceremony

This ceremony is held to represent the passing of command from one commander to another. Depending on how large the unit and high-ranking the commander, the ceremony may be either a large, elaborate affair with hundreds of people attendant or a small one with just a few dozen. The flag is passed from the outgoing commander to the incoming one, while the people under his command stand at attention. Visitors watch from chairs on the sidelines. Flowers are often presented to the commanders' spouses.

Aboard Ship

The Navy offers a lifestyle unique in many ways from that of its sister services. One of the things that sets it apart is the custom of having some social affairs aboard ship. While the same rules of dress—casual, informal, and formal—that apply to socials ashore apply here, keep in mind that you'll be climbing steep ladders, walking drafty passageways, and stooping to get through short hatches before you get to your final destination. Therefore, low-heeled or rubber-soled shoes and slacks, if appropriate, will serve you best; bring a sweater for that breezy deck and a purse with a shoulder strap.

> Even if you don't wish to participate in socials, know the people in your Family Support Group. They're a great information source for questions such as "When will the ship arrive?" and "How do I contact my husband while he's at sea?"

If the ship is moored, you'll enter it by walking down the pier and along the gangway, in front of your husband. But if it's anchored in the harbor, you'll ride a motorboat to it. Motorboats leave on a regular schedule from the fleet landing. The stern seat, considered the "seat of honor," should be left for the senior woman. When you step onto the quarterdeck, introduce yourself to the officer of the deck. If your husband has not accompanied you aboard and is unable to meet you, an escort to the wardroom will be provided.

Every rule regarding manners and propriety that applies to shore applies here, plus a few more. Don't come aboard ship without an invitation, and when you do come, leave Fido at home. When you are aboard, remember that you are in the single sailors' home and act accordingly. *Never* wander about unescorted; many areas are restricted. Remove your hat if you're wearing one, and don't smoke unless you specifically ask and are granted permission.

> **Q:** Why are Navy promotion parties called "wetting downs"?
> **A:** Wetting downs got their name from the tradition of pouring salt water over the new stripe to make it match the old, tarnished ones. Today a whole new set is sewn on, however, as tarnished stripes are considered shabby.

Alcohol is not served aboard ship, being against Navy regulations. Don't bring a camera aboard unless you've been given permission.

You'll probably want to visit your husband aboard ship when he has duty. That's fine, but since sailors consider one person's guest to be everyone's guest, you will wear out your welcome if you do it too often.

Coffees, hails and farewells, receptions, teas, and banquets are but the main types of social affairs encountered in military life. There are many more affairs common to all services, to only one service, and even just to a particular branch of that service. There are MASH parties for hospital staffs, all-hands parties, potlucks, promotion parties (or "wetting downs" in the Navy), commissioning ceremonies, the Air Force Birthday Ball, the Marine Corps Birthday Ball, and parades. There are dinings-in and dinings-out, luncheons, and brunches. Customs vary from base to base, so when in doubt, just follow the lead of the senior people there.

Of course, there are also unofficial parties and social gatherings that go on among friends. If you meet people at an affair and would like to get to know them better, invite them to dinner. When you accept an invitation to dinner at someone's house, you owe them one to yours. It is good manners to bring a small gift to your host, such as a potted plant, fresh-cut flowers, a trinket, or a bottle of wine. Offer to open any wine you bring at the table.

Socials offer opportunities to dress up, have fun, and make life-long friends. They are for your pleasure and morale. Take advantage of them; they're a great fringe benefit of military service.

≡ Calling Cards

At officers' receptions, you might find a silver tray for leaving a calling card. Calling cards were introduced into this country after the Civil War, reached a heyday in the early 1900s, and disappeared for the most part after World War II. They were used for the numerous official and social calls that officers made. Traditionally, an officer would leave his card on his first social call. If the people he was calling upon weren't home, he would leave his card with the servants and receive "credit" for that call.

Very few officers have servants anymore, but in some places the tradition does remain that cards are left on some calls, such as attending a formal Christmas reception at a high-ranking officer's home. A man leaves a card for every adult member of the family that he is calling upon, including children over eighteen. More than three cards should not be left by one person, however. Cards should be left in the tray upon arrival or depar-

HAROLD LOUIS NEATE

LIEUTENANT
UNITED STATES ARMY

CAPTAIN NOAH MATTHEW JACKSON
AIDE-DE-CAMP TO MAJOR GENERAL SECREST

UNITED STATES ARMY

LIEUTENANT COLONEL AND MRS. NATHAN MENZO NEELY

Edna Trude Shope

Colonel
United States Army

Sample calling cards.

ture, never handed to the host. Note that today, "calling card" simply refers to a servicemember's business card (see the accompanying examples). It is called a calling card when used for a social purpose. It is not a card printed especially for social visits.

You can order cards through your exchange or a stationery shop.

≡ A Military Wedding

What's the difference between a military and a civilian wedding? Not much, really. The military wedding, like most civilian weddings, is held in a chapel and the ceremony is performed by a clergyman of your faith. A military wedding simply has some service traditions added.

If your wedding will be held in a military chapel, contact the chaplain's office. Most chaplains schedule weddings as first-come, first-served. Some chapels, such as the historic one at Fort Myer, Virginia, are in such demand that you may need to make reservations as much as a year in advance. Service academy chapels have their own scheduling system to accommodate the many weddings they have after graduation. A military wedding may be held at a civilian church as well, but the people there must be instructed in military protocol.

Just like a civilian wedding, a military one requires a civil marriage license, a blood test, and religious counseling or classes. As a courtesy, most base hospitals will give you the blood test at no charge.

> My father has his own saber, and my brother, who was part of the honor guard, used it instead of a chapel loaner. At the reception we used it to cut the cake.

> When you leave the saber arch, don't be surprised if a saber bearer whacks you with the flat side of the saber and says, "Welcome to the U.S. Army!" It's a tradition!

Invitations may include the parents' military rank. If the parent is retired, (Ret.) follows the name. As a courtesy, you should send invitations to the service-member's commander and spouse and all the people in the unit and their spouses. This is true even if you're not getting married where your fiancé is assigned.

You'll need sabers for the honor guard detail. Don't buy these; you can borrow them from the base chapel, an ROTC detachment, a military preparatory school, or a service academiy. If you need saber bearers, cadets are often willing to assist.

The uniforms the military groomsmen and saber bearers wear depends on how formal your wedding is. At an informal one (where the bride wears a short dress or simple gown), the servicemembers wear service or dress uniforms with long (four-in-hand) ties. At a formal wedding (where the bride wears a long gown with a veil and train), dress or mess uniforms with bow ties are worn. The best man and ushers wear the same uniform as the groom. Civilian wedding party members wear a business suit or tuxedo, whichever is more appropriate.

The base protocol office will be able to answer questions on dress or any other aspect of the wedding.

≡ Further Reading

Baldrige, Letitia. *Complete Guide to Executive Manners*. New York: MacMillan, 1993.

———. *Complete Guide to the New Manners for the 90's*. New York: MacMillan, 1990.

Swartz, Oretha. *Service Etiquette*. Annapolis, MD: Naval Institute Press, 1988.

5

Your Own Career

If you work outside your home and a permanent-change-of-station (PCS) move is on the horizon, one of the first things you will want to know is the job situation at your new locale.

Many wives believe that employment is difficult, if not impossible, to find simply because employers don't want to hire military. This can be true for organizations that promote from within, but it is certainly not the general rule. Defense Department surveys on spousal employment show that 60 percent of people married to active-duty servicemembers work.

The average tour of duty served by most military members is three years. In three years the employee turnover in any civilian work setting—law office, engineering firm, or hardware store—is likely to be quite high. America is a mobile society.

> Try not to adopt a "short-timer's" mentality when working. If you act like a short-timer, you'll be treated like one. Act as though you are going to be there forever.

> Active-duty spouses contribute 12 percent of the $82 billion yearly income of active-duty households.

Meet Rosemary Rothlein, a woman who spent eleven very successful years as an agency personnel recruiter before marrying her Army husband. They moved to Germany, where she promptly landed a job as director of the job information center at the civilian personnel office in Mainz-Kastell.

When asked how easy it was to place a wife who moved every three years because of her husband's military career, she replied, "In eleven years of placing, I can't remember an employer ever asking what

As a career counselor in a military town, I can say that some military wives have a problem getting jobs with the private sector—those who constantly change jobs *within* tours. Those whose résumés state, "Three months here. Six months there. One year here. Four months there, then my husband got orders. So now I'm here, looking for another job." I see this a lot, particularly with wives who have worked for the federal government. They change for a variety of reasons—higher GS level, closer to home, looks more interesting—but for whatever reason, such a pattern will lead an employer to conclude that the applicant really doesn't know much of anything. How could he think otherwise? Three months at a job—even six or nine—is just not enough time to learn it.

Ask for a written recommendation from your present employer to include with your résumé to the potential employer.

the applicant's husband did. It wasn't an issue. There's a tremendous amount of transferring in the civilian world. You see it all the time on applications: 'husband transferred.' Or 'divorced husband.' The only difference between them and a military wife is that the military wife would say, 'husband got orders.' If an applicant has good skills and background, she can be placed. If a young wife who comes to me is well groomed and has a professional image and good attitude, I can place her in a week."

When there are jobs to be had, qualified people who know how to market themselves get them whether they're military spouses or civilian. Remember this when talking to someone who is negative about your chances. Did she or a friend try for work unsuccessfully? When people say something is impossible, it often just means it was impossible for them.

For military wives, though, one thing is certain: Getting employment, especially the type we want, requires more assertiveness and flexibility than might otherwise be necessary. How successful you'll be in maintaining your career concurrently with your husband's is directly proportional to the amount of those qualities you have. Plus, of course, how good you are at marketing yourself.

So, assuming you already have the skills needed for the job you're looking for, let's proceed.

Success through Flexibility

You can make your transiency work to your advantage. If you show you are someone who can apply old skills to new jobs, build upon your storehouse of knowledge with each job, and bring this knowledge successfully to the next, your experience and obvious adaptability will work in your favor.

Say you worked as a budget analyst at an insurance company. If you visit an insurance company at your new station and apply for the same position and there are no openings, you'll be turned away.

> Acquire multiple skills. Take any opportunity to learn something useful, from carpentry to bookkeeping. You never know when it will come in handy.

But if there's an opening for something that might be a distant cousin to what you've done, analyze your skills to see how they fit. Did you supervise or manage? Did you juggle figures, write reports, balance accounts? Such skills apply to all kinds of jobs at all kinds of places. Give the personnel department a résumé written in general terms but with enough descriptive adjectives to show why you fit the bill. It's not unheard of for an employer to advertise for a certain type of person and end up hiring someone entirely different on the basis of that person's ability to sell him- or herself. Be careful to tailor your résumé to the position you're applying for in particular, not to it and three others in general.

You needn't look at each job as starting at the bottom again. Show your employer why your new salary and responsibilities should be commensurate with your experience. If the work is challenging and if you're learning new things and building upon your storehouse of knowledge, you are maintaining a career.

Rather than just sending out résumés and waiting for answers, actively seek the job you want. A very large job market exists—some career experts estimate it at 85 percent—that is not and never will be in the help-wanted pages. Following are several methods that can result in a successful job hunt.

≡ Be Creative

Find employers in the best reference book available—the local phone book. Write down all employers listed under your specialty, then add others that might have one or two people from your field on their staff. Jobs in all fields exist in all types of places. Carpenters work in hospitals, writers work for oil companies, reporters work on Army posts, and lawyers are employed by engineering firms. It's called *in-house labor,* and it is used when the services of such people are needed so frequently that it is

> There are job opportunities wherever you go. It's up to you to find and grab them. Moving a lot is stimulating. It keeps you flexible and creative.

more cost-effective to keep them on board than to constantly contract their services. And it's very common.

→ Once you've compiled your list, call each place and ask to speak to the person who has the power to hire. The best times to call are first thing in the morning and late in the afternoon; during the rest of the day this critical person is usually hard to reach. Once you get her on the phone, introduce yourself. Briefly explain your qualifications and background and ask whether the company could use someone like you. If not, ask whether she knows someone who might. Leave your name and number, and request that she keep you in mind if she hears of anything.

Start your search even before you get to the new town. Write to the chamber of commerce and the local state employment office to ask what is available. Write to the newspaper for Sunday editions and to the phone company for a local phone book (your library might have a collection of nationwide phone books). Write letters to the companies that interest you, introducing yourself and saying you'll be in touch when you get there. Don't do this any earlier than one month ahead, however. A visit before your actual move might even be in order to investigate something particularly promising. Write to your college for a list of alumni in the area; they may be able to help. Also, take advantage of any employment assistance programs offered by your base's family support center.

→ Temporary agencies are great resources for employment. The larger ones even offer training and benefits. Some temporary jobs have turned into permanent ones for employees who proved valuable. Temporary agencies place everyone from secretarial, clerical, and factory workers to architects, doctors, engineers, and lawyers. One woman tells her story:

"I obtained both my jobs through a temporary agency. In my first I worked for a rust company in New York supervising shareholder relations accounts for multinational corporations. It was a terrific job. When my husband got orders to D.C., the recession was in full force and I couldn't find a job on my own. I went to the same temporary agency, which placed me with a defense contractor in a congressional lobbying office. My job included the responsibilities of office manager, legislative research assistant, and facility security officer. In my office there were many retired high-ranking officers, and through them I met members of Congress and staffers. What terrific contacts I made!

→ *"If you use a job service agency, I recommend that you use a fee-paid (meaning the hiring company pays the fee) one or an agency that collects payment only after it finds you a job. Be wary of agencies that want payment up front, whether they find you a job or not."*

The transition assistance office conducts workshops on the job search process. It's open to spouses, active-duty personnel, Reservists, and civilians subject to a reduction in force.

Check out the Spouse Employment Assistance Center at

your Family Services office. Staff there assist in résumé writing and interviewing, and offer tips on job hunting and the civil service.

≡ Develop Contacts

Get to know the local population. The referral network is very powerful. Someone always knows someone who knows someone who is hiring, and that gives you the advantage of saying, "Mr. Hammond from First National suggested I call." How do you plug into this network? Ask working military wives what's available. Get to know the civilian community. Attend the meetings of the local professional society of the field in which you're interested. Most towns have an organization of professional and businesswomen. Find out what societies and organizations are in your town by reading the local newspaper or calling the chamber of commerce. Instructors who teach in your field at the local university are good sources of information. Take a class in your field to develop contacts. Church committees, the Jaycees, town council meetings, investment clubs, and the YMCA's pool or racquetball court during lunchtime are just some of the places you're likely to meet people with the power to hire and people who know people with the power to hire.

Try to make contacts during house-hunting trips.

If you're on the West Coast, check out the Military Spouse Business and Professional Network, P.O. Box 80744, San Diego, CA 92138-0744. On the East Coast, its address is 1400 Winding Ridge Lane, Centreville, VA 22020.

Career America provides taped job information. Call (912) 757-3000.

═ Volunteer

Volunteering in your field will lead to contacts more quickly and more easily than anything else. Is your degree in social work or psychology? Army Community Services, Navy Relief, or the local center for distressed youth will welcome you. Are you a physical therapist? Any nursing home will love you. Are you a speech therapist? The Special Needs program would like to meet you. Do you have a degree or experience in the recreation or leisure services field? See whether you can help out at the local park district.

Volunteering gives you contact with the people who hire, keeps your skills sharp, and enables you to attend workshops and seminars, sources of more contacts. If something does open at the place you're volunteering, your name will be at the top of the list. You don't need to volunteer five days a week; even working just several hours a week, you can make contacts while keeping in touch with your field.

Marketing Volunteer Experience

When job hunting, don't overlook volunteer experience. Many people have beaten out competitors on edges obtained strictly from volunteer work. Some general tips:

To be most effective, volunteer work must be done regularly and seriously. Emphasize the time you put into it. It demonstrates potential dedication to a paying job.

Never take the attitude that you were "just a volunteer." That you didn't earn a salary is completely irrelevant. Volunteer work is work. Show how your experience relates to the job at hand, just as your competitors must.

Keep a file of all volunteer documentation: thank-you notes for a job well done; letters of reference and recommendation; newspaper clippings that mention your name and projects you worked on; log sheets and copies of time cards if hours were counted. Don't count on the organization for which you were a volunteer to keep records for you; turnovers are high, and if an employer calls to check on you, no one there may remember you. Such a file is also helpful when filling out a résumé.

When filling out job applications, describe your work experience as precisely as salaried employees describe theirs. Don't expect everyone to know what the cookie chairman of the Girl Scouts does. *You* know that it was an organizational nightmare, but you must also let your prospective employer know.

Commute

While stationed at Fort Campbell, Kentucky, I was offered a good job in Nashville, over an hour away. At first I didn't want to take it because of the commute, but then I thought, what am I presently doing the time I'd be commuting? Sleeping? Watching the *Today* show? Complaining to my friends that I can't find a job? Driving ten minutes to a job I hate? Once I put it all in perspective, commuting didn't look so bad.

Many duty stations are in small communities. Since there isn't much commerce in small towns, job opportunities are limited. But many of these small communities are a short drive from big communities where lots of opportunities exist. If you want to work and can't find anything outside Gate 1, you may have to commute.

Don't want to drive that much? Don't have the time? Too hard? Your car gets terrible mileage?

You can talk yourself out of commuting pretty fast. But if you truly want to work at a job you consider suitable, at some stations you'll have to commute. It's part of the need to be flexible. If your car gets poor mileage, sell it for a more efficient one or carpool to split expenses. Put an ad in the paper for other commuters. Surely you're not the only person in town who wants to work in the big city.

One enterprising young wife literally made a business of commuting. She was offered a job she couldn't turn down in a city an hour's drive away. She drove solo for a while, then realized that a lot of other women—both military wives and locals—were also commuting. This twenty-five-year-old woman, who had two children at home and was four months pregnant, bought herself a used forty-seat commuter van, taught herself to drive it, got a chauffeur's license and insurance, distributed fliers advertising the service in mall and discount store parking lots, and was in business. She picked everyone up at a common point, dropped them off along a route she devised, then went to her own job. At 5:00 P.M. she picked them all up again and drove them home. Within a month she had her entire van filled and a waiting list so long she bought a second van and hired one of her riders to drive it. When it came time to move, she sold the service to a local businessman.

Get Going

An important note about the search for meaningful work: The sooner you start, the better. Taking months to settle in before starting your search will eat into the precious time needed to schedule information interviews, make personal contacts, and do everything else that lands a job. It's a fact that the currently employed have an easier time finding new work than the unemployed. So update your résumé and start your search as soon as your husband gets his PCS orders. The more time you devote to the search, the better

> I'm a great believer in luck. And I find the harder I work the more I have of it.
> —THOMAS JEFFERSON

Tell potential employers that you don't need relocation money. That will make you equally competitive with local applicants.

If you gave up a great career to marry your servicemember, apply yourself to your new lifestyle the way you applied yourself to your job. You're bound to be successful.

your chances are of finding something you want. If you approach job hunting as a full-time endeavor, your chances of getting a good job increase exponentially. People who seem lucky are often just people who actively seek to control the elements that bring luck within their grasp.

Lori Stanton
1 Juniper Lane, Apt. #4
Fayetteville, N.C. 28304
(302) 555-1234

Objective

Office management in a small to mid-size office

Education

Avila College, Overland Park, Ks. 66210, 1986–1990
Bachelor of Science in Business Administration, 1990
G.P.A.: 3.4/4.0
Scholastic Achievements: Named to Dean's List two years. Graduated in top 10 percent of class.

Work Experience

1993 to present: Office Manager, Ryan Foods, 43 Madison St., Fayetteville, N.C. 28304. Helen Gomez, supervisor.

• Supervise 10 employees in a computerized inventory-control department
• Administer automated inventory-control system
• Review and evaluate existing system and procedures
• Wrote procedure manual covering inventory control, warehousing, requisition, purchasing, receiving, shipping

1990–1993: Assistant Office Manager, Gem Foods, 5 Harris Lane, Nashville, Tn. 37205. Mark Decatur, supervisor.

• Assisted in supervising seven employees
• Responsible for accounts payable and receivable, bookkeeping, additional administrative duties
• Prepared annual administrative budget
• Implemented salary review program
• Acted as substitute Benefits Administrator and Office Services Manager

1988–1990: Assistant Inventory Control Trainee, Dwyer Food Corporation, 211 Oak Ave., Overland Park, Ks. 66210. Ann Kirkpatrick, supervisor.

• Prepared and implemented inventory-control and management systems
• Assisted with requirements planning, procurement, maintenance of automated system, and order processing for company with annual volume of 15 million units

A sample résumé.

≡ Résumés and Interviews

When interviewing, I keep my military connections to myself in case the interviewer has any negative opinions about hiring military spouses.

Since whole books are devoted to these topics, we won't discuss them in detail. But a few words are in order.

Résumé-writing services are everywhere, but if

June 5, 1995

Lori Stanton
1 Juniper Lane, Apt. #4
Fayetteville, N.C. 28304

Jill Kribbs, Personnel Director
Holloway Food Marketers
1 Plumtree Dr.
Chicago, Ill. 60653

Dear Ms. Kribbs,

I am an office manager with five years of experience at food corporations. Since I will be relocating to the Chicago area in October 1995, I am seeking employment there in this same capacity.

I saw your advertisement in the Chicago *Tribune*. It sounds like an interesting position and I would like to learn more. I have enclosed a copy of my résumé outlining my qualifications. My present earnings are within the range of the salary described in your advertisement, and I would welcome the opportunity to discuss with you in person my background and objectives and how I could be of benefit to the company.

Thank you for your time.

Sincerely,

Lori Stanton

Lori Stanton

A sample cover letter.

you invest a little time reading a book on résumé writing, you can write a good résumé yourself and save the (often hefty) fee. Besides, some professional résumé writers really outdo themselves and give you a product so slick it's recognized as ghost-written and promptly tossed.

Colored paper, photos, and other gimmicks are distracting and unprofessional. Use cream or heavy white bond paper, and use the same type for both your cover letter and résumé. Professional printing is unnecessary; what is important is that the papers be neat, have no spelling or grammatical errors, and briefly describe all relevant data. Type it or print it on a laser or ink-jet printer.

Dress up for your interview. Jeans may be appropriate for the employee, but they're not appropriate for the applicant. First impressions in a job interview are everything; no matter how misleading they may be, they're all an employer has.

Keep good records of your work experience. Certificates of education, training, awards, and volunteer work should be kept handy in document protectors. Since dates of employment, beginning and ending salaries, and addresses and telephone numbers of past employers are included on a résumé, keep a record of them.

Make the interview a lively dialogue, not a situation in which you just answer questions. If you're interested in the job, you will have questions too. What are the duties of the job? What possibilities exist for additional responsibilities and promotion? How long has the organization been in business here? Is there a growing market for the product in this town? Who's the competition? Ask about the staff turnover rate; a high one indicates that it's a poor place to work. Such questions show that you're concerned about finding a good place to work. Make clear that you want a job where you can remain for your entire tour. Don't ask about benefits and salary, though; that comes later. Don't dwell on your weaknesses or lack of skills, either. If you make an effort to learn something about the job and give reasons why you want to work there instead of somewhere else, it will favorably impress your interviewer.

≡ Don't Get Discouraged

Some states give unemployment benefits to spouses who had to quit jobs because of a PCS move.

Military wives are not the only people who have to look for work in a new city. Dual-professional couples wrestle with this all the time, as do people who choose their locations for health, family, or other reasons. The need to make choices exists for any couple where both people are meaningfully employed. If you've been trying hard to find suitable employment and still keep banging into brick walls, remember that your situation isn't unique. These days, it takes persistence, strategy, and sometimes real ingenuity to find a job in any field, whether you live in Altus, Oklahoma, or New York City. The proliferation of employment agencies and advice books wouldn't exist if there weren't a need.

Does it all sound like a lot of work? It is. You're engaged in the job of marketing yourself, and there are no shortcuts. But keep trying, and you'll eventually hear those wonderful words, "When can you start?"

≡ The Federal Civil Service

If you're interested in a job with the federal government, you'll have to learn its complex hiring system. There are many rules and regulations on how, where, when, and for what you can apply and who has priority. Federal bosses can't pick the person they want as easily as those in the private sector can.

> When you leave a federal civil service job because of a transfer, try to get leave without pay (LWOP) if you intend to seek another civil service job. If you land another job before your LWOP runs out, you'll maintain your career status.

The reason it's so complicated is summed up in one word: accountability. The taxpayer pays federal salaries, and the taxpayer wants a fair system of hiring. Without regulations, jobs might be given to friends and relatives, and promotions could be made on the basis of popularity, not merit. So the complex system of regulations exists to protect everyone. Bureaucracy is the result of this need for accountability.

There are two funds from which salaries of government jobs are paid: appropriated (AF) and nonappropriated (NAF). Congress appropriates tax dollars to pay AF salaries, but NAF salaries are paid from the locally generated proceeds of Morale, Well-being, and Recreation (MWR) activities and the exchange. NAF jobs are not civil service; they're governed by Department of Defense policies.

To be interviewed for any position, you must first be referred to the interviewer by the Civilian Personnel Office (CPO). To get this referral, submit Standard Form No. 171 (SF-171) for AF jobs or a separate application for NAF jobs. (See accompanying sample SF-171 form.) These forms are used in lieu of a résumé. A staffing specialist will review your application and rate you qualified or not qualified for the position. Let's look at CPO's rating system, a very misunderstood aspect of federal hiring.

The rater is a person who knows a great deal about the requirements for the job for which she is rating an applicant. She gets this information from the *U.S. Qualifications Standards,* a book that describes in great detail all the education, experience, and combinations thereof needed for the job. These standards are written in Washington. They are a fact of law and cannot be downgraded or waived. The rater must match the applicant's qualifications as described on the SF-171 to the qualifications spelled out in the Standards Book. Although some leeway in interpretation does exist, the basic standards must be adhered to.

You can't just apply for jobs that interest or intrigue you or that will "hold you over" until something better comes up. Your background must match the qualifications standards. When you have been hired for a job for which you are qualified, the government will pay to send you to courses to improve your knowledge in that field. But if your background doesn't qualify you, the government will not train you. In fact, the civilian personnel office keeps a list of classes allowed for each job category, and once you're working and are registered for one, the list is scanned to ascertain that the course is appropriate for your field.

The following comment from one CPO worker is worth noting:

"Some family members submit 171s to us like tickets in a lottery. They apply for every job on the roster whether they're qualified or not, whether they intend to take it or not. Many times we've offered jobs to family members just to hear, 'Well, I really don't want that one; I'd rather have the other one I applied for. What's the status on that?'

"There are many complaints that CPO is slow; it's precisely things like this that make it slow. Every application has to be carefully evaluated, and the number we get from people who aren't even marginally qualified for the job they're applying for or who have no intention of taking it creates a giant drag on the system. If we received applications only from people who really had a shot at the jobs they applied for and who took them when we offered them, we'd have them rated and back in a day."

How do you submit an application? Look at a list of job vacancies, available from the CPO on base and from your regional Office of Personnel Management (OPM; formerly the Civil Service Commission). Selected listings are also carried in *Federal Career Opportunities* and *Federal Times,* newspapers available at your base library. Even though the CPO usually goes to the regional OPM only when it has no qualified applicants in its own inventory, it is a good idea to keep applications at both places since hiring is done from both. The accompanying list shows all regional OPMs. Visit or call the one nearest you for a recorded job listing. They are not mailed to prospective applicants. If you have a personal computer and modem, dial (912) 757-3100, code 9999, for access to the Federal Job Opportunity Board.

Most people can apply only for what's advertised, but applicants for certain professional and upper-level positions may submit even if there are no current openings. Since the government often has a hard time filling such positions, it will keep these applications on file. But for the vast majority, only applications that correspond to advertised positions are accepted. If there is no advertised opening, there is no authority to hire.

There are two types of openings: *one-times* and *open continuous* (OC). For one-times, current openings are announced and there is an application cutoff date. OC means there are no current openings but some are anticipated, so applications are accepted. Apply for OC announcements, because CPO doesn't always post all vacancies; some are filled through special announcements or the OC inventories. Since CPO accepts OC

U.S. Office of Personnel Management Federal Employment Information Centers

ALABAMA
Huntsville:
520 Wynn Dr., N.W. 35816-3426
(205) 837-0894

ALASKA
Anchorage:
222 W. 7th Ave., #22, Rm. 156 99513-7572
(907) 271-5821

ARIZONA
Phoenix:
Century Plaza Building, Rm. 1415
3225 N. Central Ave., 85012
(602) 640-4800

ARKANSAS:
(See San Antonio, TX, listing)

CALIFORNIA
Los Angeles:
9650 Flair Dr., Suite 100A
El Monte, 91731
(818) 575-6510

Sacramento:
1029 J St., Rm. 202, 95814
(916) 551-1464

San Diego:
Federal Building, Room 4218
880 Front St., 92101-8821
(619) 557-6165

San Francisco:
211 Main St., 2nd Floor, Room 235
(mail) P.O. Box 7405, 94120
(415) 744-5627

COLORADO
Denver:
12345 W. Alameda Pkwy., Lakewood
(mail) P.O. Box 25167, 80225
(303) 969-7050
For forms, call (303) 969-7055

CONNECTICUT
(See Massachusetts listing)

DELAWARE
(See Philadelphia, PA, listing)

DISTRICT OF COLUMBIA
Metropolitan Area:
1900 E St., N.W., Rm. 1416, 20415
(202) 606-2700

FLORIDA
Miami:
Claude Pepper Federal Building,
Room 1222, 51 S.W. 1st Ave., 33130
(305) 536-6738

Orlando:
Commodore Building, Suite 125
3444 McCrory Pl., 32803-3701
(407) 648-6148

GEORGIA
Atlanta:
Richard B. Russell Federal Building
Room 940A, 75 Spring St., S.W. 30303
(404) 331-4315

HAWAII
Honolulu (and other Hawaiian islands and overseas):
Federal Building, Rm. 5316
300 Ala Moana Blvd., 96850
(808) 541-2791
Overseas Jobs (808) 541-2764

IDAHO
(See Washington listing)

ILLINOIS
Chicago:
175 W. Jackson Blvd., Rm. 530, 60504
(312) 353-6192
(For Madison and St. Clair, see St. Louis, MO, listing)

INDIANA
Indianapolis:
Touch Screen Service available at Minton-
  Capehard Fed Building, Room 368
575 N. Pennsylvania St., 46204
(313) 226-6950
(For additional information services in Indiana,
  see Michigan; for Clark, Dearborn, and
  Floyd counties, see Ohio listing)

IOWA
(See Kansas City, Missouri, listing)
(816) 426-7757
(For Scott County, see Illinois listing)

KANSAS
Wichita:
Touch Screen Service available at:
One-Twenty Building, Rm. 101
1∠0 S. Market St., 67202
(816) 426-7820
(For additional information services in Kansas,
  see Kansas City, MO)

KENTUCKY
(See Ohio listing)
(for Henderson County, see Michigan)

LOUISIANA
New Orleans:
1515 Poydras St., Suite 608, 70112
(504) 589-2764/24-Hour Jobline

MAINE
(See Massachusetts listing)

MARYLAND
Baltimore:
Marsh and McLennan Building
300 W. Pratt St., 21201
(Self-Service only. For mail or telephone,
  see Philadelphia, PA)

MASSACHUSETTS
Boston:
Thomas P. O'Neill, Jr., Federal Building
10 Causeway St., 02222-1031
(617) 565-5900

MICHIGAN
Detroit:
477 Michigan Ave., Rm. 565, 48226
(313) 226-6950

MINNESOTA
Twin Cities:
Bishop Henry Whipple Federal Building
1 Federal Dr., Room 501
Fort Snelling, Twin Cities, 55111
(612) 725-3430

MISSISSIPPI
(See Alabama listing)

MISSOURI
Kansas City:
Federal Building, Rm. 134
601 E. 12th St., 64105
(816) 426-5702
(For counties west of and including Mercer,
  Grundy, Livingston, Carroll, Saline, Pettis,
  Benton, Hickory, Dallas, Webster, Douglas,
  and Ozark)

Saint Louis:
400 Old Post Office Building
815 Olive St., 63101
(314) 539-2285
(For all other Missouri counties not listed
  under Kansas City above)

MONTANA
(See Colorado listing)
(303) 969-7052

NEBRASKA
(See Kansas City, MO, listing)
(816) 426-7819

NEVADA
(For Clark, Lincoln, and Nye counties, see
  Los Angeles, CA; for all other Nevada
  counties not listed above, see
  Sacramento, CA)

NEW HAMPSHIRE
(See Massachusetts listing)

NEW JERSEY
Newark:
Touch Screen Service available at
Rodino Federal Building
970 Broad St., 2nd Floor, 07102

(For additional information services in
   Bergen, Essex, Hudson, Hunterdon,
   Middlesex, Morris, Passaic, Somerset,
   Sussex, Union, and Warren counties, see
   New York City, NY; for additional infor-
   mation services in Atlantic, Burlington,
   Camden, Cape May, Cumberland,
   Gloucester, Mercer, Monmouth, Ocean,
   and Salem counties, see Philadelphia, PA)

NEW MEXICO
Albuquerque:
505 Marquette Ave., Suite 910, 87102
(505) 766-2906

NEW YORK
New York City:
Jacob K. Javits Federal Building
Second Floor, Room 120
26 Federal Plaza, 10278
(212) 264-0422/0423

Syracuse:
P.O. Box 7257
100 S. Clinton St., 13261
(315) 423-5660

NORTH CAROLINA
Raleigh:
4407 Bland Rd., Suite 202, 27609-6296
(919) 790-2822

NORTH DAKOTA
(See Minnesota listing)

OHIO
Dayton:
Federal Building, Rm. 506
200 W. 2nd St., 45402
(513) 225-2720

(For Van Wert, Auglaize, Hardin, Marion,
   Crawford, Richland, Ashland, Wayne,
   Stark, Carroll, and Columbiana counties
   and farther north, see Michigan)

OKLAHOMA
(See San Antonio, TX, listing)

OREGON
Portland:
Federal Building, Rm. 376
1220 S.W. Third Ave., 97294
(503) 326-3141

PENNSYLVANIA
Harrisburg:
Federal Building, Rm. 158
P.O. Box 761, 17108
(717) 782-4494

Philadelphia:
William J. Green, Jr., Federal Building
600 Arch St., 19106
(215) 597-7440

Pittsburgh:
Federal Building
1000 Liberty Ave., Rm. 119, 15222
(Walk-in only. For mail or telephone, see
   Philadelphia listing)

PUERTO RICO
San Juan:
U.S. Federal Building, Room 328
150 Carlos Chardon Ave.
San Juan, PR 00918-1710
(809) 766-5242

RHODE ISLAND
(See Massachusetts listing)

SOUTH CAROLINA
(See Raleigh, NC, listing)

SOUTH DAKOTA
(See Minnesota listing)

TENNESSEE
Memphis:
200 Jefferson Ave., Suite 1312
(Walk-in only. For mail or telephone, see
   Alabama listing)

TEXAS
Corpus Christi:
(See San Antonio listing)
(512) 884-8113

Dallas:
1100 Commerce St., Rm 6B10, 75242
(214) 767-8035

Harlingen:
(See San Antonio)
(512) 412-0722

Houston:
(See San Antonio)
(713) 759-0455

San Antonio:
8610 Broadway, Rm 305, 78217
(210) 805-2423
For forms, call (210) 805-2406
24-Hour Job Info: (210) 805-2402

UTAH
(See Colorado listing)
(303) 969-7053

VERMONT
(See Massachusetts listing)

VIRGIN ISLANDS
(See Puerto Rico listing)
(809) 774-8790

VIRGINIA
Norfolk:
For mail only:
Federal Building, Rm. 500
200 Granby St., 23510-1886
(804) 441-3355
For walk-in only:
Norfolk VEC Job Service Office
5145 E. Virginia Beach Blvd.

WASHINGTON
Seattle:
Federal Building, Rm 110
915 Second Ave., 98174
(206) 220-6400

WEST VIRGINIA
(See Ohio listing)
(513) 225-2855

WISCONSIN
(For Dane, Grant, Green, Iowa, Lafayette,
Rock, Jefferson, Walworth, Milwaukee,
Waukesha, Racine, and Kenosha counties, see Illinois listing, (312) 353-6189;
for all other Wisconsin counties not
listed above, see Minnesota listing)

WYOMING
(See Colorado listing)
(303) 969-7052

applications for only as long as it takes to build a suitable inventory, be prompt when applying.

After the cutoff date for one-times has expired, all applications are reviewed and rated. If you are rated unqualified, your SF-171 is returned to you. During the rating process, points are assigned for education and experience; the more you have, the higher your score. Additional points are given for veteran status. Preference is given to career employees displaced from their jobs through no personal cause, selected employees placed under the Equal Opportunity Program, selected planned career progressions of employees in developmental positions, and employees returning from overseas under the Priority Placement Program. The names of the applicants with the highest numbers of points are forwarded to the person requesting the position, who will contact the applicants for an interview.

Things get complicated now. There are a lot of different types of appointments: career, career-conditional, competitive, excepted, general schedule (GS), general merit (GM), senior executive service (SES), wage grade (WG), wage leader (WL), wage supervisor (WS), teaching professional (TP), universal annual (UA), administrative services (AS), patron support (PS), trades and crafts (NA), trades and craftsleader (NL), trades and crafts supervisor (NS), when actually employed (WAE), part-time employees performing general schedule duties, regular full-time, regular part-time, intermittent regularly scheduled, intermittent on call. Then there are different types of government agencies: legislative, quasi-governmental, judicial. We'll just take a look at general schedule (GS) and NAF types of jobs, as they are the ones held by most military spouses.

GS jobs are assigned grade levels ranging from 1 to 18. Levels 1 through 4 are clerical; 5 through 8, clerical supervisor; 9 through 12, midlevel administrative; and 13 through 15, senior positions. Levels 16 through 18 are held by appointees. A federal employee's pay is determined by the level of the job, not by the person's qualifications. Though you may have qualified for a GS-7, if you are occupying a GS-5 slot, you will be paid a GS-5 salary. GS jobs run the occupational gamut from custodial worker to nuclear physicist.

NAF jobs are usually of a Morale, Well-being, and Recreational nature, as almost all NAF money an installation receives is for quality-of-life projects. Typical NAF jobs are club manager, child-care worker, cashier, cook, bartender, and day-care worker. (Incidentally, base facilities like the clubs, shoppette, commissary, and exchange are great employers of military spouses.) Office-type positions (such as clerical and accounting) that support these activities fall under the NAF universal annual category; workers receive the same pay rates as GS rates, and they're the same worldwide. Other NAF rates are based on local wage surveys.

Civilian personnel offices operate one-stop job information centers that bring a variety of services to aid the job hunter under one roof. One-stops offer seminars, informational pamphlets, and help in filling out the SF-171. Many even offer workshops on interviewing and résumé writing and tips on finding a private-sector job. For information on the different types of appointments, as well as transfer programs, intern programs, reinstatement programs, the Priority Placement Program, and more, visit your CPO. Books and newsletters that discuss ways to get a job with the federal government are on the market, but much of the information they contain is already available to you, free, from the CPO.

Standard Form 171

Application for Federal Employment

*(Formerly **Personal Qualifications Statement**)*

Read the Following Instructions Carefully Before You Complete This Application

- **DO NOT SUBMIT A RESUME INSTEAD OF THIS APPLICATION.**
- TYPE OR PRINT CLEARLY IN DARK INK. If you need more space for an answer, continue in item **47** on page 4 or use a sheet of paper the same size as this page. On **each** sheet write your name, Social Security Number, and the announcement number or job title. Attach all sheets to this application at the top of page 3.
- If you do not answer **all** questions fully and correctly, you may delay our review of your application and lose job opportunities.
- Unless we ask for additional material in the announcement or qualification information, **do not attach** any materials, such as: official position descriptions, performance evaluations, letters of recommendation, certificates of training, publications, etc. Any materials you attach which we did not ask for may be removed from your application and will **not** be returned to you.
- We suggest that you **keep a copy** of this application for your use. If you plan to make copies of your application, we suggest you leave items **1, 2, 48** and **49** blank. Complete these blank items each time you apply. **YOU MUST SIGN AND DATE, IN INK, EACH COPY YOU SUBMIT.**
- **If you are applying for a specific Federal civil service examination** (whether or not a written test is required):
  - Read the announcement and other material provided. Make sure that your work experience and / or education meet the qualifications described.
  - Make sure that you are allowed to apply at this time. Civil service examinations may be closed to receipt of new applications for specific types of jobs, grade levels, and / or geographic locations. Follow any directions on "How to Apply".
  - If a written test is required, follow the instructions on your admission card (for example: "Bring a completed SF171 to the test").
  - If a written test is **not** required, mail this application to the address in the announcement.
  - Include all forms required by the announcement.
- **If you are applying for a specific vacancy in a Federal agency:**
  - Study the vacancy announcement to make sure that you meet the qualifications for the job **and** are allowed to apply. Some jobs are limited to people who work for the Federal Government, have worked for the Federal Government in the past, or have an application on file with the Office of Personnel Management.
  - Mail this application to the address in the vacancy announcement.
  - Include all forms that are required by the announcement.
- If you change your address, notify all offices that have your application. Always include your Social Security Number.

Work Experience (Item 24)

- Carefully complete each experience block you need to describe your work experience. Unless you qualify based on education alone, **your rating will depend on your description of previous jobs. Do not leave out any jobs you held during the last ten years.**

- Under **Description of Work**, write a **clear** and **brief**, but **complete** description of your **major** duties and responsibilities for each job. Include any supervisory duties, special assignments, and your accomplishments in the job. We may verify your description with your former employers.
- If you had a major change of duties or responsibilities while you worked for the same employer, describe each major change as a separate job.
- Write in each experience block your name at that time. If it is different from the name you currently use, show your former name in parentheses on the first line under **Description of Work**.

Veteran Preference (Item 22)

- DO NOT LEAVE **22** blank. If you do **not** claim veteran preference, place an "X" in box number **1**, "NO PREFERENCE".
- You **cannot** receive veteran preference if you are retired, or plan to retire, at or above the rank of major or lieutenant commander, **unless** you have a service-connected disability (see "10-POINT PREFERENCE" below).
- Some Vietnam Era and disabled veterans qualify for special hiring programs. More information is available from any Federal Job Information Center.
- **5-POINT PREFERENCE.** If you claim 5-point preference you must have:
  - Received an honorable or general discharge *(a clemency discharge does not meet the requirements of the Veteran Preference Act)*; **and**
  - Served on active duty anytime between December 7, 1941, and July 1, 1955; **or**
  - Served more than 180 consecutive days of active duty, any part of which was after January 31, 1955, and before October 15, 1976 *(do not count active duty for training under the "6-month" Reserve or National Guard programs)*; or
  - Served in a military action for which you received or were entitled to receive a Campaign Badge or Expeditionary Medal. Write the names of your Campaign Badges and Expeditionary Medals in **47**.
  If you claim 5-point preference place an "X" in box number **2**, "5-POINT PREFERENCE".
- **10-POINT PREFERENCE.** If you claim 10-point preference you must meet the requirements for **one** of the groups below, as described in the Standard Form 15, Application for 10-Point Veteran Preference (SF-15). The SF-15 is available by mail from any Federal Job Information Center.
  - Non-Compensably Disabled or Purple Heart Recipient;
  - Compensably Disabled (less than 30%);
  - Compensably Disabled (30% or more);
  - Spouse, Widow(er), or Mother of a deceased or disabled veteran.
  If you claim 10-point preference, place an "X" in the box that applies to you (**3** or **4** or **5** or **6**). ATTACH A COMPLETED SF-15 TO THIS APPLICATION, TOGETHER WITH THE PROOF REQUESTED IN THE SF-15.

DETACH THIS PAGE • NOTE ADDITIONAL WORK EXPERIENCE BLOCKS ON BACK

Standard Form 171. Application for Federal Employment.

Standard Form 171-A—Continuation Sheet for SF 171

Form Approved:
OMB No. 3206-0012

• Attach all SF 171-A's to your application at the top of page 3.

1. Name (Last, First, Middle)	2. Social Security Number

3. Job Title or Announcement Number You Are Applying For	4. Date Completed

ADDITIONAL WORK EXPERIENCE BLOCKS IF NEEDED

☐ Name and address of employer's organization (include ZIP Code, if known)

Dates employed (give month and year)	Average number of hours per week
From: To:	
Salary or earnings	Place of employment
Starting $ per	City
Ending $ per	State

Exact title of your job	Your immediate supervisor	Number and job titles of any employees you supervised
	Name Area Code Telephone Number	

Kind of business or organization (manufacturing, accounting, social service, etc.)	If Federal employment (civilian or military), list series, grade or rank, and the date of your last promotion	Your reason for leaving

Description of work: Describe your specific duties, responsibilities and accomplishments in this job. If you describe more than one type of work (for example, carpentry and painting, or personnel and budget), write the approximate percentage of time you spent doing each.

For Agency Use (skill codes, etc.)

☐ Name and address of employer's organization (include ZIP Code, if known)

Dates employed (give month and year)	Average number of hours per week
From: To:	
Salary or earnings	Place of employment
Starting $ per	City
Ending $ per	State

Exact title of your job	Your immediate supervisor	Number and job titles of any employees you supervised
	Name Area Code Telephone Number	

Kind of business or organization (manufacturing, accounting, social service, etc.)	If Federal employment (civilian or military), list series, grade or rank, and the date of your last promotion	Your reason for leaving

Description of work: Describe your specific duties, responsibilities and accomplishments in this job. If you describe more than one type of work (for example, carpentry and painting, or personnel and budget), write the approximate percentage of time you spent doing each.

For Agency Use (skill codes, etc.)

THE FEDERAL GOVERNMENT IS AN EQUAL OPPORTUNITY EMPLOYER

PREVIOUS EDITION USABLE   NSN 7540-00-935-7157   171-209

Standard Form 171-A (Rev. 3/84)
Office of Personnel Management
FPM Chapter 295

Standard Form 171 *(continued)*.

Application for Federal Employment—SF 171

Read the instructions before you complete this application. *Type or print clearly in dark ink.*

Form Approved:
OMB No. 3206-0012

GENERAL INFORMATION

1 What kind of job are you applying for? *Give title and announcement number (if any)*

2 If the announcement lists several job titles, which jobs are you applying for?

3 Social Security Number

4 Birth date *(Month, Day, Year)*

5 Name *(Last, First, Middle)*

Street address or RFD number *(include apartment number, if any)*

City   State   ZIP Code

6 Other names ever used

7 Sex *(for statistical use)*
☐ Male   ☐ Female

8 Home Phone
Area Code | Number

9 Work Phone
Area Code | Number | Ext.

10 Were you ever employed as a civilian by the Federal Government? If "NO", go to 11. If "YES", mark each type of job you held with an "X".
☐ Temporary   ☐ Career-Conditional   ☐ Career   ☐ Excepted
What is your highest grade, classification series and job title?

Dates at highest grade: FROM   TO

11 Do you have any applications for Federal employment on file with the U.S. Office of Personnel Management? If "NO", mark here ☐ and go to 12. If "YES", write below and continue in 47 the information for each application: (a) the name of the office that has your application; (b) the title of the job; (c) the date of your Notice of Results; and (d) your rating.

DO NOT WRITE IN THIS AREA

FOR USE OF EXAMINING OFFICE ONLY

Material	Entered register:
☐ Submitted	
☐ Returned	
Notations:	

Form reviewed:
Form approved:

Option	Grade	Earned Rating	Preference	Aug. Rating

☐ 5 Points (Tent.)
☐ 10 Pts. (30%) Or More Comp. Dis.
☐ 10 Pts. Less Than 30% Comp. Dis.
☐ Other 10 Points
☐ Disallowed

Initials and Date

☐ Being Investigated

FOR USE OF APPOINTING OFFICER ONLY

Preference has been verified through proof that the separation was under honorable conditions, and other proof as required.

☐ 5 Point   ☐ 10-Point—30% or More Compensable Disability   ☐ 10-Point—Less Than 30% Compensable Disability   ☐ 10-Point—Other

Signature and Title

Agency   Date

ANNOUNCEMENT NO.
APPLICATION NO.

AVAILABILITY

12 When can you start work? *(Month and Year)*

13 What is the lowest pay you will accept?
Pay $_____ per _____ OR Grade _____

14 Are you willing to work:
	YES	NO
A. In the Washington, D.C., metropolitan area?		
B. Outside the 50 United States?		
C. Any place in the United States?		
D. Only in *(list the location(s))*		

15 Are you willing to work: A. 40 hours per week (full-time)?
B. 25-32 hours per week (part-time)?		
C. 17-24 hours per week (part-time)?		
D. 16 or fewer hours per week (part-time)?		
E. In an intermittent job (on-call/seasonal)?		
F. Weekends, shifts, or rotating shifts?		

16 Are you willing to take a temporary job lasting:
A. 5 to 12 months (sometimes longer)?		
B. 1 to 4 months?		
C. Less than 1 month?		

17 Are you willing to travel away from home for:
A. 1 to 5 nights each month?		
B. 6 to 10 nights each month?		
C. 11 or more nights each month?		

MILITARY SERVICE AND VETERAN PREFERENCE

18 Have you served on active duty in the United States Military Service? If your only active duty was training in the Reserves or National Guard, answer "NO". If "NO", go to 22.
YES	NO

19 Were you honorably discharged from the military service? If your discharge was changed to "honorable" or "general" by a Discharge Review Board, answer "YES". If you received a clemency discharge, answer "NO". If "NO", explain in 47.

20 Did you or will you retire at or above the rank of major or lieutenant commander?

21 List the dates, branch, and serial number for all active duty service.
FROM	TO	BRANCH OF SERVICE	SERIAL NUMBER

22 Place an "X" in the box next to your Veteran Preference claim. Mark only one box. See the instructions for eligibility information.

☐ **1** NO PREFERENCE
☐ **2** 5-POINT PREFERENCE—You must show proof when you are hired.

10-POINT PREFERENCE—If you claim 10-point preference, you must complete a Standard Form 15, which is available at any Federal Job Information Center. ATTACH THE COMPLETED SF 15 TO THIS APPLICATION, TOGETHER WITH THE PROOF REQUESTED IN THE SF 15.

☐ **3** Non-compensably disabled or Purple Heart recipient.
☐ **4** Compensably disabled (less than 30%).
☐ **5** Spouse, widow(er), or mother.
☐ **6** Compensably disabled (30% or more).

THE FEDERAL GOVERNMENT IS AN EQUAL OPPORTUNITY EMPLOYER

Page 1   PREVIOUS EDITION USABLE   NSN 7540-00-935-7150   171-106

Standard Form 171 (Rev. 2/84)
Office of Personnel Management
FPM Chapter 295

Standard Form 171 *(continued).*

23 May we ask your present employer about your character, qualifications and work record? A "NO" will not affect our review of your qualifications. If you answer "NO" and we need to contact your present employer before we can offer you a job, we will contact you first....................

YES ☐ NO ☐

24 READ WORK EXPERIENCE ON THE INSTRUCTION PAGE BEFORE YOU BEGIN
- Describe your current or most recent job in Block A and work backwards, describing each job you held during the past 10 years.
- You may sum up in one block work that you did more than 10 years ago. But, if that work is related to the type of job you are applying for, describe each related job in a separate block.
- If you were unemployed for longer than 3 months, list the dates and your address(es) at that time in 47. Do not list unemployment that was more than 10 years ago.

- INCLUDE VOLUNTEER WORK (non-paid work)—If the work (or a part of the work) is like the job you are applying for, complete all parts of the experience block just as you would for a paying job. You may receive credit for work experience with religious, community, welfare, service, and other organizations.
- INCLUDE MILITARY SERVICE—You should complete all parts of the experience block just as you would for a non-military job, including all supervisory experience. Describe each major change of duties or responsibilities in a separate experience block.
- IF YOU NEED MORE EXPERIENCE BLOCKS OR MORE SPACE TO DESCRIBE A JOB— For more blocks, use the SF 171-A or sheets of paper the same size as this page (be sure to include all information we ask for in A or B below). On each sheet show your name, Social Security Number, and the announcement number or job title. For more space continue in 47 or on a sheet of paper as described above.
- IF YOU NEED TO UPDATE (ADD MORE RECENT JOBS), use the SF 172 or a sheet of paper as described above.

A

Name and address of employer's organization (include ZIP Code, if known)	Dates employed (give month and year) From: To:	Average number of hours per week
	Salary or earnings Starting $ per Ending $ per	Place of employment City State
Exact title of your job	Your immediate supervisor Name Area Code Telephone Number	Number and job titles of any employees you supervise(d)
Kind of business or organization (manufacturing, accounting, social service, etc.)	If Federal employment (civilian or military), list series, grade or rank, and the date of your last promotion	Your reason for wanting to leave

Description of work: Describe your specific duties, responsibilities and accomplishments in this job. If you describe more than one type of work (for example, carpentry and painting, or personnel and budget), write the approximate percentage of time you spent doing each.

For Agency Use (skill codes, etc.)

B

Name and address of employer's organization (include ZIP Code, if known)	Dates employed (give month and year) From: To:	Average number of hours per week
	Salary or earnings Starting $ per Ending $ per	Place of employment City State
Exact title of your job	Your immediate supervisor Name Area Code Telephone Number	Number and job titles of any employees you supervised
Kind of business or organization (manufacturing, accounting, social service, etc.)	If Federal employment (civilian or military), list series, grade or rank, and the date of your last promotion	Your reason for leaving

Description of work: Describe your specific duties, responsibilities and accomplishments in this job. If you describe more than one type of work (for example, carpentry and painting, or personnel and budget), write the approximate percentage of time you spent doing each.

For Agency Use (skill codes, etc.)

Standard Form 171 (continued).

EDUCATION

25 Did you graduate from high school? *If you have a GED high school equivalency or will graduate within the next nine months, answer "YES".*

YES ☐ If "YES", give month and year of graduation: _____
NO ☐ If "NO", give the highest grade you completed: _____

26 Write the name and location *(city and state)* of the last high school you attended

27 Have you ever attended college or graduate school?
YES ☐ If "YES", continue with **28**
NO ☐ If "NO", go to **31**.

28 NAME AND LOCATION *(city, state and ZIP code)* OF COLLEGE OR UNIVERSITY *If you expect to graduate within nine months, give the **month** and **year** you expect to receive your degree.*

| | MONTH AND YEAR ATTENDED | | NO. OF CREDITS COMPLETED | | TYPE OF DEGREE *(e.g. B.A., M.A.)* | YEAR OF DEGREE |
	From	To	Semester Hours OR Quarter Hours			
1)						
2)						
3)						

29 CHIEF UNDERGRADUATE SUBJECTS
Show major on the first line

| | | NO. OF CREDITS COMPLETED |
		Semester Hours OR Quarter Hours
1)		
2)		
3)		

30 CHIEF GRADUATE SUBJECTS
Show major on the first line

| | | NO. OF CREDITS COMPLETED |
		Semester Hours OR Quarter Hours
1)		
2)		
3)		

31 Have you completed any other courses or training **related to the kind of jobs you are applying for** *(for example, trade, vocational, Armed Forces, or business)?*
YES ☐ If "YES", give the information requested below *(More courses?—Use a sheet of paper)*
NO ☐ If "NO", go to **32**.

	MONTH AND YEAR TRAINING COMPLETED	TOTAL CLASSROOM HOURS	SUBJECT(S)	NAME AND LOCATION OF SCHOOL *(City, state, and ZIP code, if known)*	CERTIFICATE, DIPLOMA, etc *(if any)*
1)					
2)					
3)					

SPECIAL SKILLS, ACCOMPLISHMENTS AND AWARDS

32 List your special qualifications, skills or accomplishments that may help you get a job. *Some examples are: skills with machines; most important publications (do not submit copies); public speaking and writing experience; membership in professional or scientific societies; patents or inventions; etc.*

33 How many words per minute can you:

TYPE?	TAKE DICTATION?

Agencies may test your skills before hiring you.

34 List **job-related** licenses or certificates that you have, such as: *registered nurse; lawyer; radio operator; driver's; pilot's; etc.*

	LICENSE OR CERTIFICATE	DATE OF LATEST LICENSE OR CERTIFICATE	STATE OR OTHER LICENSING AGENCY
1)			
2)			

35 Do you speak or read a language other than English *(include sign language)?* *Applicants for jobs that require a language other than English may be given an interview conducted solely in that language.*
YES ☐ If "YES", list each language and place an "X" in each column that applies to you.
NO ☐ If "NO", go to **36**.

| LANGUAGE(S) | CAN PREPARE AND GIVE LECTURES | | CAN SPEAK AND UNDERSTAND | | CAN TRANSLATE ARTICLES | | CAN READ ARTICLES FOR OWN USE | |
	Fluently	With Difficulty	Fluently	Passably	Into English	From English	Easily	With Difficulty
1)								
2)								

36 List any honors, awards, or fellowships you have received. For each, give the year it was received.

REFERENCES

37 List three people who are **not** related to you and who know your qualifications and fitness for the kind of job(s) for which you are applying. **Do not** list supervisors you listed under **24**.

	FULL NAME OF REFERENCE	PRESENT BUSINESS OR HOME ADDRESS *(Number, street, city, state, and ZIP code)*	TELEPHONE NUMBER(S) *(include area code)*	BUSINESS OR OCCUPATION
1)				
2)				
3)				

Page 3

Standard Form 171 *(continued).*

Place an "X" in the proper column for each question below

	YES	NO

38 Are you a citizen of the United States? If "**NO**", write the country or countries you are a citizen of: _____

> **Important note about questions 39 through 44:** We will consider the date, facts, and circumstances of each event you list. In most cases you can still be considered for Federal jobs. However, if you fail to tell the truth or fail to list all relevant events, this failure may be grounds for not hiring you, for firing you after you begin work, or for criminal prosecution (18 USC 1001).

39 During the last **10 years**, were you **fired from any job** for any reason, did you **quit after being told that you would be fired**, or did you leave by mutual agreement because of specific problems? If "**YES**", use 47 to write for each job: *a) the name of the employer; b) the approximate date you left the job; and c) the reason(s) why you left.* ......

> **When answering questions 39 through 44 you may omit:** 1) traffic fines of $100.00 or less; 2) any violation of law committed before your 18th birthday, if finally decided in juvenile court or under a youth offender law; 3) any conviction set aside under the Federal Youth Corrections Act or similar State law; 4) any conviction whose record was expunged under Federal or State law.

40 Have you **ever** been convicted of or forfeited collateral for **any felony**? ....

> A felony is defined as any violation of law punishable by imprisonment of longer than one year, except for violations called misdemeanors under State law which are punishable by imprisonment of two years or less.

41 Have you ever been convicted of or forfeited collateral for any **firearms** or **explosives** violation? ....

42 During the last **10 years** have you forfeited collateral, been convicted, been imprisoned, been on probation, or been on parole? Do **not** include violations reported in **40** or **41** above. ....

43 Are you **now** under charges for **any** violation of law? ....

44 Have you **ever** been convicted of a **court-martial**? If no military service, answer "NO". ....

> **IF YOU ANSWERED "YES" TO 40, 41, 42, 43, or 44, GIVE DETAILS IN 47.** For each violation write the: 1) date; 2) charge; 3) place; 4) court; and 5) action taken.

45 Do any of your relatives work for the United States Government or the United States Armed Forces? Include: *father; mother; husband; wife; son; daughter; brother; sister; uncle; aunt; first cousin; nephew; niece; father-in-law; mother-in-law; son-in-law; daughter-in-law; brother-in-law; sister-in-law; stepfather; stepmother; stepson; stepdaughter; stepbrother; stepsister; half brother; and half sister.* ....

If "**YES**", use 47 to write for each of these relatives, their: a) name; b) relationship; c) department, agency, or branch of the Armed Forces.

46 Do you receive, or have you ever applied for retirement pay, pension, or other pay based on military, Federal civilian, or District of Columbia Government service? ....

ADDITIONAL SPACE FOR ANSWERS

47 Write the number to which each answer applies. **If you need more space**, use sheets of paper the same size as this page. On each sheet write your name, Social Security Number, and the announcement number or job title. Attach all additional sheets at the top of page 3.

SIGNATURE, CERTIFICATION AND RELEASE OF INFORMATION

YOU MUST SIGN THIS APPLICATION. Read the following carefully before you sign.

A false statement on any part of your application may be grounds for not hiring you, or for firing you after you begin work. Also, you may be punished by fine or imprisonment (U.S. Code, Title 18, Section 1001).

> I **understand** that any information I give may be investigated as allowed by law or Presidential order;
>
> I **consent** to the release of information about my ability and fitness for Federal employment by employers, schools, law enforcement agencies and other individuals and organizations, to investigators, personnel staffing specialists, and other authorized employees of the Federal Government.
>
> I **certify** that, to the best of my knowledge and belief, all of my statements are true, correct, complete, and made in good faith.

48 SIGNATURE (Sign each application in dark ink)

49 DATE SIGNED (Month, day, year)

✩ U.S. GOVERNMENT PRINTING OFFICE: 1988-201-760/60309

Standard Form 171 *(continued).*

═══ The SF-171

The SF-171 is to the government what the résumé is to the private sector. The SF-171 gets the government interested, then you may be contacted for an interview. In fact, some jobs are filled on the basis of the SF-171 alone. What's on your SF-171 will determine whether you get past the first hurdle of being rated "qualified" for the position you want.

It's imperative that your SF-171 clearly and completely describe all experience, education, skills, and performance appraisals (if you have prior civil service) that pertain to the job you're applying for. Literally hundreds of applications pass over a rater's desk every month, and in some places every week. If something on your form is ambiguous, the rater has neither the time to call you nor the authority to make assumptions about what you meant.

Say you're applying for a secretarial position. The *U.S. Qualifications Standards* lists the requirements: so much experience in typing, so many words per minute, a knowledge of office machines, and so on. Your last job was as executive secretary to the president of Texaco, so that's what you write on your SF-171: "Last job held: executive secretary to the president of Texaco." You don't describe what you did because it's obvious what you did. And since everyone knows that Texaco presidents don't hire slouches for secretaries, the rater will dash to mark you "qualified!" Right?

Wrong. Unless you've painstakingly detailed everything you did, the rater has nothing to match to her qualifications standards and will simply pass you over. Don't ever assume she knows what secretaries do, or what budget analysts, accounting technicians, payroll clerks, or any other personnel do. It's your responsibility to bring your qualifications to her. You must show why your skills match the advertised opening. Even if she knows what executive secretaries do, she must be able to tell an auditor why she rated you "qualified."

To avoid a lot of frustration with the application process, first find out the conditions for the position in which you're interested. The standards book is available for your perusal; read it, then start writing. Don't just copy the requirements onto your SF-171; a rater will see through that in a minute. If you're truly qualified for a job, you'll be able to write its qualifications yourself and show why what you've done applies to it.

CPO puts out fliers that give tips on filling out the SF-171. After you've filled it out, make an appointment with a staffing specialist to review it. They'll offer assistance and advice; it's part of their job. It's not unusual for a person to have been rated "not qualified" for a job, get advice on how to make her application more accurately reflect her qualifications, then resubmit and get rated "qualified." It happens all the time.

Some SF-171 guidelines:

- Separate applications must be used for each job you apply for. Prepare a master SF-171 and photocopy it, leaving certain items blank, so that you may apply for different jobs and save yourself the trouble of filling out this lengthy form more than once.
- Block 6: Under "other last names ever used," put your maiden name. This will aid the staff when verifying employment at places you worked when single.
- Block 9: If you don't work, supply your husband's work phone number. CPO will try only two or three times to reach you; if unsuccessful, they will pass over your application.
- Block 11: NAF jobs do not count as "previous federal employment."
- Block 12: "Current application filed with OPM" applies only if you submitted one to an OPM and received a rating. Attach the notification of rating.
- Block 20: Under "veteran preference," if applicable, attach a copy of your discharge papers.
- Block 21: Fill this section out in much more detail than you would a résumé, being very specific about what you did. Credit is given for volunteer work. Account for all periods of unemployment of three months or more.
- Block 22: Attach copies of all licenses, registrations, or certificates you hold that pertain to your job. Testing of typing or stenography skills is often required.
- Block 23: Attach college transcripts. If you don't have them, ask for Form 60-R0481, which serves in lieu of transcripts. Government-sponsored training classes count, as do correspondence courses.
- If an item doesn't apply to you, write "NA" (not applicable) to let the rater know you read the question. Never leave anything blank.
- Ask CPO what papers you need to submit besides the SF-171. There are often a lot of them.

≡ Federal Job Fairs

OPMs sponsor federal job fairs, which are sessions where applicants can be rated, interviewed by prospective supervisors, and hired on the spot. These fairs are held when a large number of positions are open and need to be quickly filled. Job fairs often revolve around a theme, such as medical, engineering and technical, or clerical. They are open to the public and are usually advertised in the classified section of the local paper.

Keep in touch with your area OPM so that you'll know when a local job fair is being held. If you sent an SF-171 to your area OPM for a position and were rated, you usually will be sent a flier advertising the fair. If one is scheduled but you are unable to attend, you can be considered if you send your SF-171 directly to the OPM and mark on it "Job Fair Announcement No. XXX" and the occupation for which you are applying. Check the deadline by which the OPM must receive it.

≣ Employment Overseas

As any wife stationed overseas knows, finding a job can be tough. There are three main reasons for this. Federal jobs are extremely limited, and in remote areas they are practically nonexistent; they are limited by law and by agreement with the host nation. You are competing with a group that has equal or greater priority for these federal jobs: citizens of the host country. And if you don't speak the language, the federal government is about the only employer available to you.

Employment procedures overseas must meet legal, regulatory, and mission requirements and must uphold host government agreements. The government has only the jobs required to accomplish its mission, and there are far more applicants than jobs. Congress places limits on the number of DOD civilians allowed overseas; it's virtually a no-growth market.

For what jobs there are, qualified host citizens have as much right as you do. Their rights are spelled out in Status of Forces Agreements (SOFA) the United States enters into with each host country, agreements that, among other things, discuss the number of jobs the United States must provide for the host citizenry.

U.S. law requires SOFAs, not Department of Defense policies. Showing how our presence benefits the local economy is one of the ways we persuade countries to keep us there. More than one base has been saved from being shut down simply because our hosts were reminded how many people would lose their jobs. Furthermore, local nationals bring stability and a knowledge of the language to the job, which most military spouses don't. For many jobs, such characteristics are essential.

You can prepare for overseas employment while still stateside by asking your sponsor or the Public Affairs Office at the new location for the address of the overseas CPO serving it. Then write that CPO to ask about the job situation and for details on submitting applications. Those interested in teaching opportunities at overseas DODDS schools should write the Department of Defense, Office of Dependent Schools, 2461 Eisenhower Ave., Alexandria, VA 22331-1100.

If you've made an effort to learn the language, not only will it make life much easier, but it also might enable you to get a job on the local economy. This is a wonderful way to broaden your horizons. Market yourself the same way you would in the States.

In addition, countries where many American multinational companies operate usually have an American Chamber of Commerce. Check the local phone directory or ask at the CPO, which should have a book that lists all American companies in the country, with addresses, points of contact, and phone numbers.

≡ The Military Family Act

Something of particular interest to military spouses is the Spouse Hiring Preference of the Military Family Act (Public Law 99-661), passed by Congress in 1985. This act requires that, when the spouse is qualified and the job is in the same commuting area as the servicemember's duty station, military spouses get preference for federal civilian positions. (Coast Guard spouses are not included, as the Coast Guard is not considered part of the armed forces for the purpose of this act. The Coast Guard has its own program for spouses of active-duty personnel.) The jobs affected are GS-2 through 15, comparable wage system (blue-collar) jobs, and NAF jobs level UA-8 and below. Spouses who teach in DODDS schools are also included.

Q: Under the Spouse Employment Preference Program, am I restricted to applying to the same branch of service that my husband is in?
A: No.

Stateside, this law applies from thirty days before you arrive at the new duty station to six months before the tour is up. At foreign duty stations there's no time limit. You may file your application with the overseas CPO thirty days before you move, but you won't receive preference until you actually arrive. Whether you're overseas or stateside, placement into any job that lasts one year or more ends your preference eligibility (whether you were placed via the preference or not) until you move again. If you're offered a job for which you had indicated availability but decline, your preference for that move is ended.

This act does not mean that you can walk into your old job at the new duty station. For priority consideration to have any effect, a vacancy for which you're qualified must already exist. The government will not create a job for you. There is no guarantee that the job you held at the last station will be available at the new one. Also, the preference applies only to external recruitments, not noncompetitive ones.

≡ Work for Yourself

Some military wives with transportable skills set up home offices. This is a trend that is gaining popularity in the civilian sector, as more women attempt to maintain careers while staying home with their children, or just because they prefer a convenient, more flexible routine. Only the motivated and self-disciplined can make this work, however.

One Marine Corps wife with secretarial skills started her own business with a word processor on a kitchen table. She advertised in the newspaper classifieds, church bulletins, and the yellow pages business listings and attracted clients that owned businesses but could not afford full-time secretarial help. She worked during preschool and late-night hours and had a drop box on her front door for clients to leave materials. Her contract specified what hours she was available to them.

If your children need pocket money, ask if the YMCA or base Family Services center has a "Hire a Teen" program, which matches teens and their perpetual need for money with adults who have money but little time. Some Family Services and state job services hold job-hunting workshops and fairs for teens. Ask the high school counselor about the Stay in School and cooperative education programs. Restaurants, hotels, resorts, amusement parks, and summer camps employ teens, as do the commissary and recreation facilities on base. The Boys and Girls Clubs of America also might help.

An Army wife turned her love and knowledge of oriental rugs into a business. She found a wholesaler and exhibited her rugs at coffee groups, officers' clubs, and the local merchandise mart. Because her overhead was minimal, her prices were cheaper than those of oriental rug stores. Word-of-mouth advertising spread quickly, and her business thrived.

An Air Force wife skilled at sewing went into business making costumes for Olympic skating champions.

A Navy wife who had given up her job as a second-grade teacher when she moved launched a successful business teaching etiquette classes to little girls.

Another Navy wife provided child care, and cleaned offices and houses on weekends. She generated so much business she hired four helpers.

One Air Force wife sold real estate at every station she moved to, until her husband received overseas orders. There, she contacted the Education Center, where they gave her a job giving real estate seminars for military personnel. The day-long seminars were offered every month and were very well attended. It wasn't as lucrative as selling real estate (which she resumed upon return to the States), but she enjoyed herself and made contacts that came in handy later.

Another Air Force wife, a licensed physical therapist, searched for a job after a move. Unsuccessful, she did volunteer work for nursing homes and eventually found herself in business ministering to homebound senior citizens and sick young people. Her clients were all referred by the nursing home patients and staff.

If you don't want to operate a full-fledged business, there are many things you can do just for pocket money. Do you speak Spanish? Are you good in math? Tutor students having difficulty in these subjects. Ask at a local school for details. Also ask about substitute teaching; you don't always have to be a teacher to do this. Post notices offering your services for waxing cars and washing windows. Sit for children, plants, pets, and houses. Think of all the servicemembers you know who detest polishing their boots and ironing their uniforms; let them know that for a price, you'll do it. Many dual-income families would love to come home to a clean house and ready-made dinner. Arrange your schedule to accommodate them. Can you sew? Lots of people like custom clothes, slip-covers, and drapes. Sew for them—or give sewing lessons! Teach arts and crafts, faux painting, wallpaper hanging, music, or cake decorating. Teach dancing to children. Advertise your typing skills at the local college. Don't underestimate what you can do; a skill you consider mundane may be valuable to someone else.

Arrange parties or bartend at them. Cater. Arrange theme food baskets and sell them. Perform magician's tricks at children's parties. Advertise your skill at photography or camcorder operation. Do you know calligraphy? Locate people who favor personalized stationery. Are you good at household handy work? There are lots of drippy faucets and creaky doors out there. Run errands for people who are homebound. Barter your services: Swap mending for guitar lessons, haircuts for typed résumés, or baby-sitting for house-sitting.

I sell Pampered Chef products. Multilevel marketing firms like Amway, Melaleuca, Discovery Products, and Avon can be great ways to earn side money. The initial investments are low, you can do it wherever you are, and you can work it around your schedule as wife and mother. My activities with the wives' club provide a built-in network to discuss the products. I use them when entertaining, and this has led to requests for shows. You have to work at this like any other job, but it can pay off.

Defense Department regulations permit spouses to operate non-professional businesses from government quarters. Read the pamphlet

Operating Home-Based Businesses in Military Housing, available from the Military Family Resource Clearinghouse, Suite 903, 4015 Wilson Blvd., Arlington, VA 22203. If you live off base, you'll need to research local zoning laws to see whether home businesses are permitted and if a license or permit is required.

Ensure that your business property is adequately insured. Consider liability coverage for any injury or property damage that might occur from your business. Your present homeowner's or renter's insurance might provide some coverage.

You will need to obtain a state sales tax number. Keep good records of your income and expenses. You'll need them for billing clients and for the Internal Revenue Service. Since taxes won't be taken out of the checks you receive from clients, you'll probably pay them on a quarterly basis. Talk to a tax lawyer or accountant about legitimate deductions.

Take small-business courses at the local community college. Join a professional association in your field. You'll meet potential clients and possibly get discounts on merchandise and insurance. The three-volume National Directory of Associations, available at your library, can give you an address.

Direct Selling Organizations

No doubt you're aware of multilevel and direct selling organizations that market cosmetics, jewelry, and household goods through home parties and other means. A great many people sell such products for side money. While most of these companies are honest, some are not. The Direct Marketing Association is an organization that monitors and imposes a code of ethics on the companies that belong to it. Write to the association at 1101 17th St. N.W., Washington, DC 20036-4704 for a list of its members and pamphlets with tips on buying, selling, and avoiding fraud. Plenty of other reputable direct selling organizations don't belong to the association, though. You can check those out with the Better Business Bureau.

Beware of Frauds

Be *very* suspicious of newspaper advertisements that offer huge sums of money for little effort. Except for lotteries, there's no such thing. Con artists are everywhere, and their targets are low-income and disabled people and those who need extra money but find it impossible to work outside the home. Most of their advertised schemes are outright frauds. You send your hefty "initial investment" (a tip-off to fraud right there), and they send you a kit for one item, explaining that you must demonstrate your skill before they'll contract with you. But no matter how cleverly you sew those baby booties, how skillfully you appliqué that apron, or how well you varnish that wooden toy, it will never be good enough to "satisfy the tastes of our discerning customers." The "discerning customers" don't exist—or if they do, *you* have to find them.

As for stuffing envelopes, that perennial favorite of con artists, while it is true that a great deal of mass mail is sent out, companies that send it use sophisticated techniques and equipment that you cannot compete with.

≡ Further Reading

Barkin, Carol, and Elizabeth James. *Jobs for Kids*. New York: Lothrop, Lee and Shepard Books, 1990.

Bastress, Frances. *The New Relocating Spouse's Guide to Employment Options: Strategies in the U.S. and Abroad*. Manassas Park, VA: Impact Publications, 1994.

Bibliography of References on Work/Income. Available from the Military Family Clearinghouse, 4015 Wilson Blvd., Suite 903, Arlington, VA 22203-5190, (703) 696-5806 or (800) 336-4592.

Bolles, Richard Nelson. *What Color Is Your Parachute?* Berkeley, CA: Ten Speed Press, 1995. Revised annually.

Elkstrom, Ruth B., et al. *How to Get College Credit for What You Have Learned as a Homemaker and Volunteer*. Princeton, NJ: Educational Testing Service, 1988.

Federal Jobs Digest. *Working for Your Uncle*. Ossining, NY: Breakthrough Publications, 1994. (800) 824-5000.

French, Albert L. *How to Locate Jobs and Land Interviews: A Complete Guide, Reference, and Resource Book for the Job Hunter*. Denver: High Pine Publishers, 1991.

Henderson, David G., *Job Search: Marketing Your Military Experience*, 2nd edition. Mechanicsburg, PA: Stackpole Books, 1995.

Merchandising Your Job Talents. Booklet published by the Bureau of Labor Statistics. Available from the Consumer Information Center, Department MB, Pueblo, CO 81009.

Merchandising Your Volunteer Service for Job Credit. Available from the volunteer counselor at your Family Services office.

6

≡ Financial Affairs

Money! Is there a subject that intrigues or perplexes us more? How to earn it, spend it, make it work for us . . . it's the subject of books, magazines, and arguments.

It's also the subject of this chapter. Though I'm not going to promise to make you rich, I am going to discuss ways to keep you from getting poor.

≡ The Leave and Earnings Statement

Before you can know whether you're living within your means, you must know what your means are. For most active-duty families, the primary source of income is the servicemember's paycheck. Each paycheck is accompanied by a Leave and Earnings Statement (LES). It details what was earned and what was deducted, where allotments were sent and how much they were, what allowances and special monies were paid, and how much vacation was taken and accrued. This is the information upon which your family's financial planning is built. Reservists receive an LES also, with drill and retirement information.

The military paycheck is calculated from information fed into a computer. Neither the people who enter the informa-

We were at Altus Air Base for nine months before we realized that our allowance was being calculated at the "without dependents" rate instead of the appropriate—and higher—"with dependents" rate. Moral of the story: Check your LES!

Use a budget to see if you're putting your money where you want to. If your goal is to finance your kids' college, make sure frivolous spending isn't keeping you from this goal.

tion nor the computers that process it are infallible, especially since the Pentagon uses 227 different accounting and finance systems! It's your responsibility to review the LES every month to make sure your family is getting what it's supposed to and to bring any problems to your finance office's attention. If you can't read the LES, inquire at your Family Services office, where classes are often held to explain the LES. If there are no classes, there should at least be a brochure.

LES entries describe leave (vacation time) and money. Let's look first at leave, which is requested through supervisors or commanders.

══ Leave

The following are the basic types of leave:

Annual Leave. Vacation time accrued at the rate of 2.5 days for each month of active duty. Up to sixty days may be accumulated; after that a servicemember must "use or lose."

Advance Leave. "Loaned" annual leave for servicemembers who need to take leave but don't have enough.

Excess Leave. Leave without pay given in emergency situations when the servicemember doesn't have enough leave accrued but is unable to pay back borrowed leave.

Emergency Leave. Counts as annual leave when taken but can be used only for a family emergency. It's usually given for up to fifteen days but can be approved for thirty. The Red Cross must verify the emergency before emergency leave can be granted.

Convalescent (Sick) Leave. Given if a servicemember is under special medical care or recovering from an operation.

Environmental and Morale Leave. Offered to servicemembers in remote, isolated locations where transportation is not easily available.

Special Leave. Thirty days for servicemembers who voluntarily extend their tours in hostile fire areas for six months.

Permissive TDY or TAD. Given so that servicemembers can attend semiofficial meetings and take house-hunting trips prior to PCS moves. TDY means "temporary duty," TAD means "temporary additional duty." Both TDY and TAD involve duty or schooling off base, usually at another base.

There are leaves for special situations like maternity, R & R (rest and recuperation), rehabilitation, delay en route, and sick-in-quarters. There are also leave awaiting orders, military academy leave, and proceed time. Passes or liberties are short amounts of time that do not require annual leave and usually do not exceed seventy-two hours. For any kind of leave, Saturdays and Sundays are counted; a vacation from Wednesday to Wednesday is counted as seven days off, not five.

Pay

Basic Pay. Basic pay is the first entry in this part. Since 1790 every servicemember has received basic pay, a simple wage that covers a twenty-four hour, seven-day workweek. The intent of basic pay is to show that every job is important; that is why everyone with the same rank and time in service gets the same basic pay.

Special Pay. But not all jobs are equal, and that's where the fifty-six types of special pay come in. Special pay recognizes critical skills, helps compensate for unique hardships, and persuades servicemembers to reenlist. Special pay can take the form of enlistment bonuses, selective reenlistment bonuses, pay for hazardous duty, submarine duty, nuclear duty, foreign duty, or demolition duty. It shows up as flight pay, sea pay, pay for proficiency in foreign languages, and pay for jobs with chronic manpower shortages. Medical professionals, divers, engineering and scientific officers, and people who serve in hostile fire zones and in combat receive special pay. Special pay is also given to people stationed in some overseas areas to persuade them to remain there.

Reserve families may claim a child-care tax credit if someone must be paid to baby-sit while the Reservist drills. To qualify, the children must be under fifteen or disabled, and the spouse must be working or attending school full-time.

Reservists may stay free in government lodging while drilling. Off-base lodging is not reimbursed, but such expenses associated with drills may be tax-deductible.

Junior enlisted families should investigate the Expanded Federal Earned Income Tax Credit. It allows families who make less than $23,755 per year and have at least one child to take home up to $2,000 more of their pay than what they did prior to 1994.

Up to 25 percent of the military paycheck may be withheld, or *garnished*, to pay child support, alimony, or other debts.

Allowances

Allowances are money to help pay food and housing costs. Allowances are not intended to completely cover the expenses they're designed for; it's up to you to maintain a standard of living your allowances can support.

You might find the following types of allowances on your husband's LES.

Reservists may receive incapacitation pay if injured while drilling.

Basic Allowance for Subsistence (BAS).
In the early days, three meals a day came with a military paycheck. Where mess halls weren't available, servicemembers were given money to buy food—or "subsistence." This evolved into the basic allowance for subsistence, an allowance for food. When a servicemember is deployed or moves into the barracks, he does not receive a BAS, since the government feeds him.

Basic Allowance for Quarters (BAQ).
The basic allowance for quarters is paid to most families who don't live in government quarters. The amount given depends upon rank and family size. People who live in quarters pay for them by giving up the BAQ. If you live in quarters that are considered substandard because of size, condition, or location, however, you get to keep part of the BAQ. BAQ is computed at 65 percent of the average national housing costs for homes typically rented by people in each rank.

Variable Housing Allowance (VHA).
The variable housing allowance is a supplement to help close the gap between what the government pays you to live off post and what housing costs in that area actually are. Newly inducted or enlisted servicemembers receive a VHA based on where their families currently live, not on where the inductee is assigned.

Overseas Housing Allowance (OHA).
The overseas housing allowance is the same as the VHA, but for overseas stations. It helps compensate for fluctuating foreign currency exchange rates.

Dislocation Allowance.
The dislocation allowance is two months' BAQ to help defray moving expenses.

Temporary Lodging Allowance (TLA).
For overseas moves, the temporary lodging allowance helps defray temporary living expenses while you are waiting to move into a permanent residence. It used to be that servicemembers who started their tour unaccompanied but later changed it to accompanied would not get TLA. Now they may, if housing is not immediately available for the family when it arrives. TLA is not granted for family members acquired after the effective date of the orders overseas, however.

Temporary Lodging Entitlement.
The temporary lodging entitlement is the same as the TLA, but for stateside moves.

Cost of Living Allowance (COLA). The cost of living allowance is a basic pay supplement given to people living overseas to help compensate for higher prices. COLA payments are given regardless of whether you're living in quarters or on the economy, vary with location and rank, and are pegged to local currency exchange rates.

Family Separation Allowance. The family separation allowance is money paid at a daily rate for expenses that involuntary separations cause.

Clothing Allowance. Officers receive a one-time clothing allowance payment after commissioning with which to purchase uniforms and insignia. Enlisted members are issued items when they come on active duty and are given lump-sum maintenance allowances thereafter.

Continental Cost of Living Allowance (ConUS). ConUS is money given to people living in areas that are 8 percent or more above the national cost of living. About twenty areas qualify. The exact amount is pegged to the servicemember and the area.

Lodging Plus. Lodging plus is a per-diem reimbursement for TDY travel based on the actual daily amount the traveler pays, up to the ceiling established for the TDY location.

═ Other Details of the LES

What else will you find on an LES? Under "deductions," you'll find withholdings for FICA (Social Security) and federal and state income taxes. There will be a deduction for SGLI (Servicemen's Group Life Insurance) and the military dental insurance plan, if you subscribe. If you're making debt payments, they'll show up under "allotments" or "other collections." A small deduction is made from enlisted paychecks to support the military's retirement homes.

Keep in mind that military compensation isn't the simple dollar amount brought home every month. Exchange and commissary privileges, space-available travel, low-cost recreation facilities, medical care, and life insurance add to the total compensation package. There are tax breaks, too: BAQ, BAS, VHA, COLA, clothing, and family separation allowances are not taxed. State income taxes are paid to the state listed as your home of record, not the state where you're living. And did you know that in some states, if a servicemember buys a car, he doesn't pay tax on it if that state is not listed as his home of record? The car dealership just needs a copy of his orders, and he will be exempted from the tax. (Licensing fees, however, must be paid.) So what a servicemember really makes is a

If you, the spouse, work outside your home, don't forget to figure your own expenses into the budget. Child care, transportation, clothes, lunches, pocket money, and office gifts all add up. Dual-income couples also tend to spend more money on high-cost convenience foods. Then there's "guilt spending"—extras for the children because you feel bad about leaving them!

Write the due dates for payments—car, rent, insurance—on your calendar. Due dates for most payments can be changed upon request to come soon after payday.

Keep a Rolodex of frequently called business numbers, such as your bank and insurance company and your account numbers.

In our thirty-year marriage, my husband and I have always been financially stable. Here are our secrets:

- We quickly retire all consumer debt.
- We pay ourselves 10 percent of our paychecks.
- We put all we can into tax-deferred instruments like 401K plans and IRAs.
- We keep an emergency fund of three to six months' living expenses.

I buy batteries, film, paper products, and food in bulk at warehouse clubs. I buy all my Christmas needs December 26. My lawn furniture was purchased in October, my fur coat in May.

---

combination of actual cash paid plus how much he and his family save by using what's available.

Paychecks arrive the first of each month, or the first and fifteenth for those on the bimonthly plan. You can receive yours in the mail or have them directly deposited into your bank account. Servicemembers on unaccompanied tours overseas have a split-pay option; part can go to the servicemember, and the rest to his family.

≡ Setting Your Financial Goals

All well-run households have financial goals and plans for managing their money. As an ancient Roman put it, "Even with fair winds, you won't reach port if you don't know where it is." Goals give you something to look forward to. They're also a powerful mental tool for saving. Nobody likes passing something up because they can't afford it, but to pass it up because you're saving for something better makes saving easier.

Where would you like to be in five years? Are you interested in college? Do you want to buy a house, a boat, new furniture? To have a great vacation? Work out a budget to help you achieve these goals. Keep it flexible; like diets, the rigid ones never work. It may take you several months to find one that does. But, like diets, budgets get easier to stick to once they've been followed for a few months. And you'll see what a useful tool they can be. Study the accompanying budgets for ideas on how to set up one of your own.

Comparison shop for large purchases. Don't buy from a store simply because its advertising has convinced you it's a better buy. Many stores simply create a *perception* of savings with their ads.

If you feel that a lot of money is coming in each month, but you don't have much to show for it, carry a notepad around with you. Jot down all purchases, from 60¢ candy bars to $60 sweaters. You may be surprised at how much you spend on little things. Do you run errands to a convenience store twice a week? Perhaps you should buy more at the commissary when you go. What are your variable monthly expenses, such as household items, food, and restaurants? Look for places to make cuts. Expenses you perceive as fixed, such as transportation, may actually be variable, if you explore alternatives.

Budget counselors offer the following spending guidelines. If you increase in one area, you must decrease in another.

- 30 percent on housing (rent or mortgage, property tax, homeowner's insurance, home improvements).
- 5 percent on utilities (gas, electricity, telephone, water, trash pickup).
- 20 percent on food (groceries, eating out, buying food at work).
- 2–4 percent on essentials (laundry, dry cleaning, postage, toiletries).
- 5 percent on medical (insurance premiums, drugs, medical bills).
- 7 percent on clothing (including accessories like purses).
- 15 percent on transportation (car payments, car insurance, maintenance, and gas).
- 4 percent on recreation.
- 8 percent on savings.
- 2 percent on mad money (money unaccountable to anyone).

Budget Counseling

Although setting up a budget may seem easy, a surprising number of people have trouble doing it. While the specific reasons for financial problems are myriad, they all basically boil down to two things: over-enthusiastic use of credit and poor checkbook habits. It's ironic, because advice on managing money, planning a budget, using credit, and balancing a checkbook abounds for service families. The Family Services financial

Master Monthly Budget

	Payment Due Date	Amount
A. Living Expenses		
Rent/Mortgage Payment		
Food		
Utilities:		
Electricity		
Gas		
Sewage		
Telephone		
Trash		
Water		
Other Utilities		
Gasoline For Auto		
Automobile Maintenance (oil, tune-up, etc.)		
Automobile Repairs		
Laundry and Dry Cleaning		
Haircut and Beauty Shop Expenses		
Clothing Expenses (including uniform replacement)		
School Costs: Books, Tuition, and Lunches		
Insurance:		
Automobile		
Life		
Other Insurance		
Alimony/Child Support		
Child Care and Baby Sitting		
Church and Other Charity		
Entertainment Costs		
Cigarettes/Tobacco		
Medical and Dental Expenses		
Out of Pocket Expenses		
Other Living Expenses		
A. Total Living Expenses		
B. Bill Paying Expenses: Total bill paying expenses from schedule and record here.		
C. Set Aside for Savings and Major Purchases: Total from attached schedule and record here.		
Grand Total of Monthly Budget: This figure is the total of A, B, and C. It must equal the monthly net income. If this figure exceeds the monthly net income, you must cut expenses somewhere.		

Schedule of Creditors

Name, Address, and Telephone Number of Creditor	Account Number	Payment Due Date	Monthly Payment
1.			
2.			
3.			
4.			
5.			
6.			

Total Monthly Payment to Creditors

Enter in block **B** of the monthly budget . . . . _____

Monthly Set Aside for Savings and Major Purchases

1. Monthly savings set aside . . . . _____
2. Item desired _____
   Estimated cost _____
   Monthly set aside . . . . _____
   Total set aside to date _____
   Month when set aside goal is reached _____
3. Item desired _____
   Estimated cost _____
   Monthly set aside . . . . _____
   Total set aside to date _____
   Month when set aside goal is reached _____

Total Monthly Savings and Planned Purchase Set Aside

Enter in block **C** of the monthly budget . . . . _____

planning office exists solely to help with such matters, and many service credit unions offer seminars and advice. Unfortunately, most people who see budget counselors are command-referred, not there of their own initiative or free will, and by the time they go, they are so far in debt all the office can do is arrange a debt liquidation* plan.

There are preventive measures you can take before landing in this unhappy situation. Some families seeing themselves headed this way do seek help and are later greatly relieved that they did. You don't have to wait until you're in trouble to see a counselor; professional advice is worthwhile any time, if only to confirm your good judgment. It's especially useful at major changes in your life; moves, the birth of a child, even spousal employment can cause major upheavals with your finances. If you're newly married, a counselor can suggest ways of combining your two previously separate households into one. He can assist in setting up a household budget, help show where your money is going, and discuss methods of money management.

Amy Dacyczyn, a former Navy wife, self-styled "frugal zealot," and author of *The Tightwad Gazette* book and newsletter, made a shrewd observation of people's spending habits. The following is an excerpt from *Military Lifestyle*, reprinted by permission of Navy Editor Service:

> "During the time the Dacyczyns were active-duty military and living in base housing, Amy was aware that her neighborhood was like a little economic test tube. 'Here was a group of people who basically had the same incomes, same

---

As a budget counselor, I've seen many ways in which people get messed up. Some seize new credit, not realizing what the additional payments will do to their disposable income. Many get advance pay when they move and spend it quickly, but the allotments remain.

People get in trouble with their checkbooks. They don't balance them, they write checks and don't subtract the amounts. Then they must ask the tellers for their balances instead of referring to their own ledgers. Some "float" checks that reach the bank before their paycheck does.

If you are a newlywed, or even just engaged, some planning is in order. Discuss what each of you is financially bringing to the marriage and how you'll manage your money. Do you want to pool your assets or keep them separate? Pay bills promptly or wait for notices? Shop more than save or vice versa? Who will pay the bills?

When couples bicker over money, the lack of it is often less a factor than differing ideas on managing it.

---

*Not to be confused with debt *consolidation*, which is entirely different. Debt consolidation is rolling all your debts together and paying just one, easier to manage, bill every month. Many counselors do not recommend this, as it is too easy to be lulled into thinking everything's under control and start accumulating new debt.

benefits, same housing, two cars in their driveways, most had kids, everything was identical.' But the disparity Amy saw between some of those families was like night and day.

"'We were saving $700 a month during that time,' she says. 'We had four kids, two paid-for vehicles and no debts. There were families working two jobs, moonlighting and still couldn't make ends meet. Families need to pay attention to that, see that they can live cheaper. I was just so amazed to see people who couldn't make ends meet, when I knew their incomes were the same as mine or better.'"

≡ Your Personal Finances and the Military

Though being able to manage one's money well is an important trait for anyone, it's particularly important for servicemembers. Bounced checks and other bad debts are brought to the attention of commanders. An excessive amount of such notices can break a career; indeed, hundreds of people are involuntarily separated each year for their inability to manage money.

Bankruptcy should never be considered as anything but a last resort to solve money problems. It will remain on your credit record for up to ten years. During that time it will be difficult, if not impossible, for you to get a loan for a car, house, college tuition, or furniture. Landlords may not rent to you, and employers may shun you (it is legal and increasingly common for employers to check the credit records of potential employees). A bankruptcy filing can also effectively terminate a military career.

Why should something as personal as our finances have any bearing on the job? Isn't that an invasion of privacy? What business is it of anyone's but our own if we have excessive debts or write bad checks? These are good questions. There are, however, equally good answers.

> If you're a two-income family, don't set your expenses at the level of both your incomes. The spouse's income may be unpredictable. Try to live on one and save the other.

> Teach your children about saving money by making a game of clipping the bright-colored coupons from the Sunday papers. I show my kids the register receipt of my savings after each grocery trip we make, and share some of the money with them.

As we all know, being a servicemember is not an ordinary office job. There are unique duties, risks, and responsibilities. Many service jobs involve a knowledge of classified secrets. Most jobs involve, to some extent, either

Here are some savings tips:

- Save by payroll deduction. Money taken directly out of the paycheck is money not missed. Use it to make regular purchases of U.S. savings bonds or put it in an out-of-town savings or money market account; don't make it too accessible for impulse withdrawals.
- Buy in bulk when things are on sale. A freezer is a good investment.
- Offer gifts that won't cost you anything, like baby-sitting or house-cleaning.
- Save a dollar every day, more if you can afford it. Save pocket change.
- Look through junk mail and newspapers before throwing them out. Many contain discount coupons for video rentals, dry cleaning, fast food, car maintenance, film developing, and other goods and services you might use regularly.

a knowledge of sensitive items or an accessibility to areas where they are kept. Because of this, service-members—and their families—are of special interest to people who would like this information. Thus the service must be concerned with potential vulnerabilities of its members, such as severe indebtedness, mental or emotional problems, drug or alcohol abuse, criminal or sexual misconduct, or anything else that could lead to a potential exploitative situation. Such concern is not intended to pry into people's lives; it is meant to protect everyone.

The ability to manage money is also considered critical to good leadership abilities. If a person cannot manage his own money, how can he manage other people? How can any NCO or officer properly do his job with money troubles on his mind?

Another reason is that each of us represents the service as a whole. Many civilians judge the entire military on the conduct of the two or three with whom they may have had contact. You have only to notice the way many local newspapers report traffic accidents involving service-members: "There was an accident on Interstate 40 involving a soldier stationed at Fort Campbell and a resident of Clarkesville." Why the resident of Clarkesville's occupation is left out but the servicemember's—who is *also* a resident of Clarkesville—is considered newsworthy is peculiar indeed, but this demonstrates the high visibility we have in the local community.

Savings and Emergency Accounts

It is easy to let the regularity of steady pay lull us into living from paycheck to paycheck, but if you direct a certain amount every pay period into a savings account, you'll look forward to payday for the sheer pleasure of watching that account grow. Treat a monthly contribution to a savings account like a bill itself instead of something made at the end of the month if anything is left over. Build up one month's pay as a buffer to cover car repairs, plane tickets, and other unexpected expenses. Emergencies can cut a big chunk out of healthy savings; when you have none at all, either you end up at the emergency aid office, which may or may not be able to help, or you fall into a hard-to-escape credit trap.

Once you get your emergency account established, build another for all those bargains, great buys, and ordinary "wish" items we all come across. Use this account to pay cash for as much as you can. Credit card interest rates currently range from 9 to 21 percent; it's ridiculous to pay such rates if you can possibly avoid it. Yet many families keep a balance in a regular savings account and a balance of thousands of dollars on these credit cards. With savings accounts currently paying only about 4 percent interest, it doesn't take much figuring to see that these families are receiving four cents on the dollar on one hand and paying out over three times that on the other.

≡ Credit

Despite its high cost, credit isn't a bad thing. It can be wonderful when you have unexpected expenses and don't yet have an emergency account or when you just want a luxury that isn't too extravagant for your income. Just remember that credit is not a right; it is a privilege. Used judiciously it's an asset; misused, it can wreck your financial health.

If you're interested in obtaining credit, there are several things you can do to show your trustworthiness. Start a savings account; they're looked upon as evidence that you're able to manage money. If you need a loan, borrow against this account; the interest you pay will be partly offset by the interest your account earns. If you don't need a loan, you might consider taking one out to establish a credit history but depositing the money into your savings account. Since you're earning interest on the deposit while you pay off the loan, it cuts down the cost of the loan. Get a department store credit card and pay your bills promptly. If you pay during the thirty-day grace period, no interest is charged.

For the price of a stamp you can get the Consumer Information Catalog, which lists more than 200 free or inexpensive government publications. Contact the Consumer Information Center, Pueblo, CO 81009, phone (719) 948-3334.

Know the return policies of stores where you shop. Merchants are not legally obligated to take back nondefective merchandise. Those that do only do so to maintain customer goodwill.

If you are unable to obtain a loan by yourself, see if a close friend or relative will cosign with you. That means you make the payments, but if you default, the cosigner is responsible for the balance.

A terrific resource for money management is the public library. There are shelves of books on this subject. Also, your county agricultural extension office has home economists who can assist with budgeting and offer tips on nutrition, smart shopping, and saving money, free of charge.

You'll then develop a credit history, a record of which will be kept with one or all of the major credit-reporting agencies in the United States: TransUnion Corp., P.O. Box 7000, North Olmstad, OH 44070, (610) 690-4909; TRW, P.O. Box 72409, Dallas, TX 75374, (800) 682-7654; and CSC-Equifax, P.O. Box 740241, Atlanta, GA 30374, (800) 879-4094. Included in this history will also be a record of your past and present employment and of your debts and how well you paid them. You might even find court judgments, spousal employment, and a list of businesses to which you might have applied for (and been denied) credit. Any derogatory notes about your repayment of debts are noted. If you've been turned down for credit, you are entitled to a free credit report from the agency that supplied the would-be creditor with the information. Review it carefully. In fact, it's a good idea to review your credit record once a year, especially if you have a common name, and at least six months before making a major purchase. TRW supplies a free credit report each year. Your request must include your full name, spouse's first name, current and previous home addresses in the past five years, Social Security number, birthdate, and signature.

How Much Credit Can You Afford?

Study your budget. Your disposable income is how much money is left after expenses are paid, not this amount plus how much you can borrow. Credit is not more money; it is merely a convenience that lets you enjoy now what you'll have to pay for later.

Before buying on credit, analyze the item you want to buy. Property appreciates in value, furniture depreciates, and vacations disappear altogether. Where does your item fit? Would you think it a ridiculously extravagant purchase for your monthly disposable income? If so, chances are it is just as ridiculous on installment payments—or even more so, because with interest, it will cost you more. Does its purpose justify time payments?

If you experience problems meeting your installment payments, contact your creditors immediately. It's always better to contact them before they contact you.

Obtaining a Major Credit Card

A major credit card is one that is accepted by many different businesses for goods or services. Examples are MasterCard, VISA, Discover, and American Express. Nonmajor credit cards are cards issued and accepted only by one merchant, such as a department store or gas station.

To obtain a MasterCard or VISA (the most common and widely accepted major credit cards), call any bank. It can be in your area or out of town. You don't have to have an account there to apply. You will be sent an application. It is free; you will not be asked to pay any processing fees. The local bank doesn't actually issue the card. It handles the application, but the issuer is a large major bank such as Citibank, Chase Manhattan, Chemical, or Manufacturers Hanover. Competition among issuers is intense, and consumers with good credit can find many attractive incentives. Lower interest rates, waived annual fees, a rebate of a percentage of the total yearly amount spent, and insurance are just some of the things offered. A convenient way to comparison shop is to contact the Bankcard Holders of America, a nonprofit consumer education group that keeps a list of banks that charge low interest and annual rates. Its phone number is (703) 389-5445. A small fee is charged for the list.

— Staying out of Trouble

Staying out of financial trouble can be difficult just because you *are* a service family. The glittering array of stereo shops, furniture stores, used-car lots, and insurance agencies that form "the strip" outside every military base attests to what attractive sales targets we are. We hear, "Easy credit! We finance E-1 and up! No deposit, no down payment! Just bring your LES!" ad nauseam on the radio and TV and see it in newspaper ads. Each place boasts lower finance rates than the next, and all, of course, "know our special needs."

Keep track of addresses of mail-order firms to which you send checks by writing the address on the "memo" line on the check. When the check is canceled, you'll have a record of where it was sent.

There are good reasons for targeting us like this. In today's volunteer force, with competition for members keen from both the civilian and educational sectors, servicemembers are paid more now than ever before. The pay is steady, many essential expenses are

Don't shop at the last minute. A common shopping mistake is to wait until the last minute to purchase a badly needed item. But then you're apt to purchase it with price as a secondary consideration. The more costly the item, the farther in advance you should plan to buy it.

covered, much of our income is tax-free, and use of the exchange, commissary, and low-cost recreational facilities leaves us with more disposable income than we might otherwise have. The single servicemember has virtually an entire paycheck free when living in the barracks, eating in the mess hall, and taking advantage of the free medical and dental care.

Many servicemembers are young, newly married, and experiencing their first time away from home. There's so much we want and need: clothes, furniture, a nice TV, baby items. For many, the fact that this is our first time making money is an added incentive. We want to spend it. It's fun to spend money, and the urge to buy doesn't stop with just one item. Debts of $25,000 to $30,000 are not uncommon to military budget counselors. So before making additional credit purchases, ask yourself whether, rent or mortgage aside, your whole debt is (or will be) more than 20 percent of your yearly take-home pay. If so, it is bad news. In franker terms, if tipping the bagger at the commissary puts a strain on your budget or if taking your children to the zoo is impossible because you can't afford the admission fee, something is wrong. No one enjoys living like that, and no one in the military should have to. And it certainly does nothing to enhance a marriage.

Cordless phones don't keep secrets. They operate over radio waves, so anyone with a scanner, or a nearby neighbor with a phone on the same frequency, can listen in. Thieves eavesdrop with scanners for credit card numbers, vacation plans, and other sensitive information.

Don't pay for information you can get free. Ads are often run by private companies that promise, for a fee, to tell you how to buy valuable government surplus property and items seized from drug dealers. You can get the same information by calling the General Services Administration. Look in your phone book for the GSA's regional address. You can get on its mailing list for upcoming auctions.

≡ "Credit Assistance" and Other Scams

Con artists that promise credit assistance (loans) and prizes through postcard solicitations and 900 numbers have proliferated in the past few years. Since many people are cheated, some words are in order.

≡ Credit Assistance Companies

TV and newspaper advertisements abound by companies who promise to repair bad credit ratings, and to help people with poor credit histories get bank loans and major credit cards. While it isn't against the law for independent companies to charge consumers a fee for putting them in touch with banks that offer VISA and MasterCard or loans, these companies don't have any inside track on getting them.

They just know how to develop mailing lists of consumers who have problems getting credit cards or loans and how to write convincing ads. Once you pay your fee, these companies simply contact a few banks and ask them to send you a credit card or loan application. That doesn't mean the bank will approve it. The ads always state that the fee will be refunded if you don't get a credit card or loan, but actually *getting* the refund often proves difficult.

Companies that promise to repair a bad credit rating for a fee are outright lying. No one can remove bad credit reports that are accurate from your file. What can be done, and you don't have to hire anyone to do it, is to obtain a copy of your credit history and contest any derogatory reports you feel are erroneous. If the report is in error, it is removed. If not, it stays.

The Consumer Credit Counseling Service is a civilian, nonprofit organization that helps people solve credit problems. Look up the local CCCS under "credit" or in the white pages of your phone book.

900 Numbers

At one time or another you've probably received a postcard saying that you have won a valuable cash prize or free gift and instructing you to call a 900 number for more information.

No business can operate by giving away valuable cash prizes and free gifts to thousands of people. The intent of these postcards is to make money for the business by getting people to call the 900 numbers; these are calls that you, the caller, pay for. Do not confuse them with 800 numbers, which are toll-free. While many businesses use 900 numbers honestly, some do not. They charge outrageous fees for each call—$100 is not unheard of—or they charge per minute. On the per-minute calls, you'll often find yourself on hold for ten minutes, then given a lengthy recorded message. The "cash prize" will often turn out to be discounts on purchases from an overpriced merchandise catalog the company will send to you, and the "free gift" costs the price of the call.

The phone company does not receive the money from 900 calls; a 900 number is simply a service it provides to businesses that request it. If you feel that you have been victimized by a 900 number, complain to your local phone company. If the call was billed through them, they will sometimes remove a questionable charge from your bill and instruct the company to deal with you directly.

Be wary of phone solicitors. Con artists cash in with telemarketing scams that promise everything from credit cards and loans to jobs in Europe. They particularly exploit people with bad credit ratings and bankruptcy histories. Examples of common scams include "free" gifts that require you to pay shipping charges or "gift taxes," solicitors that give an unfamiliar name or just a post office box for an address, recorded messages that direct you to a 900 number for more information, and promises to find loans for large advance fees. *Never* give your credit card or bank account number to an unsolicited caller, and be wary of solicitors who don't want you to send money via U.S. mail. Con artists don't like the postal service because mail fraud carries stiff penalties. Thus, they'll often require you to use Federal Express or another private carrier.

☰ Service Credit Unions

Most bases have a credit union you can join. The main difference between a bank and a credit union is that anyone can open an account at a bank, but only a select group of people can join a credit union. There are credit unions for teachers, policemen, university students, and many other groups of people who share a common interest or profession.

A credit union pools deposit money to pay monthly dividends and make loans to its members. The interest on these loans is usually lower than interest on bank loans. Monthly service charges are also lower; in fact, because you receive dividends, you usually earn money on your checking or "share" account every month. Some credit unions offer IRAs and certificates of deposit, and many service credit unions allow you to remain a member even after you move or leave the service.

On bases where there is both a bank and a service credit union, the credit union usually gives overall better terms. Compare them before opening an account.

☰ Buying or Leasing a Car

When shopping for a car, think about how much you'll be using it. If you'll be putting a lot of miles on it each year, buy one that gets good mileage and is relatively inexpensive to fix. Try to buy one that can be paid off quickly, too. Compare the difference in total cost of the car if paid off in one or two years versus four or five. It could be thousands of dollars. Also factor in the cost of insurance when choosing a car. Some cars carry higher insurance costs.

My dad always told me that when a person drives a fancy car it doesn't necessarily mean he has more money than you. It usually just means he *owes* more.

If you aren't sure which model you'd like, you might want to rent a car for a month to give it an extended test drive.

A car that gets good mileage makes good sense for the working military wife, since the job at the next tour might be a considerable commute away. Good mileage can make all the difference when deciding whether the salary makes it worthwhile.

Leasing has become a popular option for many buyers. Educate yourself on its pros and cons. Leasing requires you to be responsible for taxes, insurance, registration, and repairs. Banks may require "gap" insurance in case the car is worth less at the end of the lease than originally anticipated, and excessive mileage is costly if you decide not to purchase the car at the end of the lease period. At the end of your lease, you will not get the break on sales tax you would if you traded in an owned car on another car. If you break your lease, you'll face heavy financial penalties, and negative marks on your credit record. Finally, know that most lessors don't permit a leased car to be taken overseas.

If you don't like haggling over car prices, there are services that haggle for you, whether you buy or lease. Many banks and insurance companies offer this service.

Q: What's a "run-through"?
A: On a car trade-in, you don't pay sales tax on the whole price of the new car; you just pay it on the difference between the new-car price and the value of your trade-in. If you have a private buyer for your car, many dealerships will permit you to sell your car to them and they, in turn, will sell it to your buyer so that you will still get a trade-in sales tax break when you purchase another car from them. This transaction is called a "run-through" or a "pass-through."

≡ Where to Get Financing

You've considered an expensive item you'd like to buy and have decided it justifies time payments. Where should you finance it?

Your bank or credit union should be your first choice. It might take some time to approve and process your loan, but you will get the lowest interest rate possible.

A bank exists to lend money, and it makes its profit by collecting interest on the loans. But a bank must feel reasonably sure that an applicant can repay the loan promptly and according to the terms agreed upon. When you apply for a loan, the bank examines your credit history before making its decision. Years of experience help the bank officers determine who is a good risk and who isn't. They must decline those they believe are bad risks so that the bank can continue to offer low interest rates. If a bank turns you down, it means its confidence in your ability to repay is low; your current disposable income is not up to the new purchase.

So if you're considering financing with a merchant, loan company, or other place because the bank turned you down, some questions are in order.

1. With the above in mind, are you still willing to take the chance that you can handle it?

When you finance directly from the merchant or a loan company, you pay a high interest rate, usually 18 percent or more, sometimes as high as 28 percent. Merchants and loan companies frequently will finance you even though you're a poor risk—that's why their rates are so high. And unlike banks, merchants are in the business of selling the items you buy. If you default on the payments, the merchant will repossess your item and resell it. Some businesses intentionally sell merchandise to people they know can't afford it. They receive a hefty down payment, some monthly payments, and the item back to resell. More than one car dealer has been declared off limits to military personnel because of this tactic.

2. With the price of this item so high you have to finance it in the first place, are you willing not only to make installment payments but to make them at high interest rates?

≡ Abuse of the Military Allotment System

A common abuse by merchants and loan companies is using the military allotment system for installment payments on furniture, trips, cars, stereos, and other expensive items. This is illegal. The military allotment system can be used *only* for family support, life insurance premiums, U.S. savings bonds, repayment of a loan obtained to buy a home or house trailer, credit to a savings account, or contributions to certain military relief organizations and the American Red Cross.

The allotment system was not set up so that private companies could use the military finance system to collect payments. But since doing so reduces credit risk and cuts bookkeeping costs, some merchants have the servicemember make out an allotment to have money put in a savings institution in his name. The merchant then attaches a line of credit to the account. The servicemember usually doesn't receive a bankbook, checkbook, monthly bank statement, or even the address of the bank where his money is going. Worst of all, many such accounts are "open," allowing the savings institution to continue transferring money to the private firm after the loan has been paid off. When this happens, it's up to the service-member to get his overpayment back. This can be difficult, even with professional help.

≡ Pawn Shops

Military towns are full of pawn shops. A glance in many will show brand-new merchandise, much of it still in original boxes, from people who thought they could handle the payments. Pawn shops can be great places for the wise buyer, but they're pretty grim for the seller.

≡ Door-to-Door Sales

Anyone who lives in an apartment or government quarters is familiar with door-to-door solicitors, people who sell everything from oil paintings to time shares. Such solicitation is not permitted in government quarters. Solicitors are permitted in quarters by appointment only. They make these appointments by telephone or by approaching people in common public areas such as the exchange or commissary parking lots. (Soliciting appointments in areas used for processing and housing transient personnel is not permitted.) If a solicitor comes to your quarters uninvited, the installation police should be called.

If you do make an appointment, ask to see the solicitor's permit before discussing the product. Solicitors must be authorized by the appropriate authority on your installation. To get this authorization, they undergo a background check. Be aware that standards vary for these checks, and the applicant cannot always be investigated as thoroughly as we might wish. Final "authorization" rests with you, the buyer.

It's critical that you thoroughly understand the product you're buying, whether it's from the exchange, a civilian store, or a door-to-door solicitor. Only then can you assess if its price is reasonable, if its quality is what you're looking for, and if it truly fits your needs. *Knowledge is your greatest protection against being ripped off.*

If you plan to buy a product, give yourself a few days to cost-compare. At the very least, you'll confirm that what you're buying is a good deal. If you're told the offer is a "one-time special" that you can only take advantage of immediately, forget it! Truly good deals are seldom accompanied by sales pitches like that; they sell on their own, whether on the spot or after days of careful consideration. The term *fly-by-night* evolved from precisely that—high pressure to buy a one-time special right now because this is the seller's "last day in town."

≡ Getting out of a Sales Contract

If you sign a contract with a door-to-door solicitor, the law gives you seventy-two hours to cancel the contract if you change your mind. If the purchase involves a contract signed in a store and you change your mind—you feel the product was misrepresented, you've decided you can't afford it, or you got a good look at the interest rates—the laws that apply vary from state to state. Some hold a contract signed by a spouse with no income of her own as not legally binding; in other states it is legally binding. Some have grace periods during which you can get out of the contract; others don't. See your legal officer. If you sign a contract with a business, such as a health spa, where monthly payments are made over several years, make sure there's a clause in it that will release you in case you move.

Some people don't seek help because they're afraid of looking stupid. They've made a mistake and don't want anyone to know, or they don't want word to get back to their commanding officers. There have even been cases of military personnel being threatened by merchants when they tried to get out of the contract. Don't be intimidated, just seek help. Don't ruin your budget for an expensive product you don't want.

≡ The Soldiers' and Sailors' Civil Relief Act

The Soldiers' and Sailors' Civil Relief Act was enacted by Congress at the beginning of World War II to protect servicemembers who entered or were called to active duty. Typically their military paychecks were lower than the civilian ones they were used to; thus, they were not able to pay their bills. So Congress required creditors to arrange new payment plans or even to defer payments until the servicemember was off active duty. This protection also applies to Reservists.

The act's protection begins when the servicemember receives orders to report for active duty and ends shortly after he is released. Protection is not automatic; a servicemember must let his creditors, such as banks, finance companies, and courts, know that he has been activated. Then new payment plans can be negotiated. Interest rates over 6 percent can be reduced to 6 percent per year for installment contracts, including real estate, if the servicemember can show that his ability to pay is materially affected by his active-duty service. Statutes of limitations for any legal disputes the servicemember was involved in before activation can be lengthened.

A servicemember may terminate a lease as long as the lease was signed before entering active duty, was for a home or business, and the servicemember and/or his family had actually been occupying it for a home or business. You must give the landlord written notice, and you are entitled to the return of your security deposit and any unearned portion of the rent.

The act also helps active-duty servicemembers who are sued while away on temporary duty. Before the act, default judgments had been entered against many servicemembers simply because they couldn't get back to defend themselves. The act calls for court proceedings to be postponed until the servicemember is able to return.

The act does not relieve a servicemember of obligations, nor is it concerned with obligations incurred *after* one comes on active duty. It simply helps the servicemember in situations that may be beyond his control. If you are in a situation where you think the act may apply, visit your legal office.

≡ Life Insurance

If you don't know anything about insurance and a persuasive sales agent comes to your door, it is easy to buy too much and the wrong kind. This is far more common than not having any at all. In fact, many families make themselves "insurance poor" by buying elaborate insurance with unnecessary frills.

The purpose of life insurance is to enable you to continue your present lifestyle after the loss of a breadwinner. So look at your budget and list your expenses. These determine how much life insurance you need.

Say you are a young couple without children, both of you work, and you haven't yet accumulated a lot. You have some new furniture and a car on which you're making payments. Maybe you have a small balance on a credit card. And that's it.

If your husband dies, you'll have some burial expenses; you'll need money to make your furniture and car payments; you'll need to continue paying on the credit card; and you'll need money to live on. How will the lack of your husband's paycheck affect your ability to meet these obligations?

If your insurance need is $50,000, don't get talked into a policy of $100,000 or more. The higher the amount, the higher the monthly payment. Why pay for something you don't need?

If you've been married longer, own a home, have children, and don't work, obviously you'll need a lot more than the person described above. Figure out your needs the same way. Again, buy only the anticipated needed amount. If it's $100,000 or $250,000, don't buy a policy for $500,000.

Give careful thought before buying large amounts of insurance on your children. Although such a loss would be devastating emotionally, it would not be devastating financially. Coverage equal to the cost of funeral and final expenses is appropriate. Life insurance for yourself, even if you're a nonbreadwinner, is a good idea if you have children. If something were to happen to you, your husband would have day-care, and possibly cooking and cleaning, expenses.

Once you've decided how much insurance you need, decide what kind to buy.

Types of Life Insurance

There are two major types of life insurance: whole life (also called permanent or regular) and term.

Whole Life.   When you purchase whole life, you're actually purchasing three separate items: insurance, a savings account, and the ability to borrow money. Agents push whole life the hardest since it's the most expensive and thus earns them the highest commissions. They justify the cost by saying that you build a cash value, you can borrow against the policy, and the premiums remain the same for the duration of the policy. For the first two or so years that you hold your policy, however, you'll build no cash value at all; the money goes to pay the agent's commission. When a cash value does start building, it is given a very poor interest rate, usually about 2.5 percent. And every cent you pay is one cent less the insurance company contributes when the insured dies. For example, if your husband took out a $20,000 policy and died after building a cash value of $15,000, the $20,000 you'd get would be the $15,000 he put in plus $5,000 more from the insurance company.

As for being able to borrow against your policy, you are limited to the cash value you've built up. You're charged interest on this loan at a rate considerably higher than the rate your cash value is given. And if the insured were to die before the loan was paid off, you would get the amount he was insured for *minus* the amount outstanding.

So before you decide to purchase whole life, consider whether your interests would be better served by buying term insurance, opening up an ordinary savings account, and going to a bank if you need a loan.

Term.   Term is the cheapest insurance available. A small premium each month buys you far more coverage than a higher whole life premium does. No cash value is built up, thus you can't borrow against it. Term insurance is guaranteed renewable every year, so it's yours to buy until you decide you no longer want it. The premiums stay the same until you reach a certain age (usually thirty), then they increase slightly. They continue to increase throughout the years, while the coverage you get decreases. This is based on the very logical premise that the older you get, the less insurance you need. Certainly the retired couple, with the children grown, mortgage paid, and nest egg built, needs less money in case of a partner's death than the young family with small children, a new house, and numerous debts.

Other Types.   Some companies offer hybrid policies, such as universal life, that fall somewhere between whole life and term. They combine a premium cheaper than that of whole life with a cash value buildup. Exact details about how long it takes to build a cash value, how much interest is paid, and so on vary from company to company, so you should cost-compare. These policies are a recent development that came about in response to general consumer dissatisfaction with whole life.

Annuities

An annuity is a financial instrument issued by life insurance companies. You can buy it through the company or through banks. There are major differences between it and life insurance. You usually don't have to pass a medical exam to buy one, as you do with most life insurance policies. And whereas insurance pays benefits to your survivors after your death, you can receive proceeds from an annuity while still alive. An annuity's tax deferral feature makes it a good retirement vehicle. Under some circumstances an annuity can substitute for life insurance. After your death, the proceeds go directly to your beneficiaries.

Servicemen's Group Life Insurance

All active-duty personnel and drilling Reservists are entitled to Servicemen's Group Life Insurance (SGLI), a term policy offered by the government. An automatic $100,000 coverage for $9 per month is issued to the servicemember upon joining the military. SGLI also offers lesser amounts of coverage for smaller premiums. The cost is 90¢ per $10,000. You may buy a maximum of $200,000 coverage for $18 per month. Although it is not mandatory, you won't find another policy that offers so much for so little. There are no eligibility requirements or medical questionnaires to fill out if you sign up for the insurance when entering the military. Coverage continues after retirement for both active-duty and Reserve personnel. Talk to the people at your base finance office about enrolling if you're not enrolled already. Premiums are deducted from the military paycheck.

Servicemembers are also entitled to insurance offered by the Military Benefit Association and the Uniformed Services Benefit Association, nonprofit organizations that offer different types of term insurance. Premiums are low and based on age and the coverage you buy. Write MBA at 108 North Center St., P.O. Box 549, Vienna, VA 22180-0549 and USBA at P.O. Box 418258, Kansas City, MO 64141-9258.

War and Aviation Clauses

Beware of war or aviation clauses in any policy you buy. A war clause exempts the insurance company from paying off if the insured is killed in war; an aviation clause exempts it if the insured is killed in a plane crash in which he was a crewmember. These clauses are contained in many private policies—including some offered by companies who solicit the military. Considering the job, such clauses appear to negate any other desirable factors the policy might have. Before purchasing any insurance, read the policy carefully, note all exemptions, and look particularly for clauses. And cost-compare! Prices for life insurance vary drastically.

Auto Insurance

In today's litigious society, the sky's the limit for how much auto liability coverage you might need. The amount required by law in each state might not be enough if you're involved in a serious accident. Buy as much as you can comfortably afford. It's ironic that the average sum needed for auto liability insurance is usually much higher than the average sum needed for life insurance. Know whether your insurance will still cover you when you move to another stateside location or overseas. Insuring your car overseas is much more expensive than it is stateside.

It often makes financial sense to take the highest deductible (the amount you, not the insurance company, pay in case of accident) that the company offers. For example, if you have a choice between paying the first $100 or the first $200 of car repairs, opt to pay the first $200. The premium for that policy will be the lower of the two. In some cases, the difference in price between the two premiums is greater than the difference between the deductibles. Check prices carefully before choosing a deductible.

The Military and Civilian Employee Claims Act

Service families who live in government-owned or leased quarters or in overseas off-base authorized rentals are given free personal property coverage under the Military Personnel and Civilian Employees Claims Act. (The act does not cover stateside off-base rentals.) Under this act, the government will compensate you in case of fire, theft, flood, or other unusual damage to your quarters or overseas authorized rental, as long as the damage didn't result from personal negligence. The act also compensates you if your automobile is damaged or if property is stolen from it while it's parked on military property, in front of your overseas authorized quarters, or being used for temporary or other military duty. Coverage is limited to an overall $25,000 with specific limits for 150 individual categories. If you have an extensive collection of anything, check with your legal office to find out what the limits are. If your possessions are worth more than the amount for which the act will compensate you, consider buying private insurance. If you have a private insurer and loss or damage occurs, you must file with that insurer first, but in certain cases the government will pay for the policy's uninsured portion (the deductible).

The phrase *authorized rental* is very important. If, when overseas, you decide to live on the economy, you need to go through the base housing office. Although this isn't always enforced, to be covered under the act you must have a form on file with Housing that shows the office has approved where you're living. Even if the rental is something Housing would authorize, you're not covered if you haven't gone through this formality.

≡ Financial Services

Military personnel, particularly officers, are heavily solicited by financial services agents. And as bewildering as the choices for insurance may be, the choices for financial services are even more so. Banks, brokerage firms, mutual fund houses, even insurance companies offer a cornucopia of investment choices from passbook savings and money market accounts to stocks, bonds, mutual funds, and more. If you wish to purchase a financial planner's services, consult a fee-only one. Many planners earn commissions from the investment products they sell you, which may not make their advice truly objective.

It is important that you know what financial instruments you're buying before you buy. Although a detailed discussion of them is beyond the scope of this chapter, here's a look at the two basic types usually offered.

═ Money Market Accounts

In a money market account, your money is merged with millions of dollars of other people's money. The institution you deposited it with uses this large pool to buy short-term government and corporation debt notes, such as certificates of deposit (CDs), treasury bills, and government agency bonds.

> I buy my eleven-year-old shares in stocks of companies he's interested in, like McDonald's, Disney, Toys R Us, and Wrigley, to spur an interest in investing.

Money market accounts compete with passbook accounts for people's savings funds. The idea for both is the same: You get back the amount of money you put in plus interest. Money market accounts, however, also offer a check-writing feature and slightly higher interest, and your share of this interest is credited to your account daily. Unlike bank deposits, money market accounts aren't federally insured, but the notes they buy have very little risk of default.

Mutual Funds

As with a money market fund, in a mutual fund your dollars are pooled with millions of other people's dollars. But in this case, the fund manager buys corporate stocks. Over 1,500 different kinds of stock mutual funds exist. There are funds that concentrate on gold stocks, oil stocks, auto stocks, stocks of major American companies, stocks of overseas companies, and stocks of financially unsound companies. Whatever your needs and desires in a fund are, you can probably find one that meets them. Keep in mind that when you buy into a mutual fund, you are buying shares of the fund, not the actual stocks themselves.

Mutual fund shares are bought in hopes that they'll increase in value. Many pay dividends, so while you're holding them you're earning money. They are professionally managed and thus good for people who want to invest but have neither the time nor the knowledge to buy individual stocks on their own. Mutual funds are also liquid; unlike real estate or collectibles, they can be quickly and easily sold at market price.

All funds have a prospectus, which describes, among other things, fees. Watch out for these. Regardless of the type of stocks they hold, all mutual funds are grouped into three fee types: no-load, low-load, and loaded funds. (*Load* means "fee.") No-loads don't charge a fee for buying into the fund. Low-loads charge a small fee, usually around 1 to 3 percent of the purchase price. Loaded funds charge much more, usually 8 percent or more. This 8 percent does not guarantee better money management; in fact, over the years, most no-load and low-load funds have consistently outperformed most loaded ones. Some funds also have maintenance and "backend" (redemption) fees, charged when you sell your shares. Combined with a load, they can eat up any profits you might make from share appreciation and dividends. It's important for you to ask about loads and fees when solicited for mutual funds, because the types of funds salespeople offer are usually loaded as well as full of fees.

We work so hard for our money, and servicemembers take so many risks for it, that we owe it to ourselves to spend and invest it the best way possible. This means researching and reading about all purchases—life insurance, car insurance, mutual funds, or anything else. The inherent conflict of interest between a salesman's desire to invest your money in the best way for you and the need to earn a living for himself is too great to leave such decisions entirely in his hands.

Salespeople's oft-made assertion that they know the "special needs" of "military money" is absurd—there's no such thing as "military money." Aside from the unique risks and sacrifices we make to earn it, the money service families earn is no different from the money that anyone else earns, and we want it working for us in the same way that doctors, lawyers, accountants, and other people want their money working for them.

So take out any papers you have that deal with investments and insurance and look them over. See whether you have what you truly want and need. No one cares about your financial well-being as much as you do.

Q: What are treasury bonds?
A: Treasury bonds, bills, and notes are some of the nation's most popular investments. They are government backed and offer conservative interest income that is free from state and local income taxes. There are no fees or commissions when you buy them directly from the government. You can buy them through payroll deduction or through a program called Treasury Direct. Obtain an application through your nearest federal reserve bank (ask your local bank for the address).

Bonds mature over ten years, and the minimum purchase is $1,000. Notes mature in two to three years or four to ten years, and the minimum purchase is $5,000. Treasury bills mature in three, six, or twelve months, and the minimum purchase is $10,000.

≡ Further Reading

Applegarth, Ginger. *The Money Diet: Reaping the Rewards of Financial Fitness.* New York: Viking Press, 1993.

Berner, J. Kevin, and Thomas Daula. *Armed Forces Guide to Personal Financial Planning,* 3rd edition. Mechanicsburg, PA: Stackpole Books, 1994.

Dacyczyn, Amy. *The Tightwad Gazette.* New York: Random House, 1992.

———. *The Tightwad Gazette.* Monthly newsletter available from RRI Box 3570, Leeds, ME 04263. Subscription $12 per year.

Dominquez, Joe, and Vicki Robin. *Your Money or Your Life.* New York: Viking Press, 1992.

Investor Swindles: How They Work and How to Avoid Them. Booklet available from the Consumer Information Center, Pueblo, CO 81009, phone (719) 948-3334.

Ortalda, Robert A. Jr. *How to Live within Your Means and Still Finance Your Dreams.* New York: Simon and Schuster, 1994.

"Scams, Schemes and Deceptive Offers," "Promises: Check 'Em Out!" "Consumer Fraud by Phone or Mail," "Pyramid Schemes: Not What They Seem." Pamphlets available from the Direct Marketing Association, 1101 17th St. N.W., Washington, DC 20036-4704.

Tax Information for Military Personnel, Publication 3. Pamphlet from the IRS, Forms Distribution Center, P.O. Box 85074, Richmond, VA 23261-5074, telephone (800) 829-3676.

7

Home Is Where the Military Sends You

Looking for a place to live? Study the classifieds, talk to agents, pound the pavement . . . there are a lot of choices out there! There are town-houses, co-ops, condos, custom-builts, and more, but since living in quarters or renting an apartment or house are the most viable for military families, those are the ones we'll discuss. Make your decision carefully: The military pays only for moves from duty station to duty station, not any moves in between.

> During PCS moves, a lot of women send their husbands out alone to find a place to live, and join them after they're settled. This may be easier on the nerves, but I think it's a bad idea. You're going to have to live in the place, so surely you'll want to give input.

Living in Government Quarters

Base housing—quarters—runs the gamut from large, airy houses to small, cramped apartments. It depends where you are. Some are newly constructed, some are old; some offer lots of privacy, some very little; some have yards, some don't; and floor plans, window sizes, closet space, and construction all vary. Some quarters, because of their poor location, condition, or construction, are considered substandard, and tenants get to keep a portion of their housing allowances. Most quarters are on base and government owned; however, the government also rents privately owned apartments, which it uses as quarters. These require a security deposit. Advance pay (discussed in chapter 8) may be used for this purpose.

> If you live in furnished quarters, read every item listed on the hand receipt, such as draperies, furniture, and humidifiers, before signing it. At moving time you will be held accountable for everything on the list whether it was actually in the quarters or not, and you will have to pay for damaged or missing items.

Quarters aren't always available; the supply is low and the demand is high, and it's getting higher with each base closure. Waiting lists can range from two weeks to two years. Your place on the list is established by the date you signed up, the number of bedrooms you require (family size determines this), and servicemember rank. (Officer and enlisted families live in separate areas.) Because quarters are not assigned on the basis of income or personal need, all eligible personnel have an equal shot at them. Since they are in such short supply, they're usually limited to people who have some seniority; thus E-1 to E-3 families are often ineligible or low on a long list. If quarters are available, you might be required to live in them or forfeit your housing allowance. People in key jobs are often required to live on base.

Here are the major points of base housing. You decide which are advantages and which are disadvantages.

- There are no rent or utility checks to write; all you pay for is the phone. Quarters are not free, however; a servicemember pays for them by giving up his housing allowance. Higher-ranking people pay more for the same set of quarters than lower-ranking ones, because they give up a greater allowance.
- When things break down, the base engineers fix them at no charge. Just call the housing office.
- Yardwork—mowing, raking, weeding, sidewalk shoveling, and so on—is your responsibility. So is keeping common areas clean.
- Quarters are close to work and base facilities. They're regularly patrolled by the installation police.
- You need to do heavy cleaning before vacating. The standards are tough; a tiny patch of baked-on food in an otherwise sparkling oven or a speck of dirt on a light fixture is cause for clearance disapproval. You can pay a private cleaning team to do the job for you, but you are ultimately responsible for the work.
- You live close to a lot of other military families. You're surrounded by them!

═══ Flexibility and Communication

This last point is what really makes or breaks living in base housing for many. While some people form lifelong friendships with their neighbors, others find getting along with the Joneses a problem of major proportions. Though there are infinite reasons for the squabbles people get into, most can be blamed on a lack of flexibility and communication.

No two families live alike. In any multitenant living situation, on base or off, it is important to understand this. Some families have children, others don't; some sleep late on weekends, others don't; and everyone has different standards for cleanliness, loud music, and the supervision of children. It's necessary to bend.

Lack of communication can turn the pettiest problem into a dramatic incident. If another resident is doing something that bothers you, tell her. Knock on her door, be friendly, explain the problem and why it's affecting you. Calm, rational assertions usually bring calm, satisfactory solutions. It's pounding on the ceiling, shouting out the window, and running to the building supervisor that create animosity. Often the person is not even aware that what she's doing is annoying you, and if you never say anything, she may assume everything is fine. If the problem can't be worked out between the two of you, use your housing area chain of command. But first try on your own. Know that family members who are a chronic problem or danger to others in the community may be required to leave. This has happened with teenagers.

Housing communities hold periodic "town hall" meetings where problems, complaints, and comments can be heard. If you have any, attend and make them known.

Make friends with your neighbors. If a neighbor invites you over for a Coke and a five-minute chat, go and enjoy the break. Being friendly will make your neighbors more tolerant about things *you* do that annoy *them*. When you move into a building, take advantage of the newcomer's prerogative and knock on doors. Introduce yourself. Do the same thing when someone else moves in. Many people say they're too shy to introduce themselves but would love it if their neighbors did.

Quarters can be a fun place to live. The oldest, most run-down buildings can be great when the relationships among the residents are great.

≡ Renting

Rental apartments or houses are the usual option when quarters are unavailable. Before you look for a place to rent, check with the housing

Before apartment hunting, know the total allowance amount you'll be given if quarters aren't available. Keep your rent under this amount, because you'll have to pay utilities, too. Otherwise, you'll spend money out-of-pocket.

Pay your rent on time, and leave the place the way you found it. That way you'll have a good reference if you need it, and it will be easier for the next military family to rent it.

At each place I live I like to plant a shrub, small tree, or flowering perennial as a reminder that I was there.

office. Under the Federal Fair Housing Law of 1968, no service-member may rent from a landlord who discriminates on the basis of race, sex, or religion. The housing office will give you a list of land-lords who don't discriminate and who have a history of good relations with military tenants.

A lease is usually required for a rental, binding you to the property for a specific length of time. Read it carefully for pet or child restrictions; some places don't allow either. Make sure there's a military clause that will release you without loss of the security deposit in case of sudden transfer orders, but know the clause's limitations. For instance, it does not apply to renters who wish to move simply to go on base or buy a home. It may not apply if the PCS move isn't far away, or for less than 179-day TDY/TAD orders. Finally, some states don't require it for landlords who only offer four-, six-, eight-, or twelve-unit dwellings. Your lease should describe how much money, if any, will be deducted from your deposit for ordinary wear and tear, what will be charged or deducted for other damages, and who pays for what repairs and services. It should also note when the landlord may enter the property.

If you really want to live in quarters but the wait is long, you can rent a furnished apartment and arrange with the transportation office to keep your household goods in storage. In this case, try to negotiate a lease that will release you when quarters become available, or one that will rent month to month. Servicemembers who make midmonth moves continue to receive their VHA or OHA (see chapter 8) for up to thirty days after they move into quarters, to help offset the effects of breaking a lease.

Clashes can and do arise between landlords and tenants over many different things. Getting your security deposit back is never a sure thing. Certain problems can be avoided by completing a written inventory and condition statement, available at most housing offices, before moving in. (See accompanying sample form.) These statements note items that are worn, damaged, or missing, and are signed by both you and the landlord. Ask what is expected from you in the way of maintenance and upkeep of the interior and exterior.

Rent and utilities can easily exceed a servicemember's housing

DWELLING UNIT CONDITION INSPECTION RECORD

UNIT NO.			ADDRESS			
NAME OF TENANT					DATE ASSIGNED	

	ITEM	CHECK IN	REMARKS	CHECK OUT	REMARKS
L I V I N G R O O M	CEILING				
	WALLS				
	FLOOR				
	WINDOWS				
	DOORS				
	ELECTRICAL				
D I N I N G R O O M	CEILING				
	WALLS				
	FLOOR				
	WINDOWS				
	DOORS				
	ELECTRICAL				
K I T C H E N	CEILING				
	WALLS				
	FLOOR				
	WINDOWS				
	WALL CABINETS				
	BASE CABINETS				
	RANGE				
	REFRIGERATOR				
	SINK				
	ELECTRICAL				
P O W D E R R O O M	CEILING				
	WALLS				
	FLOOR				
	COMMODE				
	LAVATORY				
	ACCESSORIES				
	ELECTRICAL				
	DOOR				
S T A I R W E L L / **HALL**	CEILING				
	WALLS				
	CLOSET				
	ELECTRICAL				

Sample page from a premises condition/inventory form.

allowance. Bargaining over the exact monthly rent is not unheard of, however, as is doing yard and handy work in exchange for partial rent payments. Alternatives to the standard apartment are one-room efficiencies, a room in a private home, or a room in exchange for work. You can also work as a resident manager of an apartment complex in exchange for free rent.

Off-base living allows you to integrate better with the local civilian

ITEM		CHECK IN	REMARKS	CHECK OUT	REMARKS
E X T E R I O R	ROOF				
	SIDING				
	STEPS				
	WALKS				
	GARAGE				
	STORM DOOR				
	STOREROOM				
MISCELLANEOUS	HEATER				
	UTILITY RM.				
	GAS LINE				
	A/C				

CODE LETTERS:

M-MISSING   DU-DAMAGED-USABLE   R-REPAIR OR REPLACE   ✓ -OCCUPANT RESPONSIBILITY

REMARKS:

CHECK-IN INSPECTOR	CHECK-OUT INSPECTOR
SIGNATURE	SIGNATURE
I hereby certify that the above Check-in Inspection (subject to comments in remarks column) represents a true record of the condition of the unit upon my initial occupancy.	I hereby certify that the above Check-out inspection (subject to comments in remarks column) represents a true record of the condition of the unit upon my vacating and I agree to pay for damages incurred or items missing during my occupancy, reasonable wear and tear excepted, noted hereon.
DATE	SIGNATURE OF TENANT	DATE	SIGNATURE OF TENANT

☆U.S. GOVERNMENT PRINTING OFFICE: 1982 — 509-281/528

Sample page from a premises condition/inventory form.

population and experience the lifestyles of different localities, which, of course, is one of the great benefits of military life. Overseas, living on the economy gives a true flavor of what life in another country is like, something not always obtainable in the "little America" societies of government housing.

⚌ Renter's Insurance

If you rent, consider purchasing renter's insurance. Although landlords have insurance on their property, it rarely covers *your* possessions. In case of burglary or fire, you would need to replace all your things. Estimate the replacement costs of your furniture, TV, VCR, stereo, kitchen and bathroom items, coats, clothes, video camera, pictures, lamps, closet and cabinet contents, and knickknacks. Most people could not afford to replace all these things at once. Policies vary, but generally they are written for the replacement, not the depreciated, value. Items don't have to be in your home to be covered; they may be in a storage shed, a friend's garage, a mover's truck, or another temporary situation.

Most renter's insurance policies also extend coverage to protect you against people injured while on your premises or using your possessions, or who are even inadvertently injured by you. For all this, such insurance usually costs between $10 and $20 per $12,000 of coverage.

For those living overseas, if your car is burglarized or damaged while on government property, or if your housing-office-approved rental is burglarized, you may be able to file a claim against the government for your damages. See your legal officer.

≡ Financing a House

Buying a house is beyond the scope of this book; if you're considering such a purchase, read books on the subject. The following is a look at several financing options available to servicemembers.

Unless you have the money to pay cash, you'll need to finance your house with a mortgage loan. There are a lot of different types—VA, FHA, owner-financed, adjustable rate, balloon, and more—but all are obtained the same way: by going to a lender and applying.

Banks, mortgage companies, credit unions, savings and loans, mutual savings banks, even insurance companies all offer mortgage loans. Shop among them carefully. Interest rates, down payment required, length of repayment time, and points vary tremendously. (A real estate point is 1 percent of the sale price. Since lenders don't make as much money from low-interest loans as they do from high ones, they charge points to bridge the gap. And since military families often use lower-interest VA and FHA loans, we're often charged points.)

A check will be run on your credit history. If you have a history of bad debts or are up to your ears in current ones, finding someone to lend you more money will be extremely difficult. "You can't believe how many people I've had to turn away, either because they have a history of paying their bills late or because their current debt-to-income ratio is so bad," says one loan officer in San Diego. "Many people want to buy a house but have little savings, and their credit cards are charged to the limit. The computers tell all."

Have your financial records in order; the amount of paperwork needed for a mortgage loan is large. It will typically include bank and brokerage statements, references from landlords or utility companies, the VA Certificate of Eligibility, proof of income and debts, credit reports, and proof of past employment.

There are many different types of loans, but Department of Veterans Affairs (formerly the Veterans Administration), Federal Housing Authority, and conventional loans are the ones most practical for military families. If you take out a VA or FHA loan, be aware that their rules constantly change. The rules of the FHA even vary from area to area. Don't count on your agent to know them all; it's your responsibility as a home buyer to find out for yourself. Call the VA or FHA office serving your town.

Department of Veterans Affairs Loans

The VA or (GI) loan is a product of the Serviceman's Readjustment Act, passed by Congress in 1946 to help servicemen readjust to civilian life. Active-duty personnel, veterans, and Reservists with six years of service or ninety days of active-duty service during times of combat (e.g., the Persian Gulf War) are eligible. IRR service does not count, however.

The word *loan* is a misnomer. What the VA does is *guarantee* 80 percent of the loan. The money comes from a bank, mortgage company, or other lender. But if the borrower defaults, the lender can collect the amount guaranteed by the VA. Since this greatly lowers the lender's risk, he is willing to loan to people he might otherwise turn down.

The VA loan guaranty can be used to buy a site-built house, condominium, or prefabricated home with or without a lot; build a new home; repair or improve an existing home; or refinance an existing home loan. The owner must live in the property. VA loans cannot be used for commercial property, although the owner may live in one unit of a property and rent the other units.

As long as the purchase price doesn't exceed the appraised value of the home, the VA doesn't require a down payment. The VA also doesn't require principle and mortgage insurance, something banks require until the owner has 20 percent equity in the home.

VA loans can be fixed rate or adjustable. Fixed rate means that the rate remains the same for the life of the loan; adjustable means that it fluctuates with market conditions. Both types have pros and cons. A fixed rate is good if you plan to own the house for a long time and want to lock in a specific rate. If you plan to own the house only a few years, however, an adjustable rate offers lower starting interest. There are all kinds of adjustable-rate mortgages. The rate may remain the same for one, three, even seven years. Some change rates only once; others change year to year. Adjustable-rate loans do come with ceilings—the maximums to which the rates may rise. For VA loans, federal law requires that the increase cannot be more than 5 percent over the life of a loan and not more than 1 percent each year.

Interest rates, points, and standard fees vary greatly from lender to lender, so shop around when obtaining a mortgage.

When the time comes to sell, if you allow someone to assume your VA loan, make certain that the buyer signs papers releasing you from the VA obligation. Failure to do so can mean you may still be responsible for the loan if the buyer defaults. It may also prevent you from obtaining another VA loan until the first one is paid off.

Contact the VA's Loan Guarantee Division at (800) 827-1000. Counselors there will help you determine your qualifications to obtain a mortgage loan.

Federal Housing Authority Loans

The FHA loan program was started in 1934 to give people of limited income a chance to buy a house. Again, the word *loan* is a misnomer. The FHA guarantees a large percentage of the loan, but the money comes from the lender. A small down payment is required, and borrowers must purchase insurance against default. The FHA sets a ceiling on interest the lender may charge, and the rate is usually lower than that of a conventional loan. Like the VA, the FHA doesn't set a maximum purchase price, but the lender often does. The Coast Guard will pay the mortgage insurance premiums for its members who purchase homes with FHA loans.

Conventional Loans

Conventional loans are for people who aren't eligible for or don't want the other types, or for those who don't want to wait: VA and FHA loans can take up to two months to process. A conventional loan is also needed if the house's price exceeds what the FHA or VA will guarantee. There's no ceiling on purchase price, and interest charged is the going rate. Down payments are needed, and the standards the borrower must meet are generally stricter than for VA or FHA borrowers. The interest rates for conventional loans are better than VA rates.

Some Questions to Ask about Any Loan

■ Is it assumable? In other words, when you sell your house, can a buyer assume (take over) your loan? A buyer may want to, especially if the interest rate you're paying is lower than the current one. Assumability can be a big selling factor.

- Who would be eligible to assume your loan? Would they have to meet the same requirements you had to meet?
- What fees do the VA and FHA forbid buyers and sellers to pay?
- 'What about renting? With a VA or FHA loan, you have to promise you'll live in the house; buying for business purposes is forbidden. How does this affect your renting the house out in case you move and can't sell it?

The person who buys a house for a short period of time needs to look at financing differently than does the person who's planning to live in it for the next twenty years. If you plan to own the house forever and ever, it's worth your while to put a lot of money down and pay the balance off in as short a time as possible. The difference in interest between a fifteen- and a thirty-year mortgage is astonishing.

If you plan to own the house for just a few years, you might be better off with an adjustable rate or making as small a down payment and getting as long a mortgage as possible. That way, your money can remain in savings, earning interest, and since your monthly payments will be low, the loan will look more attractive to a prospective buyer who might wish to assume the loan. Plus, since the buyer must buy out your equity, the less you've got in, the less he must come up with.

For Air Force and Coast Guard families making PCS moves, the Air Force Aid Society and Coast Guard Mutual Aid Association make loans to cover closing costs.

≡ Decorating Tips for Families on the Move

Can you decorate on a tight budget? Can you decorate at all when you move so much?

Yes to both! Good decorating involves a little money and a lot of research and creativity. If you bargain shop, cost-compare, and use some imagination, on any income level you can make a home you'll be proud to show off. The imaginative person never uses a lack of money as an excuse for dreariness.

If you're fixing up a house, be cautious of making improvements that please your tastes but don't really add to the house's value. People as transient as we are really shouldn't put a lot of money into redecorating, because getting our money out is never a sure thing. Tastes differ, and that perfectly good brown carpet and gold wallpaper you replaced with the blue and coral may not impress the new buyer.

But just because it's impractical to redo a place completely doesn't mean you should live with brown and gold if blue and coral is what you really want. There are economical ways to fix up a house, apartment, or quarters to satisfy your tastes.

Military households are famous for their eclecticism. We go so many places and have so many opportunities to collect so many different things, why not make a style out of that? This is not to say that you should have a wild mixture of colors and textures (although some people get that to work very well), but you can plan a scheme of your favorite colors and patterns and build on that. Coordinating all your purchases around three or four colors will pull your rooms together and allow you to interchange furniture, drapes, and rugs and add to them easily.

If you can afford to, you're better off buying your own furniture than renting it. It's good to save and pay cash for a piece at a time.

> If you want to do major construction on your house, such as finish a basement or a garage, spend money on a professional. Unless you and your husband are master craftsmen, home jobs look just that. A poorly finished room is harder to sell than an unfinished one.

> Carry samples of all your upholstery, drapery materials, and wall colors while you shop.

> Scotchgard all your upholstery. It's only a few dollars a can and will keep your furniture cleaner longer.

Here are some decorating ideas:

- Select area rugs made of heavy wool. They will stand a lot of traffic. Turn them occasionally so that they will wear evenly.
- If you buy carpeting, search for remnants. Many carpet stores sell them, and they offer terrific savings. Have the edges of the carpet or remnant bound and buy a pad to put underneath for a finished appearance.
- Craft fairs are sources for lovely homemade, folksy things such as quilts and fabric hangings for the walls. The "country" look is in, and it's an easy style to arrange and add to.
- Red bricks or painted concrete blocks along with stained planks make nice display shelves. Put your TV, compact disc player, philodendrons, photographs, and knickknacks on them. Such bookshelves can form a divider for your children's shared bedroom.
- Buy unfinished furniture. It's inexpensive, and shops that sell it often teach classes on staining and antiquing it.
- Faux painting is popular for giving an expensive, custom look to

homes. Paint can be applied with sponges and rags for marbled and other effects. Paint stores and building-supply stores often offer classes in these techniques. Paint and a wallpaper border make a dramatic change, as does a stenciled border. Many borders are prepasted and are easy to apply and remove. In the kitchen, contact paper is a popular alternative to wallpaper. Many housing offices allow you to paint quarters and don't even require you to repaint them when leaving if the new occupant accepts it.

- Nail a piece of round plywood to a footstool, cover it with nice textiles, and use it as an end table or nightstand.

- You can get terrific deals through the classified ads. A sofa bed that costs $600 new can be had several years later, still in excellent condition, for $200. So it's not the color you want? Use it while you save to pay cash for the one you do want. When you sell it, you're almost certain to get all your money back. Anything and everything can be bought used through the classifieds: furniture, appliances, computers, stereos, TVs, rugs, and household goods.

- Go to base property disposal auctions and defense reutilization sales for low-cost quartermaster furniture. Those old china cabinets, desks, and bureaus are usually newly refinished, in good condition, and very attractive. Check the thirft shop, too.

- Paint and stencil old wooden footlockers to make toy boxes and coffee tables. Since they can be locked, you can store valuables in them. Do the same with wooden cribs and dressers.

- Don't skimp on your bed. A cheap mattress full of lumps and sags is no bargain. Buy the best box spring and mattress you can afford. You can always buy the headboard and footboard later.

- Wrap fabric around cork squares and hang them up for bulletin boards.

- If you sew, make your own draperies and leave large hems for future adjustments, or puddle the extra fabric on the floor for a luxuriant look. For a valance, wrap material around a curtain rod or quilting and fabric around a board. A valance dresses up shades, draperies, or blinds. The advantage with the board-type valance is that if the windows are longer at the next place, you can hang the curtain rod lower and it's still hidden.

- Buy slipcovers. Buy the best upholstery you can afford; heavy good-quality material will last longer and give you more for your money. If you sew, make them, and check the phone book for textile factories where you might be able to obtain remnants at low cost.

- Mix and match old wooden chairs at your kitchen table for an interesting look. Paint with bright colors and spray lacquer for gloss. A painted and stenciled wooden picnic table makes a wonderful dining table for a large family.

- Freshen up tired rooms with new lampshades and throw pillows, potted flowers, and large, framed family photographs. Dye and trim the lampshades yourself for a custom look. Colorful maps and posters in discount-store frames dress up a wall, and if you cut off the words at the bottom of the posters, they'll look more like expensive prints. For an avant-garde look, cut them in quarters and frame each piece in plain acrylic frames. Plants add color to a room, especially large plants. A seven-foot ficus tree is a strong focal point, and you can take a silk one with you.

- Steam-clean your carpet and upholstery. That alone can make a big difference.

- Space in quarters kitchens is never generous, but there are things you can do to maximize it. Store spices on a wall-mounted rack, use hanging baskets for fruits and vegetables, hang pegboards on cabinet doors, hang mugs from racks, and use wall-mounted shelves for small kitchen tools. Pour cereal and spaghetti into pretty plastic containers to keep on your countertops.

- Plastic shower curtains are made with all sorts of motifs these days; a jungle or underwater scene can add zest to a small bath.

- Baskets are attractive and versatile. Use them to hold magazines, cosmetics, and baby toys. Spray-paint them to match your decor, and wrap wired silk flowers around their handles.

- Decorate a child's room by choosing a theme from his or her favorite movie and buying appropriate posters and stuffed animals.

- When buying new furniture, cost-compare. Start at the most expensive stores so that you can see what well-made furniture looks like. This will help you judge the quality of what you're buying. Pull the drawers out, turn them over, and examine them. Know about staples, dowels, dovetails, and glue blocks. Try to buy solid wood instead of veneer; unlike veneers, when solids are gouged during moves, they can be sanded and refinished. You can tell whether a piece is solid by examining it to see whether the grain is identical on both sides. If it is, it's solid.

Be careful when shopping at furniture stores that heavily solicit the military. They're far more expensive than those the general civilian population patronizes, and their goods are usually inferior.

Buy a good sofa. It's a major item in your decorating scheme. A sofa bed is a great buy; it can be used for your own bed when you first get married and as a guest bed later.

■ Buy what suits you. A mahogany dining table and eight high-back chairs may look great, but if you don't entertain formally, do you need them? If you like to read, an overstuffed recliner with a bright table lamp next to it might be a better choice than a Queen Anne wingback and a Tiffany-style shade.

Look through your library's card catalog for books on furniture buying and low-cost decorating. These are also frequent subjects in home magazines; check back issues. Whether you're living in quarters, an apartment, a house, or a Quonset hut, you can make a perfectly nice home wherever the military sends you.

≡ Further Reading

Better Homes & Gardens New Decorating Book. Lido Beach, NY: Meredith Corporation, 1990.

Franks, Beth. *Very Small Living Spaces: Design & Decorating Strategies to Make the Most of What You Have.* New York: Holt, 1988.

How to Buy a Home and *Fixing and Financing a House.* Booklets available from USAA, San Antonio, TX (800) 531-0283 (or 498-7700 in San Antonio).

How to Buy a Manufactured Home. Pamphlet available from the Consumer Information Center, Dept. 427Y, Pueblo, CO 81009.

Torrice, Antonio, and R. Logrippo. *In My Room: Designing for and with Children.* New York: Fawcett Columbine, 1989.

8

≡ On the Move

It's permanent-change-of-station time—time to pack up and move to the next place!

Moving can be viewed as military life's greatest advantage. What opportunities to see the world! What luxury to expose your children to things their civilian playmates will only read about! In the span of nine years, you can see how rural Tennesseeans, big-city Atlantans, and small-town Oklahomans live. You can visit the San Diego Zoo on one tour and Opryland on the next. You can tour Dallas, camp out in Gatlinburg, and visit Disneyland. You can ski the Alps, gaze at the Colosseum, soak in a *kur,* and admire a pagoda. Any of these places might be in your very backyard.

Moving is never easy, but it need not be an ordeal. It can be a pleasant adventure, especially if combined with a vacation. But, unless you're a newly married couple with nothing to worry about except yourselves and a couple of Swedish ivies, you must plan a move. Planning will make the difference between a happy,

Q: Why do we move?
A: There are two reasons:

1. Military success—readiness—depends on having the right people in the right places. Each year that a servicemember is in the military, he acquires new skills and may need a new job that fits those skills, a job that often is not at the base where he is stationed. Moves almost always mean a better job, or at least a different one.

2. The United States maintains installations all over the world. Some of them are in great places; others are not. But since all installations need to be maintained regardless of the lifestyle they offer, a system of rotation is observed.

As a military brat, I found going away and adjusting to college a snap after all the moves I had made.

successful move and economic and emotional ruin. Smooth moves don't just happen on their own.

≡ See Your Transportation Counselor

As soon as those PCS orders arrive, make an appointment with the Installation Transportation Office (Army), the Traffic Management Office (Navy and Marine Corps), the Personal Property Shipping Office (Air Force), or the Household Goods Shipping Office (Coast Guard) to get details and set a date for the movers to come. Often only the servicemember goes to this appointment, but it's a good idea for you to go, too, to ask the questions your husband may forget: Are hanging wardrobe boxes authorized to keep your clothes from becoming a wrinkled mess? Can a special crate be built for your grandfather clock, marble-top table, or antique piece? No two moves are ever alike, and the rules change. You'll be advised whether a do-it-yourself move is good for your situation, and what kind of storage is available. You'll also be given the pamphlet *It's Your Move*. Read it; it contains a lot of good information.

Q: Do we have any say in where we are assigned?
A: A servicemember may submit a preference for his next duty station, but whether he gets it depends on such factors as whether there's a job and a need for his skills there. Some families—for example, one with a family member in a Special Needs program—receive special consideration. There are also compassionate reassignments, given if a family member or an extended family member is extremely ill.

The month before you move, keep a copy of the PCS orders in your purse. It will be needed to make a lot of arrangements.

If you'll be handling the move by yourself, the transportation office will require a written notice from your husband saying so, plus a power of attorney. When you visit the office to set up a date, know your approximate date of arrival at the new duty station, the type of shipments you'll have (e.g., stuff from storage in another state), and any large and unusual items that you'll be shipping, and have twelve copies of the PCS orders handy.

≡ Special Pays

═ Advance Pay

Advance pay is an interest-free loan of up to three months' base pay that a servicemember can take to help with moving expenses. It can be given at the old station, the new one, or partly at both. Advance pay is not automatic; if a servicemember wants it, he must apply at the base finance office. The money is usually given a day after applying; sometimes it's given in a few hours.

The servicemember must submit a written justification to receive advance pay, describing exactly what he's going to use it for. Even if three months' pay is requested, the finance office sometimes only approves one.

Advance Housing Allowance

An advance housing allowance may also be applied for. This requires approval from your husband's unit commander and a copy of your lease. You must have already committed to a rental before applying.

Advance BAQ, VHA, and OHA

You can apply for an advance of up to three months' basic allowance for quarters (BAQ) and variable housing allowance (VHA) for stateside moves. For overseas moves, you may apply for up to twelve months' advance BAQ and overseas housing allowance (OHA).

Move-in Allowance

If you move overseas, you will find that the phrase "unfurnished apartment" takes on new meaning. Along with the furniture, you usually must also provide your own light fixtures, sinks, and cabinets! So for overseas moves, a one-time move-in allowance is often permitted to help pay the costs of these types of items. You must have committed to a rental before applying.

Dislocation Allowance

A dislocation allowance consists of two months' BAQ that is automatically issued to help pay moving expenses. The servicemember does not apply for it. It does not have to be paid back and is considered taxable income.

Dislocation allowances are not given to servicemembers leaving home for their first duty station nor to those transferring to a nearby duty station. It also is not paid to those separating or retiring.

Mileage and Per Diem Allowances

If you're driving to your new home, your husband can apply for a mileage allowance. The amount is based on the distance between the old and new duty stations. It does not have to be paid back. If you're going overseas, you can apply for a mileage allowance based on the distance driven from the old duty station to the airport.

Per diem allowances, which cover food and lodging costs, can also be applied for. They are based on flat rates for family size and are given for the reasonable amount of time it should take to arrive at your destination. If you plan to combine your travel with a vacation, you are not allotted more mileage or per diem moneys. Mileage and per diem allowances do not have to be paid back.

Temporary Lodging Allowance

A temporary lodging allowance (TLA) helps pay the cost of temporary housing and meals for servicemembers who have just moved overseas. Amount given depends, among other things, on rank and family size. It must be applied for, and it doesn't have to be paid back.

Temporary Lodging Expense Allowance

A temporary lodging expense allowance is similar to a TLA, but for Stateside moves.

In addition to special pays, the government will buy your family's travel tickets, whether they're for plane, train, or bus. If you buy the tickets yourself, you can be reimbursed. Always check with the base finance office before buying your own tickets, however, to ensure that what you're buying is an allowable expense and to verify the proper documentation.

Allotments to repay advances are taken out of the paycheck for one year (two years in case of hardship) until the amount borrowed is paid back. The servicemember will continue to get his full allowances while paying back his advances. Don't use this money to buy stereos, furniture, or new clothes; if you couldn't afford such things before, you can't now. While this may sound obvious, many military families get into financial trouble in just this way. Remember, your budget may have some catching up to do in the months after you move, and that additional allotment isn't going to help. Use advance moneys for moving expenses only, and use them judiciously.

If—and only if—you're financially sound and already have enough money to carry you comfortably through the move, a prudent use of advance pay is to pay off any debts that charge high interest rates. Since advance pay is interest-free, you're replacing an interest-bearing loan with an interest-free loan. Another idea is to put the advance pay in a savings account. That way you will earn interest on money that didn't cost you anything to borrow.

Special Leaves
House Hunting

While at the old duty station, if your husband's unit commander approves, he may take some time off to house hunt at the new location. No money allowances for house-hunting trips are provided. The Army and Navy permit ten days off; the Air Force, eight; the Marine Corps and Coast Guard, five. The federal civil service also permits time off for this purpose.

Processing Time

Processing time is a leave of absence of up to seven days at both the old and new duty stations to process in and out.

Leave en Route

Leave en route is for unforeseen delays. It must be obtained before leaving the old duty station and approved by the unit commander.

Moving and Traveling Time

Time off to move and travel is also granted and is not charged against a servicemember's annual leave.

Tax Deductions of Unreimbursed Expenses

Relocation expenses that are not reimbursed by the government include those that are necessary for buying and selling a house; premove house-hunting trips; premove spouse job-hunting trips; child care; pet transportation; phone and utility deposits; security deposits; advance rent; cleaning supplies and fees; and auto license plates, registration, and inspections. You can, however, deduct a limited amount of some of these from your yearly income tax. Accurate records with accompanying receipts are critical, so put everything in a large manila envelope until it's all placed in your permanent records. Unlike our civilian counterparts, we don't have to meet requirements for relocation distance and time in residence to make these deductions.

Here is a general list of tax-deductible PCS expenses. Tax laws change yearly, and other expenses may apply for your personal situation, so ask a military attorney or an accountant for details.

Expenses for the Move.

- Commercial transportation.
- Personal auto—gas, oil, and mileage (repairs are not deductible).
- Hotels.
- Meals.
- Child care.
- Car rental.
- Taxis.
- Parking.
- Tolls.
- Cost of traveler's checks.
- Miscellaneous.

Unreimbursed Shipping Expenses.

- Postage and shipping of items not authorized for government expense, excess weight charges, and pet travel.

Temporary Housing Expenses (thirty days maximum stateside, ninety overseas).

- Lodging.
- Meals.
- Mandatory cleaning fees.
- Miscellaneous.

Expenses to Settle or Get a Lease.

- Money lost from breaking a lease.

Expenses of Selling a Residence.

- Loan origination fee.
- Loan assumption fee.
- Title and escrow fees.
- Recording fees.
- Survey.

≡ Weight Allowance

The government hires movers to pack and move your goods for you. You can ask for a particular mover, but whether you get him depends on his schedule. You're given a weight allowance—a maximum weight that may be moved and/or stored at government expense—based on rank, family size, and whether the move is continental or overseas. The accompanying charts give general guidelines, but your transportation counselor will give you specifics for your situation.

Table of Joint Federal Travel Regulations Weight Allowances

(Pounds)

Grade	PCS Without Dependents	PCS With Dependents	PCS Weight Allowance
0-10	18,000	18,000	2,000
0-9	18,000	18,000	1,500
0-8	18,000	18,000	1,000
0-7	18,000	18,000	1,000
0-6	18,000	18,000	800
0-5	16,000	17,500	800
0-4/W-4	14,000	17,000	800
0-3/W-3	13,000	14,500	600
0-2/W-2	12,500	13,500	600
0-1/W-1	10,000	12,000	600
E-9	12,000	14,500	600
E-8	11,000	13,500	500
E-7	10,500	12,500	400
E-6	8,000	11,000	400
E-5	7,000	9,000	400
E-4 ***	7,000	8,000	400
E-4 **	3,500	7,000	225
E-3	2,000	5,000	225
E-1 & E-2	1,500	5,000	225

* TDY/Temporary Duty Station.
** More than 2 years.
*** 2 years or less.

Exception: Entitlement is limited to 2,000 pounds or 25 percent of household goods weight allowance, whichever is greater, when shipment is to/from an overseas station that has been designated by the military service concerned as a place where public quarters or private housing is furnished with government-owned furnishings.

U.S. Air Force Unaccompanied Baggage Allowances

	A	B	C
	if grade is	*and member is*	*then allowance is*
1	O–1 to O–5	PCS	600 lbs. net weight (see notes 1 & 2)
2	O–6	PCS	800 lbs. net weight (see notes 1 & 2)
3	O–7 to O–10	PCS	1,000 lbs. net weight (see notes 1 & 2)
4	E–1 to E–9	PCS serving unaccompanied tour overseas	500 lbs. net weight (see notes 1 & 2)
5		PCS serving accompanied tour overseas	400 lbs. net weight (see note 1)
6		PCS with CONUS	400 lbs. net weight
7	E–1 to E–10	PCS and authorized movement of dependents	350 lbs. net weight for each dependent 12 yrs of age or older. 175 lbs. net weight for dependents less than 12 yrs old.

Notes: 1. Single and unaccompanied members assigned to duty stations outside the CONUS have two options. They may ship the normal allowance or 10 percent of their full JFTR weight allowance by surface (700 pounds for E-1 through E-4, with 2 years or less). This surface option is also authorized for the member of a military couple not authorized household goods allowance. When the member elects surface option, the shipment may include household goods. Split shipments (part by air, part by surface) are not authorized.

2. For unaccompanied members assigned to hardlift areas, shipment of the 10 percent option by air is authorized.

Unaccompanied Baggage Weight Allowances U.S. Army Personnel

Personnel	Allowance (pounds)
Military members on permanent change of station	
General officers (0-8, 0-9, and 0-10)	1,000
General officers (0-7) and colonels (0-6)	800
Other officers	600
Enlisted members	500
Dependents of military members	
Each adult and child 12 years and older	350
Each child under 12 years of age	175

U.S. Navy and Marine Corps Unaccompanied Baggage Allowances

Navy and Marine Corps members should contact their transportation office for unaccompanied baggage allowances.

Household Goods Weight Allowances for U.S. Army Personnel Unaccompanied Overseas

	Short Tour	Long Tour
O–6 through O–10	1,000	4,500
O–5	1,000	4,000
O–4/W–4	1,000	3,500
O–3/W–3	1,000	1,500
O–2/W–2	1,000	1,400
O–1/W–1	1,000	1,400
E–9	1,000	1,600
E–8	800	1,500
E–7	700	1,500
E–6	500	1,250
E–5	500	1,000
E–4	500	800
E–1 through E-3	500	700

Aviation Cadets

Aviation cadets should contact their transportation office for authorized weight allowances.

During a continental move you may ship your entire allowance. In an overseas move your allowance often depends on the availability of government furniture overseas. The government will store free of charge what you leave behind, up to your full allowance.

Keeping within your allowance is your responsibility, not Transportation's or the mover's. The mover will give you a weight estimate, but it's not official and can't be used to refute excess weight charges. If you exceed your allowance, you'll be hit with a bill sometime later. It may be a whole year later, but it will come, and the entire amount will be withdrawn in one lump sum from the military paycheck.

A fairly dependable way of estimating your possessions' weight is to figure 1,000 pounds per room (excluding storage and bathrooms). Then add the estimated weight of large appliances and other items you might have in the garage, storage room, and basement. Another way to figure is to count the number of items listed on the movers' inventory sheets and multiply by forty. The result will be your estimated poundage.

≡ Types of Baggage

Your possessions will be categorized three ways: unaccompanied (hold) baggage, household goods, and storage.

Pack the yellow pages in your household goods. You will need to find addresses from the old homestead more often than you expect.

If friends are leaving, make a wreath to hang on their new door, or give them a surprise present to ship with their household goods and open when they're settled.

To the extent possible, physically separate items destined for these three categories. Otherwise you'll get possessions put in storage that you wanted to take with you and vice versa. If separating isn't possible, tag items with large paper labels detailing the category. Be sure to remove any stickers left from previous moves.

Things you can't ship or store are outboard motors, airplanes, gliders, sailboats, motorboats, vehicles, trailers, and parts. (Sometimes trailer homes can be stored.) Nor will the government ship or store perishable foods, live plants, pets, alcohol, cigarettes, loaded firearms, live ammunition, explosives, aerosols, flammable products, acids, cordwood, or property for resale or commercial use.

Unaccompanied Baggage

Unaccompanied (hold) baggage is a small shipment of things sent to the new duty station early so that you can set up basic housekeeping when you arrive. The following are useful items to put in it:

- Food staples.
- China, cups, glasses, silverware.
- Pots, pans, skillets, utensils, small appliances.
- TV, maybe stereo.
- Bedding and the baby's crib.
- Shower curtain, bath rug, towels, washcloths, toilet paper.
- Light bulbs.
- Clock.
- Coffee pot, coffee.
- Plastic trash bags.
- Contact paper.
- A familiar possession for a young child who may be unsettled by the move.
- Clothes. If you're moving overseas, send *lots* of clothes, because the time it takes for your household goods to arrive is much longer than for continental moves. If the seasons are changing, send what's appropriate, and pack a raincoat and umbrella for each person. Some servicemembers mail uniforms to the new address in case their household goods are delayed.

- Clothes hangers, iron, ironing board.
- Jumper cables, tools, child's car seat.

If you want to send more than your unaccompanied baggage allowance permits, mail the items to yourself at your husband's new unit address. Using third-class mail is a lot less expensive than paying the movers. Even if you don't exceed your allowance, you still might want to do this, because mail arrives more quickly than unaccompanied baggage, and it reduces the number of things you might need to carry on your person. Save your postal receipts for tax purposes.

Household Goods

Household goods include furniture and everything else you want to ship.

Storage

Storage applies to overseas moves, since restricted weight allowances may keep you from shipping everything you own. Anything you feel you can do without for the next three years goes here. When you return, your storage items will be sent to your new duty station.

You may have the government handle the storage of your property, in which case it will be inaccessible to you for the duration of the storage. You can also arrange storage with a service of your choosing, and the government will pay you as much as it would have paid to its own storage contractor.

Things to Do before You Leave

Prepare lists of things you'll need to do, and keep them in a notebook. Start a folder of costs and lists of things you wish you had done differently for future moves. Did you know that every year one out of every five Americans moves? Retirees, corporate transferees, job-hoppers, young college graduates, and the recently unemployed are, like military people, constantly on the move. Consequently, you'll find a lot of articles on moving in military and civilian magazines, particularly in the late spring. Clip the ones you find useful and put them in your folder.

Here are some items that should be on your lists:

- Close your checking accounts if that's your plan. Give the bank at least five days' notice.

Before leaving each area, take photos of your favorite places and friends to hang on the refrigerator at the new place. Buy usable items, like dishtowels and coffee mugs, to serve as happy reminders.

Bring any remaining checks, deposit and withdrawal slips, automatic teller machine cards, and a copy of the PCS orders. Bring your check register, too, so that the bank can determine which checks are still outstanding. If you know what your new bank will be, you can open an account and have your money transferred, eliminating the need to carry a large cashier's check. If you have direct deposit, go to the finance office to make arrangements for the military paycheck to be deposited with your new bank.

- Retrieve valuables from your safety deposit box. Buy a locked strongbox to keep them in while the movers are there. You might want to keep it in your car trunk. Then use it to carry them in while on the road.

- Get change-of-address cards from the post office and send them to creditors, magazines you subscribe to, and other places you do business with. Leave one with the post office so that your mail can be forwarded.

- Clean your rugs, drapes, and slipcovers and have the movers pack them in the cleaners' wrappers. It's morale boosting to have them fresh and ready when you move into your new place.

- Get things that need repairing repaired. It will take you a while to find shops at the new place.

- Pick your medical records up from the hospital and dental clinic. You need to carry them to the new duty station yourself. New schools will usually ask to see your children's records before admitting them. Keep an updated inoculation record for each member of the family.

- Have utilities disconnected the day after you leave. You'll need your phone to call the housing inspector if there's a problem with the movers, and obviously you'll want lights and running water while they're there. And make sure you *do* call the utilities. It's disheartening to get final bills with the new occupant's long-distance phone calls and electricity charges on them.

- Cancel your newspaper and any other home-delivery items you receive.

- Disconnect your gas and electrical appliances. Know that storing dishwashers, washers, dryers, refrigerators, and freezers for several years is not a good idea, as they frequently go bad or rust out. Freezers contain Freon, which goes dead after sitting idle for a while. If you move your appliances, set aside one whole day to prepare each one. Drain all water from appliance hoses, thoroughly wash the inside of your refrigerator and freezer, leave their doors open, and give them at least two days to dry out. Place several charcoal briquettes or a sock full of new coffee grounds or baking soda inside while in transit to prevent mold and mildew. The base engineers can give you more details on how to prepare appliances. If plumbing, carpentry, or electrical work is needed in disconnecting appliances, you must arrange and pay for that.

- Disconnect electronic components such as stereos, TVs, VCRs, and computers.
- Photograph all your possessions, and record serial, make, and model numbers on the backs of the photos. You might need them to verify a claim. A great way to do this is by making a video-tape. If you don't own a camera, rent one. The family shutterbug can operate the camera while someone else calls out the numbers. Have expensive items appraised. Don't ship small valuables like jewelry and coin collections. And don't pack receipts and appraisals in the same box as the items.

> When deciding whether you should get rid of an item, consider these things: Is it broken? Obsolete? Unworn for years? Does it have stains or holes that can't be repaired? Is it shabby, worn, too tight? Are the shoes worn out? Get rid of them!

- Remove pictures, mirrors, curtains, rods, lights, utensil racks, and other hardware from the walls. Take the air conditioner out of the window. Stick tags on items that belong to the apartment so that the movers won't remove them.
- Remove items from crawl spaces, the attic, and the roof (don't forget the TV antenna). Movers are not required to go into areas that aren't accessible by a stairway (ladders don't count), aren't well lit, don't have a finished floor, or don't allow them to stand erect.
- Dismantle outdoor play equipment.
- Fill all prescriptions. Base hospitals usually fill only prescriptions written by the doctors stationed there. Once you arrive, it might take a while to get an appointment. And if you need routine things like Pap smears or eye exams, and it's easy to get them where you are, do so. It may be difficult to make such appointments at the new station.
- Get a health certificate for your pet, as you might have to put him in a kennel temporarily, and kennels require such certificates. If you know your new address, get it printed on a tag for your pet's collar. You never know what will happen at a rest stop! (See "Shipping Your Pet" later in this chapter.)
- Separate professional books, papers, and equipment from the rest of your possessions. Their weight is not charged against your allowance, but they must be weighed separately and listed as "professional" on the inventory; if they get packed with everything else, their weight will be charged to you.
- Make advance reservations at hotels along the way. Major chains have toll-free numbers you can call to cost-compare. Inquire about military discounts. Try to stay at military guest houses and lodges

when possible, to save money. Your PCS orders will entitle you to priority use. Make reservations as soon as you can, because military guest houses fill up fast.

■ Call or write the housing office at the new duty station to ask about the availability of quarters, apartments, quartermaster furniture, 110V outlets (if overseas), and so on. Dan Cragg's *Guide to Military Installations* (see "Further Reading" at the end of this chapter) gives brief descriptions of all major U.S. military installations and lists addresses of public affairs offices to which you can write for further information. Base libraries and Family Services centers keep packets of brochures of all duty stations. A useful resource is the Defense Department (Pentagon) operator, who can give you numbers of military bases and offices worldwide. That number is (703) 545-6700. Finally, write the new town's chamber of commerce. Real estate agents, movers, and apartment complexes use those inquiries as leads and will send you area maps and other information.

> Standard Installation Topic Exchange Service (SITES) is a worldwide Defense Department relocation service. It is a computerized network of information on employment opportunities, housing, shopping, and services at each duty station. Visit your Family Services office to use it.

> Don't take telephone answering machines overseas; they won't work with the local systems.

■ Get rid of unwanted items. Start doing this about four months before you move. Decide what you're keeping, and get rid of the rest. Moving junk is a waste of your time and the government's money. It will also cost *you* money if you exceed your allowance. There are several ways you can dispose of items you don't want to take. Put ads for items with considerable monetary value in the newspaper. Sell lesser items at the thrift shop or hold a garage sale. If you're feeling generous, Airman's Attic, Goodwill, the Salvation Army, and the Family Services lending closets are always in need of items. Get receipts for tax purposes.

■ Pick up developed film, dry cleaning, and other items. Retrieve loaned items, and return library books and other borrowed things.

■ Give your landlord notice as required by your lease.

■ Plan meals from what's in your freezer and pantry.

■ Close out any local charge accounts.

■ Check expiration dates of any major credit cards you plan to use en route. Check your family's ID card expiration dates.

≡ Tips for a Successful Garage Sale

Inventory your house from basement to attic to see if you have enough merchandise to make a garage sale worthwhile. If not, ask friends to participate. People won't stop if the pickings look slim.

Ask the city if a permit is required. There is a cost, but the fine if you're caught without one is bigger. If you live on base, ask the Family Services office if there is an annual date for yard sales. Take advantage of the free advertising and large crowds such events bring. If the annual date won't work for you, ask for an exception to policy if yard sales are otherwise prohibited. Your first choice of sale should be Saturday, then Friday, then Sunday.

Advertise your hot sellers in the base and local papers. Children's clothes and toys, furniture, baby needs, tools, kitchen items, carpets, lamps, and small appliances are hot sellers; adult clothing is not. Put out anything and everything you don't want, even if you think it's useless; garage sales are truly proof of the old saw "One man's trash is another man's treasure." Post fliers at supermarkets, the thrift shop, the exchange, and the commissary. Specify "no early birds" if you don't want shoppers before your advertised opening time.

Put a price on everything; many shoppers hate to ask. Be realistic; if the shoppers wanted to pay a lot they'd buy it new. Write the prices on pieces of masking tape or stick-on labels. You can write "obo" ("or best offer") after the price if you wish. Hot sellers generally bring 30 percent of their new cost; poor ones bring 10 percent.

Make the items easy to browse through. If people have to bend, they often won't bother. Purchase a free-standing garment hanger at a discount store, and arrange knickknacks neatly on a table or a piece of plywood supported by two chairs.

Older children love to help and can demonstrate how the toys work. Also, it's easier to convince them to give up their possessions if you tell them they can keep the money.

Be prepared to make change. Wear a fanny pack with dollar bills and coins or a workman's apron with large pockets. Don't take it off, and don't leave a cash box lying around; these are frequently stolen. Enlist a helper to prevent shoplifting of small items like cassette tapes.

Be prepared to demonstrate items. Have an extension cord handy, and put batteries in items that need them.

Don't take checks from people you don't know, and don't let them in the house to use the bathroom. If you're holding the sale in your garage, cover items not for sale with large sheets.

Be prepared to dicker; that's part of the fun for many who attend.

Don't get huffy if offered a low price. Just say, "Try later on this afternoon; if I still have it, we'll talk." That often prompts a quick sale.

Not everything that's broken needs to be fixed, but everything does need to be clean. Most people don't want to handle grimy items.

≡ Be Ready for the Movers

The importance of being ready when the movers arrive can't be overemphasized. Time is money for them; keeping them waiting while you're making decisions and doing things you should have done in advance will get things off to a bad start. Know what will go in your unaccompanied baggage, what will go in your household goods, and what you'll carry on your person. Put the items from this last group in a closet and hang up a Keep Out sign. *Everything not in this closet will get packed.* The movers will not verify whether you need particular items—they will simply pack everything they see. Even essentials like medicine, diaper bags, glasses, and contact lenses will be packed if you haven't given instructions not to pack them. Heavy stacks of magazines and newspapers that you certainly didn't plan to waste your weight allowance on will get packed, too, if they're lying around. Anything that can be disassembled will be, so tell the movers in advance if you don't want a certain item taken apart.

In the Keep Out closet should go the following:

- Plastic bin that fits under a car seat and can be used as a trash can while on the road.
- Plastic scrub bucket, squeegee mop, broom, dustpan, and cleaning materials for final once-overs and for the new place.
- Locked box containing your jewelry and other valuables (you can store this in your car trunk).
- Briefcase with files you may need while on the road and when you first arrive: monthly bills, creditor addresses, envelopes, and related correspondence; at least ten copies of the PCS orders; family medical records; photographs and inventory lists of your possessions (they'll do you no good if they're in a box that gets lost); all papers the movers give you (you'll need them if it becomes necessary to file a damage claim).
- Makeup, soap, plastic carrying cases, blow dryer, prescriptions, contact lenses, glasses.
- Pet needs.
- Baby needs.

- "Goodie bag" for the trip: nonmessy snacks, comic books, crayons, drawing paper, puzzles, magnetic board games.
- Maps.
- Change for rest-stop vending machines.
- Thermos and foam cups.
- Plastic bags, garbage bags, twist ties, plastic plates, quart bottle, plastic utensils, assorted condiments.
- Bag of food, cooler with soft drinks and water. "Blue ice," a reusable ice substitute, works better and lasts longer in a cooler than the real thing.
- Paper napkins, packets of moist towelettes, washcloths.
- Pillows.
- Coats, sweaters, and jackets, even in the summer, for cool nights.
- Clothes and suitcases.
- Negatives of your wedding photos and other events of extraordinary sentimental value. You wouldn't want both your photos and negatives in a box that gets lost.

> If you're concerned about a special item being broken, pack and move it yourself. I rent a small trailer to move such items.

- Big envelope for receipts pertaining to your move. Save for tax purposes.
- Pet kennel.
- Telescoping clothes pole to set up in the backseat from which to hang plants or clothes.
- Flashlight, fresh batteries.
- Military-issued items that must be returned.

≡ While the Movers Are There

Moving day will go more smoothly if you get pets and small children off the premises. Those movers work fast; making sure they're packing what you want where you want and how you want will require your undivided attention. Besides, on moving day the premises aren't safe for chil-

> Packing and lifting furniture is hard work. When the movers come, have a plentiful supply of ice water, soft drinks, and sandwiches on hand. They'll appreciate it, and it will show in the care your possessions get.

dren and pets. Movers prop doors open, letting the cat out and cold drafts or hot, sticky air in. Babies can get stepped on, and toddlers can get into things. Ask a friend to watch them, make arrangements at the child-care center, or hire a baby-sitter.

Watch the movers carefully; a lot of damage can be averted just by paying attention to what's going on. Not that you should tell them how to pack, but if you see them handling things roughly or incorrectly, politely assert yourself.

Don't pack anything yourself; such items will be labeled "packed by owner," and if they are broken, you won't be reimbursed. Have the movers verify and note which appliances work so that if they get broken, you can back up your claim.

Make sure boxes are labeled with the name of the room or closet their contents came from. This will make things easier when moving into your new place. Don't let toys get mixed with towels and kitchen utensils and labeled "Miscellaneous." Rugs should be rolled, mirrors and pictures individually wrapped, furniture disassembled, and mattresses put in individual cartons.

Don't let the movers use excelsior (fine, curled wood shavings) or newsprint to wrap anything. The moving company is paid to use plastic bubble sheets and brown wrapping paper.

Have lots of copies of the PCS orders on hand, and instruct the movers to put a copy in each box before it's taped up. That way, if a box goes astray, it'll be easier to locate its owner.

All your boxes and furniture will be put into large wooden crates. Insist that this be done in front of you, not at the warehouse. By watching your things get crated, you can ensure that boxes of dishes don't get balanced on sofa arms and sharp edges don't butt into bureaus. This is how major damage occurs. After the crates are nailed shut, make sure a sealant is applied to all joints and doors to make them watertight.

If you have a problem with a mover—he won't build a special crate for your marble-top table, he's dropping and breaking things, he's drunk, or whatever—don't argue with him. Call Transportation. It's your right to request another moving team or company.

Carefully check the inventory sheets before you sign them. Make sure everything packed has been listed. If it's not listed, it can't be claimed. Expensive items should be specifically identified: "Lladró porcelain figurine," not "statue"; "Waterford crystal goblet," not "glass." Make, model, and serial number of high-priced items should be listed. Make sure stereo equipment is specifically described: A JVC equalizer, Akai compact disc player, and Sansui cassette deck shouldn't be summed up as "stereo." The same with your

Moving companies are a great source of information for repair specialists. Add their recommendations to the ones the claims division will give you. Try not to get too upset over damaged items; it's impossible to make a move without something getting broken or damaged.

TV; if your twenty-six-inch color console is stolen, you may have difficulty proving that the mover's hastily scribbled "TV" didn't mean a ten-inch black-and-white.

If you disagree with the way an item's condition is described, briefly note that on the form. At this point, your interests and the movers' are not the same. Make sure you understand all symbols used to describe damages.

Fill out the form provided by Transportation that describes your satisfaction with the way this company handled your possessions. If your experience was bad, chances are other families' were too, and enough bad reports will get a company off the government payroll.

≡ Filing a Claim

If items arrive at the new duty station damaged, you can file for their reasonable repair or replacement cost. You can do this without your husband if you have power of attorney.

When your household goods were delivered, the movers should have provided you with a pink form (DD 1840). Note all damages and missing items on it, and turn it in to the claims office within seventy days of the day your property was delivered. This form is the official notification that you are going to make a claim. You don't have to file the actual claim within seventy days; you have two years to do that. If you fail to file the official notification within seventy days, the government won't be able to collect any money from the moving company, and thus will offset your claim by the amount it could have recouped.

When you bring your DD 1840 to the claims office, personnel there will sign and date it and give you a copy. Keep this copy as proof that you did everything you were supposed to. At this time pick up a claim packet. It contains all the forms you need.

Your claim needs to be accompanied by written estimates of everything that costs more than $100 to fix or replace. For items that have to be replaced, submit either copies of catalog pages of similar items or a signed note from a department store verifying the price. Sometimes the claims office will send an inspector to see your damaged goods. The mover has the right to inspect any damage reported to them and often will ask a local repair firm for an estimate. Keep all broken items until the claim is settled, and then some. You might be asked to turn in any salvageable items for which you are paid replacement costs.

The claims system is not a substitute for insurance. The most the government will pay for any one claim is $40,000, regardless of the possessions' worth, and there are maximum amounts for specific items like jewelry, crystal, and cameras. If you have unique or particularly expensive items, you might want to take out a private policy on them. Make sure that the policy covers government moves; not all do.

≡ The Do-It-Yourself (DITY) Move

DITY movers should ask the rental truck company or another moving company for brochures and advice on packing boxes and loading the truck. A DITY move isn't a bargain if everything arrives damaged.

Q: How do I calculate measurement tons?
A: Measurement tons =
$$\frac{length \times width \times height}{40}$$

If you don't have much to move, are willing to work, or just prefer to maintain complete control over your property, DITY might be the way for you. The DITY program is a self-help one through which the government will give you 80 percent of what it would pay a commercial mover to move your things. If your move costs less than that, you pocket the difference. The average profit made by service-members who DITY is $500. If the move ends up costing more, however, you must pay the difference.

The transportation office must authorize your DITY, even if you use your own truck or trailer. They'll help arrange for rental equipment and provide you with packing materials. You pack, load, and move your own possessions.

Estimate your possessions' weight as accurately as possible before you visit the transportation counselor. This will help him or her estimate the cost of your move and give you an idea whether you'll come out ahead financially. It will also help ensure that you'll get a truck or trailer the size you need.

You'll need to get two weight tickets, one showing the weight of your truck or trailer empty and one showing it full. The exact amount of money the government pays is tied to this weight. DITY movers are entitled to travel allowance, per diem, mileage, and $25,000 insurance coverage from the government. You'll have the same weight allowances that you would if you were moved commercially.

If you want, you can pack your own things and contract with a private trucking firm to drive them to the new location. While this takes a bite out of your profit, it helps if you're relocating cars or have to drive a long distance. You can also split your possessions between DITY and the government-hired movers.

≡ Moving Your Mobile Home

If you want to move everything *and* the homestead, you can. As long as your mobile home or trailer is small enough to be self-propelled, you can receive a mileage allowance to move it yourself or have the government arrange to move it professionally. The government will pay as much to move a mobile home as it would pay to move your maximum weight allowance. You must pay anything over that. Know that it's rare for anyone to break even when shipping a mobile home; moving them is extremely expensive. What the government pays usually doesn't even cover half the cost. Transportation personnel have seen bills in the thousands presented to the servicemember.

Also know that what a mobile home can hold while sitting on blocks and what it can hold while being pulled down the interstate are two different things. People moving overloaded trailers have had them break down or even break in half en route. For this reason, a carrier may decline to move a mobile home after deciding it's overloaded, but you would then have to pay an attempted-pick-up charge.

≡ On the Road

The following are tips from wives in the VMMC (Veterans of Many Moves Club) on how to make that car trip more pleasant.

"Portable cribs for babies are a must. They're compact and can be set up in minutes at rest stops and motels."

"Plants travel well wrapped in a plastic garbage bag with a few holes punched in it for air."

"Give your kids geography lessons on the way. Show on the map where you're going. Dig up some history on the states you're passing through and discuss it as you pass through them. Get off the interstate once in a while and meander through the small towns. Make stops at tourist places, scenic vistas, and other highlights. That will make the trip seem like a vacation."

"We didn't stay at motels on the way to New Mexico. We brought our tents and camping equipment and stayed at campgrounds."

"Stay at motels that have pools. Everyone will want to work off some energy after being cooped up all day, and pools are a good place to do it."

When packing the suitcases that will travel with you, be *brutal* about what stays and what goes! Carrying around unnecessary items makes your suitcases heavier, and you waste time arranging and rearranging, folding and refolding their contents. Zip-closure bags are a must to hold bottles and tubes that might leak, pack a wet washcloth in, or store restaurant leftovers. Don't pack big supplies of things you can buy anywhere, like detergent or aspirin.

The day you vacate your home, don't throw out any good food you have left. Give it to the Family Services food locker or to the neighbors.

When our daughter was very young, we'd have her pack a "goodie box" of all her favorite things. We'd carry it in the car or load it on the moving van last so that it would be the first thing unloaded at our new home. We'd also arrange her new bedroom as much as possible like her old one. Once, when she was eleven, she looked around and said, "Mom, this looks like home." That was exactly what I was after.

"Have a good breakfast each day on the road. It makes sitting in the car easier."

"Bring games and toys to amuse babies and toddlers. Play road games with the older ones. We like to play 'geography.' I'll say the name of a town, city, country, body of water, whatever. The next person will say another place, but it must start with the last letter of the place I named. If I say 'India,' for example, the next person must name a place that starts with an 'A.' You can only use each name once. Then there's 'license plate bingo.' You make ordinary bingo cards with the names of states written in the squares. When you see a car with a license plate from a state on your card, you color in that square. We can spend hours on these games. Have prizes for the winners."

"If you're driving two cars, prearrange a signal, such as flashing your headlights, so that one can notify the other if there's a problem. Make sure both drivers know where they're going, because it's easy to get separated in traffic."

"Bring the pet kennel. If the trip is any length at all, at some point you're going to want to put your pet in it."

"In the summer, drape sheets over leather or vinyl seats. Otherwise, sitting back down after coming out of a rest stop will be painful!"

"We play games of anticipation before and during the trip. What will the new place be like? Where will we go for vacations? What sorts of activities will we get involved in there?"

"Carry a big over-the-shoulder bag with separate compartments for

your purse contents, baby needs, and goodies for the kids. Juggling a purse, diaper bag, and two or three other bags is just too hard."

"Tie baby toys on a string so that they can't get thrown around in the car."

"Many hotels provide more than just soap and towels. Ask at the front desk to borrow robes and blow dryers. Some stock personal-care items like toothbrushes and razors and will give them out free even if the gift shop is open. When making reservations, you can often arrange for a refrigerator, iron, even a humidifier in your room."

"I amused my twelve-month-old while we were driving at night by beaming a flashlight on the roof and making patterns."

"Burgers and fries and junk food on the road get boring. Stock your cooler creatively. Buy deli items, or go to a gourmet shop or exotic bakery for treats. This is a vacation! Buy variety breads such as chewy rye rolls, bagels, tortillas, or pita. Summer sausage, deviled ham, and pepperoni travel well, as do hard cheeses like Swiss. Carrots, grapes, melon chunks, kiwi fruit, cucumbers, apples, bananas, snap peas, and dry-roasted peanuts make healthy munchings. Avoid salty chips and crackers; they're fattening and will make you thirsty. Pack different drink mixes. Water is free, so refill your quart bottle at rest stops and gas stations. Stopping at a grocery instead of a drive-through takes longer, but the food is better and cheaper." If you have a baby on formula, buy ready-to-feed cans or carry bottled water, since changes in water may be upsetting."

≡ Shipping Your Car

If you're going overseas and want to ship your car, you need to find out the answers to the following questions:

1. If you lease your car, will the lessor and the financer allow you to take it overseas?
2. What will it cost to insure your vehicle in the country you're moving to? Rates vary, but you can be sure you'll pay a lot more than you're paying now. Ask your sponsor for names and addresses of companies

Don't make extensive repairs to a car you plan to sell, but have it detailed, steam-clean the engine, clean the upholstery and trunk, and tighten any loose fittings (to quiet minor rattles) to bring a better price.

When shipping your car, remove your stereo if you can. If something gets stolen, that will be it.

that insure Americans, and write for quotes. If your present insurer will continue to insure you, ask how your rates will be affected.

3. How easy will it be to get parts and repair work done where you're going? Car dealerships in foreign countries do not stock American car parts, and ordering them can take months.

4. Does the country have any laws governing characteristics of vehicles? Some restrict type, color, and optional equipment. In many countries, CB radios and radar detectors are illegal.

5. Service policy restricts vehicle shipment to some countries. Is the one you're going to one of them?

Check all this well in advance so that you'll have plenty of time to make appropriate arrangements.

Once you decide to ship your car, your transportation officer will have exact details on what you need to do. The following are some general guidelines:

Every servicemember is entitled to ship one eligible private vehicle to or from an overseas area. It must be self-propelled, be licensed to travel overland on public highways, have four or more wheels, and be designed to carry passengers or property. A motorcycle or moped may be shipped as long as another vehicle isn't shipped under the same set of orders. Commercial-use vehicles won't be shipped, nor will trailer homes. And if your vehicle exceeds twenty measurement tons in size, you'll have to pay for the excess.

Shipping a vehicle back to the States from an overseas assignment does not depend on whether one was shipped over. The entitlement to ship a vehicle overseas and the entitlement to ship one back are separate. With few exceptions, you can't ship back at government expense a foreign-built vehicle that was bought overseas. You can pay to ship a vehicle yourself, space available, on the Military Sealift Command. Naturally, it must meet all U.S. safety and emission standards before you may drive it away. Converting a foreign specification car to meet U.S. standards is very expensive, so before you buy one with this in mind, check into prices.

Get your car in the best condition possible. While the government has strict rules on the condition a vehicle must be in before being shipped, the host country's rules can be even stricter. Tire treads a millimeter too thin, rust on the exhaust, a hairline crack in the windshield, even an unadjusted light can cause your vehicle to sit at the host-country port until you can afford to correct it. The engine, windshield wipers, brakes, horn, battery, and lights must work. The exhaust system must be sound and body and fenders free of breaks or tears. Make sure your car has adequate rust protection if you're going to humid areas like Panama or the Pacific.

Don't use your car to ship property. The incidence of things getting stolen is high. Don't even leave jumper cables, tools, or a car seat in it; ship these things with your unaccompanied baggage. Compensation for lost or stolen items varies for each service and might not cover the cost of replacement.

Find out the emission control standards in the country you're shipping your car to, because you're going to have to meet them. They differ around the world. Some countries don't have any, and those of other countries are so tight they are, for all practical purposes, impossible to meet. For example, Japan's standards are so strict, and the price of converting pre-1976 vehicles to meet them so high, that the Department of Defense refuses to ship at government expense any vehicle (except motorcycles) built before March 31, 1976, there or to Okinawa. The United States has its own standards, too. Your car will be checked when you return to make sure it still complies with them.

If your car has a catalytic converter, find out if the country you're going to has unleaded gas. If not, have the converter removed. Naturally, you'll need to put it back on before your Stateside return and show proof of this before the U.S. authorities will let you drive it away. If you wait until you get back to the States to have it done, you'll have to post a bond before leaving the port. This can be up to three times the car's value.

Ports for shipping vehicles overseas are in Bayonne, New Jersey; Philadelphia, Pennsylvania; Charleston, South Carolina; New Orleans, Louisiana; Norfolk, Virginia; Cape Canaveral, Florida; Oakland, California; Wilmington, Delaware; and Baltimore, Maryland. Since port personnel will drain all gas before the car is shipped, don't fill up your tank when you get there. As for how long it will take your car to catch up with you, it usually takes twenty-eight to forty-five days to get to Europe, forty-five to sixty days to the Mediterranean, and sixty to ninety days to the Pacific areas and Africa when shipped from East Coast ports.

When picking up your car, wash it before signing the inventory sheet. Most ports have car washes on the premises. Dirt accumulated on the way over can obscure new nicks and scratches. Be careful about hiring other people to pick up your car for you; they don't know your car as well as you do and won't be as meticulous about noting new scratches. Once the inventory sheet is signed and the car driven away, scratches not noted will be difficult to claim.

≡ Shipping Your Pet

There's no need to leave Fido behind when you move overseas. You can ship him three ways: on the Air Mobility Command (AMC), on a commercial or air cargo carrier, or through a pet-shipping service. Pets don't travel at Defense Department expense, so some cost is involved.

AMC is the carrier most used, as it is the least expensive, typically costing between $10 and $85 per pet. AMC also has the most restrictions. Only dogs and cats may be shipped, two per family, and the pet plus its carrier must weigh 100 pounds or less. Pets cannot be less than eight weeks old or unweaned. Pets will not be shipped to England, Korea, or Japan because of their lengthy quarantine requirements (e.g., six months in England). Shipment is for permanent moves only, and service ends at the port of entry. You must make separate arrangements for any continuing flights, and your pet must stay with you until boarding time. Reserve space for him the same time you make arrangements for yourself, because there are usually only eight pet spaces per aircraft.

When shipped on a commercial carrier, your pet is technically considered baggage. When shipped as air cargo, he is treated more like a passenger. Both allow him to travel in a climate-controlled, pressurized compartment, but a cargo plane has more responsibility for live cargo than a commercial airline has for baggage. If you have an unusual pet, such as a snake, ferret, or horse, air cargo may be your only option. Air cargo carriers accept any animal legal to export or import.

Pet-shipping services offer shipping plus extras. You can arrange for home pickup, boarding at the airport kennels, and delivery at the cargo terminal. Naturally, the price will be commensurate with the service you receive.

All animals must be in an approved container. If the country has a quarantine, you will have to pay all associated expenses, such as lab tests and food. When your tour is over, you'll have to comply with the United States' own quarantine requirements (for instance, Hawaii has a 120-day quarantine). Ask your military veterinarian or the country's consulate about quarantines and other requirements, such as the bilingual health certificates that Japan and Germany demand.

Shipping your pet requires advance planning. Airlines require a health certificate issued within ten days of departure. That is not enough time, however, to treat some ailments that prevent certification. For instance, if rabies shots are required, they must be given between thirty days and one year before departure. Travel is stressful for animals, and they pick up diseases easily. Vaccinations for kennel cough and distemper/parvo are strongly recommended and may be necessary. Have your dog tested for heartworm and started on a heartworm preventive before you travel.

Always carry your rabies certificate during travel. If your pet bites someone while traveling, you must provide proof of current vaccinations (a rabies tag is not enough) or your pet will be impounded for ten days.

In some places, if proof of current vaccination cannot be provided, the animal may be destroyed in order to be tested.

If you're traveling by car, a health certificate is legally required to take your pet across state lines. Though this law is rarely enforced, your pet could be impounded without one.

≣ Nonconcurrent Travel

If the overseas area you're going to has a severe shortage of housing—on base and off—concurrent travel orders for you and your husband will not be issued. Your husband will still have to report to his new assignment, but you will not be authorized to travel with him. You will be issued travel authorization when the housing situation improves.

≣ Homeowner's Assistance Program (HAP)

Base closings have a devastating effect on home prices. If you are moving from a base that has announced a closure, you might qualify for the Department of Defense's Homeowner's Assistance Program (HAP). It is run by the Army Corps of Engineers and assists military people from all services and DOD civilians. HAP is not designed to make you money or even let you break even; it just softens the financial blow.

Homeowners may qualify for the program if they were employed near or at the base, and if they owned and occupied their homes when the closure was publicly announced. The occupancy requirement can be waived for homeowners stationed overseas at the time. Homes must be one- or two-family dwellings. Most mobile homes do not qualify.

HAP works like this: If you are unable to sell your house, the government will buy it for 75 percent of the prior market value or for the balance of the existing mortgage, whichever is greater. Even if you do find a private buyer, HAP can reimburse you for part of your financial loss. The government will make up the difference between the sale price and up to 95 percent of the house's value before the base closure announcement.

Some help is also available even if you already defaulted on your mortgage. If your home was foreclosed upon, the government will reimburse enforceable liabilities such as taxes, needed repairs, the mortgage balance, penalties, and other expenses needed to settle the mortgage debt.

Be aware that the IRS has ruled that when the government buys homes or pays off the mortgage, some of the money paid to you or your lender is taxable income.

If you're stuck at an airport because of a flight delay, cancellation, or missed connection, ask if there's a USO lounge where you can relax. Some airports have minihotels where you can rent a bed and bath by the hour. Some even have fitness centers.

The government spends almost $3 billion a year moving service families around, and eventually you will be one of them. So always look for the positive. If you make up your mind you are not going to like a place, you won't, no matter what it has going for it. A place is what you make of it. I've met people stationed in New York City who can't find anything to do, and people in Adak, Alaska, who can't find enough time to do all they want.

Camp out in your new home to save money while waiting for your furniture to arrive. Borrow cots, sleeping bags, pots, pans, cribs, dishes, and such things from the Family Services lending closet. Ask the housing office if they lend furniture; some do.

Pack a "goodie bag" for yourself to be used when you move in. I put bubble bath, a good book, Walkman, and favorite tapes in mine.

When you leave good friends who are also in the military, get a permanent address of a relative of theirs so that you can always stay in touch.

Moving In

Even if you're living in a hotel or military guest house for the first few weeks, contact the transportation office immediately on arrival and leave a phone number where you can be reached when your possessions come in. If you don't have a phone, give the transportation office your husband's new unit number. If your plans or duty station changed while you were en route, it's your responsibility to contact Transportation so that they can make appropriate arrangements.

Here are some things to do the day you move into your permanent home:

- Find a baby-sitter for your small children. Moving in is just as hectic as moving out.

- Accept your property as soon as possible after it arrives. Intermediate storage heightens the risk of loss or damage. It will also cost you money if it exceeds the amount of time the government will pay for.

- Know in advance where you want each piece of furniture. The movers are required to place each item only once. Make a sketch of the layout of the house or apartment so that you can decide beforehand where pieces should be placed. If you're waiting to get into quarters, get a floor plan from Housing.

- Insist that the movers bring the boxes in through one door only, and check each box off as they bring it in. Don't sign the inventory until every box is accounted for. (You don't have to account for box contents, just the box.) Otherwise, filing a claim will be difficult.

- The movers are paid to unpack your stuff. If you wish them to do so, tell them. They will not organize your house, however. Be sure to check each empty box before they cart it off; many a small item has gotten hidden in the wrapping paper and thrown out.

- Hang signs that correspond to the box labels on the door of each room, so that boxes can be put in their appropriate places.

Throughout the entire moving process, it is critical to carefully monitor the Leave and Earnings Statement. Temporary lodging, cost of living, dislocation, per diem, and mileage allowances, as well as special allowances for certain types of work, all figure into the paycheck during moves. Accidental over- and underpayments are often made during moves. Save overpayments;

Take kids on familiarity trips. Letting them see some of the houses or apartments you're considering and some of the new town's parks, beaches, museums, or anything else that gives them an idea of what their new home will be like will take away some of the mystery of the move.

Let children help make decisions. If they are involved in choosing paint or wallpaper for their bedrooms, for example, they are more likely to feel positive about things.

Allow and encourage your kids to stay in contact with their old friends through letters and phone calls. This will smooth the transition and teach them about the importance of maintaining friendships. And don't discount any of their concerns. While such things as worrying over how the new kids wear their hair may seem trivial next to your concerns, they are not trivial to your children.

Encourage your children to have portable hobbies for the same reason working military wives strive for portable careers. These hobbies will lead to jobs and friends in the new town. Invite new kids over for an outing to a park or ice cream shop.

if you don't report them, Finance will eventually find out and withhold them in one lump sum from the military paycheck.

Get acquainted with your new neighborhood and base. Go with your husband to the newcomer's briefing; it will be a good source of information about available services and facilities. Spouses are always welcome. Find out where the town library, park, YMCA, YWCA, health spa, and other leisure spots are. The local chamber of commerce and tourist or recreation office can help you with this. Actively seek friendships.

Go to your unit wives' coffee. If you're an extrovert, take advantage of the newcomer's prerogative and introduce yourself to your neighbors. If you're an introvert, hang around outside washing the car, sitting on the porch, or playing with your pet, to give someone more outgoing a chance to introduce herself. There's no better way to start a new tour than by making new friends.

≡ Making the Most of It

Some comments from people thoroughly enjoying their duty stations:

"Annapolis was a great tour. I have fond memories of boat rides down the Chesapeake Bay and of eating tasty crab cakes and oysters."

"The high altitude and low humidity at Cannon AFB, New Mexico, make for great skiing at Angelfire, and you can play golf year-round. The base has trailers for rent at Lake Conchas, for a nice weekend getaway."

"I love being stationed at Tyndall. There's lots to do in Panama City. You can rent boats at the marina and do some great fishing. It doesn't get better than sitting at the Club La Vela or Spinnakers with a drink and watching the sun set."

"Don't spend a tour on the East Coast without taking a ferry to Nantucket. So much history and beauty on one island, and unlike Martha's Vineyard, all the beaches are public."

"While stationed at the Long Beach Naval Hospital, we'd take trips to Catalina Island, where you can camp at the beach. The air is smog-free, since most cars aren't allowed. Front Street has lounges, nightclubs, restaurants, even a comedy club. It's fun for people watchers, as you see all types there."

"For something different, visit the ghost town of Gleeson while stationed at Fort Huachuca, Arizona. It's eerie! Tombstone's Boot Hill Cemetery is a 'don't miss,' and environmentalists will enjoy hiking in the Sonora Desert."

"Hawaii is a great tour for the water-sport lover. It's all here: surfing, wind sailing, scuba diving, snorkeling, fishing, and sailing. I also recommend a tourist submarine ride through Waikiki's coral reef. The kids will love seeing all the colorful fish."

"Fort Bliss, Texas, offers the opportunity to take frequent trips to Mexico.

Once you get past the border towns, it truly is another country, with its own customs and culture. You get the benefits of a foreign tour without moving to a foreign country."

"When stationed in Alaska, we took Gray Line's Grand Denali Explorer tour, and we also traveled through Denali National Park. We rafted on the Nenana River and went on wilderness safaris. People from all over the world spend a fortune to do these things that were right in our backyard. A frequent treat was the sight of people stopping their cars to let ducks and their ducklings cross the road."

≡ Further Reading

Cragg, Dan. *Guide to Military Installations, 4th edition.* Mechanicsburg, PA: Stackpole Books, 1994.

Groberman, Jeff. *The Garage Sale Book: Turn Your Trash into Cash.* New York: Prima Publications and Communications, 1987.

Guide to Military Installations in the U.S. Supplement to *Army, Air Force,* and *Navy Times* newspapers (issued annually)

Halpern, Shari. *Moving from One to Ten.* New York: Macmillan Publishing Co., 1993.

Hayes, Nan DeVincentis. *Move It! A Guide to Relocating Family, Pets, and Plants.* New York: Dembner Books, 1989.

Importing a Car. Pamphlet by the U.S. Customs Service, available from your transportation office.

It's Your Move. Booklet available from your transportation office.

Kids on the Move. Booklet available from Conquest Corporation, P.O. Box 488, Franklin, MI 48025.

The Mover's Advantage. Booklet available from Ryder Moving Company, (800) GO-RYDER.

Moving Expenses (publication 521) and *Selling Your Home* (publication 523), Internal Revenue Service.

Moving with the Military. USAA publication, available from Family Services offices.

Philbin, Tom. *Moving Successfully: Your Guide to Low-Cost, Hassle-Free Moving and Storage.* Yonkers, NY: Consumer Reports Books, 1994.

U.S. Forces Travel and Transfer Guide. Falls Church, VA: Military Living Publications, 1993.

9

Orders Overseas

Your husband has just received orders assigning him to a foreign land and authorizing you to go with him.

Lucky you! You're being given the chance to become a more knowledgeable and worldly person. You'll be able to visit places your civilian counterparts only wish they could and to see conditions firsthand instead of just reading about them in a book. You'll have the opportunity to meet citizens of another country and discuss their opinions. In other words, you can meet the people that make a foreign country foreign. That's something tourists on those ten-countries-in-twelve-days trips can never do.

In addition to the same preparations Stateside moves require, an overseas move necessitates passports, inoculations, absentee voting, permits for firearms, and storage.

Q: Why are servicemembers stationed overseas?

A: Because America's defense rests not only on its home bases but on its overseas ones as well. Overseas bases are needed to support the personnel that keep open the sea routes by which goods critical to our economy travel, such as petroleum, chromium, steel, rubber, sugar, coffee, VCRs, bicycles, stereos, cars, and ball bearings. They are also needed to support personnel sent to areas where they'd most likely be needed in case of hostilities.

You are all the luckier to be sent overseas today, as drawdown plans call for tens of thousands of troops to return to the United States, units and wings to be deactivated, and air stations to close. Here are some ways you can make the most of this chance of a lifetime.

≡ Prepare to Go

As soon as you find out where you're going, learn the language. Think of all the things you do in the course of a day, such as asking for directions, talking to phone operators, questioning clerks, or calling for information. You read bills, the classifieds, and labels on gasoline pumps. Unless you plan to live an extraordinarily limited and restricted life, you'll want to do these same things overseas, and an inability to do so will make life frustrating.

Besides making life easier, knowing some of the language will make it more fun. It's a proud feeling to be able to walk into a shop and converse with the clerk in her native tongue. You'll get better buys, because shops where English is spoken charge dearly for the service. You'll be able to read the local newspaper, which will give you insights into host citizenry thinking and new perspectives on your own country. You'll make host citizen friends more easily. Finally, knowing the language goes a long way in making the place feel like home.

When we were ordered overseas, I worried about how my six-year-old would handle the long plane ride. The day before the trip I told him to pretend we were getting on the plane. I said I'd tell him when we'd get off. He asked me several times if we were there, and I said, "Not yet." When the time came, I said, "That's how long we'll be on the plane tomorrow."

When a host citizen says he doesn't speak English, don't get upset, even if he studied it in school. How many Americans do you know who studied French or Spanish in school but still can't speak it?

If you are storing a car, investigate whether you can save money by dropping all insurance coverage except for comprehensive loss. Be sure to resume full coverage before driving the car upon your return.

Take night classes. If they don't fit your schedule, advertise for a tutor. Check out some tapes from your library, or splurge and buy a set. Play them on your car's cassette deck on the way to work, or wear a headset if you ride a bus. Instead of watching TV some nights, practice. Making it a family project will help enthuse everyone for the move.

Once you get to your new country, if your husband is required to take classes that teach phrases, go with him. Spouses are always welcome. Afterward, sign up for the low-cost courses the Education Center offers. The instructors are usually host citizens and give lots of information on the area. Ignore the people who quit after the first three weeks, complaining, "I wanted to learn the language, not grammar." It's impossible to learn a language without learning the grammar. Also ignore the people who tell you the classes are worthless because they teach High German or Castilian Spanish, and the people in the area speak Low German or Catalán Spanish. Even if it's true, you will be better off learning it than nothing at all. Besides, the high form of any language is spoken on television, and everyone understands that.

Study, too, some history of the country; at the very least, browse through the Fodor's, Michelin, or "Let's Go!" guides. You might even find something to whet your interest in specific sites. Studying the country's modern history will also help you understand what the American military presence there today is all about.

Pick up a welcome packet from the Family Services office. Go to a USO newcomer's orientation. You'll meet new friends and learn about living in your new country.

Don't compare peaches and pears. If you dwell upon all the wonderful things you left in the old country, you'll miss all the wonderful things the new one has to offer. And don't be daunted by the fact that things are different. Part of the learning experience is discovering *why* they are different.

Obtain mail-order catalogs to pack with your household goods before going overseas.

≡ Venture Out

Don't hang around the apartment waiting for your husband to come home and drive you around. Buy a city map and a pocket dictionary or phrase book, write your address on a slip of paper, and walk or get on a bus. You'll find buses all over; many countries have more-advanced public transportation than the United States has. Don't be afraid of getting lost—just show someone that slip of paper with your address. Hand signals are universal. If you get tired of bumbling around, hail a cab. If you have a car, drive. This will increase your confidence even more. You can always ask for directions at gas stations or from people on the street.

We're stationed in Mainz, Germany. I was surprised to learn that in 38 B.C., Roman soldiers set up field camps in the very area we're living! Now here I am, living with my soldier husband just like some other woman did 2,000 years ago.

There are plenty of opportunities for Reservists to perform their drills and annual training while living overseas.

Obtaining a license to drive overseas is simple. You merely present a valid, unexpired U.S. license and take a test on international symbols and signs.

Buy a wallet with separate compartments for American and local currency, and carry a pocket calculator to figure purchase prices and develop a feel for exchange rates. Go to supermarkets and department stores, browse around, and familiarize yourself with the things they sell and the way they sell them.

Pursue Your Hobbies

Buying a TV from the exchange overseas is advantageous because you can buy a multivoltage (eliminating the need for a transformer), multisystem (NTSC/PAL) set. This allows you to watch local TV, the SkyChannel, and other English-language channels, giving you a break from the Armed Forces Network.

A tour in Europe is a shopper's paradise! Nutcrackers, beer steins, David Winter cottages, Lladros, Swarozski crystal, Wedgwood china, porcelain . . . exquisite mementos can be purchased for so much less than in the States.

What do you like to do? Seek clubs where you will find other people who share your interest. The woman who paints will discover new vistas; the sewer, new patterns; the cook, new recipes. Ask your language teacher if she knows of sport or hobby clubs, or inquire at stores where the wares are sold. Check the phone book for swimming pools, health spas, and other recreational facilities. The host citizens are interested in these things, too, and they're good places for you and your family to meet them.

Participate in the local lifestyle. Ask at the public affairs office whether there's a club that brings Americans and host citizens together, like Germany's famous Kontakt clubs. Here you'll meet people who are eager to meet you and who will be able to give you information about places to go and things to do.

No Excuses

Don't use a lack of money or low currency exchange rates as an excuse to spend three years cocooned in your quarters. It doesn't take a lot of money to have fun. The host citizenry is living on the same economy that you are, and no matter how little you and your husband are paid, the great majority of them are paid even less. And they don't have the benefit of the military support systems that you do.

The best burgers I ever ate were cooked at the Nashville Club in Iteawon, Korea.

You don't need to go on expensive tours to enjoy yourself. Ordinary things make a tour fun, too. And in most locations there are fun things to do that cost very little or nothing at all. As one wife is fond of saying, "You only live once, and this ain't no dress rehearsal."

≡ Make the Most of Things

Here are some comments from people definitely making the most of things:

"Every other Saturday we go to the market by the ocean. The mama-sans and their children sell fresh fish, mussels, lobsters, clams, shrimp, and prawns. There are dozens of tiny stalls. In one you'll find soaps; in the next, mink blankets; and in the next, a small restaurant where the man cooks your food right in front of you in a wok. We take drives in the country. The houses are light, airy oriental style with tipped roofs, surrounded by vegetable and flower gardens. They're certainly different from those rows of aluminum-sided houses we left in Ohio! Once we went to where the kings are buried. The ancient Koreans would bury their kings by laying them on the ground and pouring dirt over them. There are mounds and mounds of buried kings and a display under glass that allows you to see the mummified body of one of them, with his gold and jewels strewn all around. Their temples are incredible—intricate confections with solid gold interiors.

"Last summer we went to the resort at Cheju-do Beach. White sand, blue water, big trees dripping with oranges. Cheju-do Beach fits every wallet; you'll find fancy hotels for the rich and picturesque shacks for the not-so-rich. There are divers you pay to go down and bring up oysters. If there's a pearl inside, you get to keep it. My daughter got a pearl—that made her day! She took it to school to show it off."

—ARMY E-6 WIFE, PUSAN, KOREA

"On three-day weekends we tie our bikes to the car, load up Steve's field gear, and drive to the Black Forest. We put our baby in a bike seat, strap a helmet on him, and cycle the paths to Switzerland. He's a 'go-baby,' always rolling on our bikes, in a stroller, or on my back. I can't imagine traveling without him. Everyone loves a baby, and he gets a lot of attention. In fact, he's our icebreaker! We've met Germans, Swiss, Austrians, and Italians cycling with their own babies. Other weekends we ride around town, exploring new neighborhoods and discovering parks and monuments. One monument listed all the men from that area who had been killed in World War I, and the dates and places. The first hundred or so were killed in France, but the last few were killed in nearby Kloppenheim and Wiesbaden. It illustrated very graphically how the Germans were in France for a long time but toward the end were reduced to just defending their own territory.

"We bought our bikes at the exchange, Peugeot ten-speeds. Together they cost over $500, but in terms of what they've done to our quality of life and morale, they're the best investments we've ever made. Steve uses his to get to work and keep fit at the same time."

—ARMY E-5 WIFE, WIESBADEN, GERMANY

"A tank of gas or a few dollars' worth of bus tickets will take you on a decent day trip anywhere. We take local buses and sightsee. We've been on a gondola in Venice, and we've seen the Sistine Chapel and the Colosseum. Going to Vatican City and attending services at St. Peter's was an incredibly emotional experience for me. My son has developed an interest in Roman history as a result of this tour."

— AIR FORCE E-7 WIFE, AVIANO, ITALY

"We live on the economy. Once we had a Texas barbecue and invited our Spanish neighbors. What a kick they got out of it! They talked about it for weeks before we even had it. On the big day, one wore an Australian outback-type hat he thought was a Stetson! We had lots of American food: hamburgers, fried chicken, chips, kosher pickles, and Haagen-Dazs ice cream. Two months later they were still telling us how much they had enjoyed it. They've also invited us to their homes. I can't imagine living in a place for three years and not making civilian friends, whether Stateside or overseas.

"I've been taking night classes in Spanish and have had great results using it. Americans who don't enjoy it here say, 'Well you like it because you speak Spanish!' Well, I didn't speak any more than they did when I got here, but I made an effort to learn. Our tour is up in four more months. I wish I could thank all the Spaniards who have made it so memorable. Hasta la vista."

—NAVY O-1 WIFE, ROTA, SPAIN

"This place is paradise. Olive trees, hot sun washing over stucco buildings. Simple. Primitive. And the fact that we don't get American TV is a blessing. My kids used to be glued to it, but now they read more. I get a kick out of the letters in the Stars and Stripes *from people in Germany complaining about the programming on AFRTS. One lady said she couldn't find anything interesting on during the day. Personally, I had that problem in the States."*

—AIR FORCE E-6 WIFE, THESSELONIKA, GREECE

"My husband and I go to Kontakt club meetings every Monday. The club organizes all kinds of activities: evenings at the local swimming pool or a restaurant, a day at the circus, a tour of a car factory, trips to amusement parks

and flea markets. Last Fourth of July we had a medieval weekend. We slept in a castle and roasted a boar and ate it with our hands while listening to madrigal music."
—AIR FORCE E-5, MARRIED TO AN E-5,
RAMSTEIN, GERMANY

"Even with the low dollar, the money situation isn't so bad. You just have to realize that currency fluctuations are a way of life and budget for them. I always figure my bills at less than what the dollar is trading for, to leave myself a cushion. We rent an apartment for less than our housing allowance. Nothing fancy, but it's enough. Since we don't own a car, we allot money for buses and cabs every month; bus- and cabfare is as fixed a part of our budget as rent. Having to take public transportation isn't convenient, but it's cheaper than car payments and insurance.

"This system works for us; my husband's only an E-4, but we do lots of things. We go to Madrid, climb mountains, and swim at the beaches, and we've even seen a bullfight. We also go to exhibit halls and museums, bowl, take walks in the park, window-shop, buy groceries from the local farmers' market, and stop in cafés for cups of coffee. We have an arrangement with friends to watch each other's children free. It saves the cost of a baby-sitter and enables us to have time on our own, which I feel is very important. It lowers the stress level."
—AIR FORCE E-4 WIFE, ZARAGOZA, SPAIN

"I love to cook. I spice up the offerings at the commissary with ingredients from the German food markets. I've discovered a lot of interesting things on their shelves and have made some very nice dishes. I'll miss spätzel, Italian eis, and those little cartons of strawberry milk when we go back."
—ARMY E-3 WIFE, HANAU, GERMANY

"Okinawa is extremely expensive, but that's OK because we don't buy things. We travel. From here we can take hops all over the Orient. We've hopped to Bangkok, Hong Kong, and the Philippines. It's the best remedy for island fever. We also check in to Okuma, the military R&R resort at the north end of the island, once in a while for minivacations."
—MARINE CORPS O-3 WIFE, OKINAWA

"These Bavarian villages at Christmastime are like something out of a Grimm fairy tale: cross-timbered, pointed-roof buildings topped with snow and strung with lights. I love walking through the Christkindlmarkt, smelling the hot, spicy wine and the lebküchen, and eating those sticks of cherries and chocolates and the big, soft, hot pretzels. Glittery ornaments and gold angels hang from the booths, and decorated horses and carriages ride through the town."
—ARMY E-4 WIFE, NÜRNBURG, GERMANY

"England is the greatest overseas station in the world; you get all the benefits of a foreign tour and don't have to learn a new language! London is only sixty miles away. I loved touring the Tower and seeing the crown jewels. We've been to the beaches at Brighton, too. I studied Stonehenge in school; it was fun seeing it in real life. We'll get to Scotland and Ireland before my wife's tour is up."

—Air Force E-6 Husband, Alconbury, England

"At first I was so homesick I couldn't stand it. Then I started to volunteer at the USO. I worked at newcomers' orientations, and meeting brand-new people, answering their questions, giving them tips, and helping them out made me realize I know more about this place than I thought. Also, by working at the USO I met new wives who wanted to go places with me. I now write long, interesting letters back home—I really like it here."

—Army E-5 Wife, Camp New Amsterdam, Holland

"My husband and I study Japanese together at night. As an aid, we watch Japanese TV and go to services in the Buddhist temples. The grounds around the temples are beautifully manicured, and families picnic on them after the services, so we do, too. I'm Italian-born and had to learn English when I went to the States, so having to learn Japanese now is no problem. I'm just one of 125,000 foreign-born spouses in the military, so if we can learn English, then native English speakers should be able to learn another language, too.

"Sometimes I get a bit upset about shortages at the commissary, but when I look at the spectacular, serene sight of Mount Fuji, it puts everything in perspective."

—Navy E-5 Wife, Yokota, Japan

"Since getting here, I've taken up photography as a hobby. I take pictures of uniquely English things and print, mat, and frame them myself at the crafts center. They look beautiful on my walls."

—Air Force E-5 Wife, Mildenhall, England

"My parents came over here for a month. My husband and I got time off from work, and we all went to ITT and signed up for tours to Holland, France, and Italy. My parents could never afford trips to Europe when I was growing up, but our being stationed here made it possible."

—Army O-2 Wife, SHAPE, Belgium

"What a party the night the Wall was declared a nonentity! People celebrated on both the west and east sides until the early morning. The East Berlin police were stuffy; they wouldn't smile or return handshakes or greetings. But everyone else was in a great mood! We all drank, cried, shook hands, and hugged total strangers. People took hammers and chisels to the Wall for personal souvenirs. We got our own souvenir—a big chunk with graffiti on it. It will probably be valuable someday!"

—AIR FORCE O-2 WIFE, BERLIN, GERMANY

"I loved living in the Philippines. It's a South Seas wonder of coral reefs, shimmering oceans, pearls, tropical breezes, hammocks gently swaying, and lush flowers and greenery. I was sorry when the eruption of Mount Pinatubo ended our days there."

—AIR FORCE E-7 WIFE, FORMERLY OF
CLARK AIR BASE, THE PHILIPPINES

"Islamic culture is entirely different from ours and endlessly fascinating. Boys and girls go to separate schools, even in college. When a girl turns twelve, she is considered a woman and must wear a veil and headdress. Women must cover everything from their elbows to their ankles. But those clothes really do help reduce exposure to sand, wind, and the hot desert sun. Sometimes I wear them myself! Dressing like a Saudi when shopping makes me feel a little less foreign.

"The Saudi diet is healthy. They don't eat pork or much red meat. They eat mostly lamb, chicken, and rice. They sit on the floor and eat their meals at a low table. Breakfasts are typically pita bread, cheese, and fruit such as dates.

"I've bought some oriental rugs and gold jewelry here. They're half the price as Stateside. Also, there are great schools for American kids that the oil employees use"

—ARMY O-3 WIFE, HAFR-AL-BATIN, SAUDI ARABIA

"Since moving here we've gotten into refurbishing affordable and usable antiques. We scour flea markets, particularly for old baskets, the kind with the quilted tops that are used to store potatoes and onions. We restore them and do a brisk business selling them at the Wives' Club bazaars. It's been a good family project that even our teenagers enjoy. My son sews the quilted tops and my daughter runs our booth."

—ARMY E-7 WIFE, FRANKFURT, GERMANY

"When we first got to La Mad, I isolated myself and wasn't happy. Then I got brave enough to walk out the front door, make friends, and take my chances. Some of my fondest memories are of sitting on the terrace with my landlady in the early morning with an Italian-English dictionary, sipping coffee, and teaching each other how to say things."

—AIR FORCE E-5 WIFE, LA MADDELENA, ITALY

"Do whatever you can to enjoy your overseas tour so that you won't be saying, 'I wish I had done . . .' when you return."
—USMC O-2 WIFE, OKINAWA

"Guam is fun if you like snorkeling, diving, or just wandering in the boondocks. Buy my favorite aspect of Guam was hopping to Korea to shop. It's a shopper's paradise! Reebok shoes, Starter jackets, and Dooney and Bourke purses for next to nothing."
—NAVY O-4 WIFE, GUAM

"I love going to flea markets, and Europeans have them just like Americans do. Although much of the stuff is similar to what you'd find in the States, other stuff is unique to the country. I bought wooden painted shoes in a Holland flea market, lederhosen and antique books in an Austrian market, and Russian military pins and hats in an East German market."
—ARMY O-3 WIFE, GERMANY

≡ If You Don't Want to Go

While you'll find many people enjoying their chance of a lifetime, you'll also find many who aren't. They closet themselves in their quarters, shop only at the exchange and commissary, and watch the Armed Forces Radio and Television Station channel exclusively. They don't drive, don't ride the local transportation, and don't learn the language or develop hobbies. When they leave, they know nothing more about the country than when they got there.

If you are greatly opposed to living overseas—it's a fact that not everyone can make the most of it or is even cut out for it—you do have a choice. Your husband can look into getting a humanitarian transfer or temporary deferment, which is given if hardship can be proven. Or you can send him alone, in which case you'll be moved where you want to go and he'll serve a shorter, "without dependents" tour. You can always join him later if you decide to, but you'll pay your own way, your husband won't get any increased allowances, you won't have use of the base facilities (only medical care is guaranteed), and you can't live in quarters. Command sponsorship can be applied for once you're there, but getting it isn't guaranteed.

≡ Status of Forces Agreements (SOFAs)

SOFAs are contracts between the U.S. government and the governments of the countries in which we have bases. Directly or indirectly, they will affect you.

SOFAs vary from country to country, but the subjects they cover are basically the same. They spell out such things as how many civilian jobs on base must be reserved for host citizens; what kind of commissary items must be procured from the host country; who has authority over problems between host and U.S. citizens; how large a school or hospital, and how much housing, may be built; which host country taxes and fees we're exempt from; cottage industry and commercial solicitation rules; broadcasting of the Armed Forces Radio and Television Station; and who may shop at the commissary and exchange.

Commissary and exchange shopping is regulated because many of these countries' economies are critically dependent on tourism, and every dollar you spend in an American military facility is a dollar lost to their own businesses. The host governments realize that since we're here by the hundreds of thousands and are not tourists, we need our own supply centers, so they allow us to build them. Just be aware that our facilities exist at their courtesy, and taxes are waived as a matter of diplomacy. If a lot of tourists who just happen to be military use them, that's a lot of money lost to them. So host governments may—and many do—decide which Americans may use the facilities and which may not. Even if the SOFA does allow military tourists to shop at base facilities, the commander may disallow it, as items are often limited and his primary responsibility is to his own people.

≡ Department of Defense Dependents Schools (DODDS)

Overseas schools for military children have been around since 1936, when the Navy built the first ones at Guantanamo Bay and American Samoa, but it wasn't until after World War II that married American troops accompanied by their families increased to the point where the need to provide for children's education became urgent. Schools were built, but each service operated its own, and their facilities, policies, and curricula differed widely. As the student population grew, administration and logistics became greater problems. In 1962 Congress ordered the Defense Department to study its overseas schools and recommend improvements. And the DODDS system was born.

Its mission today is to provide a free, high-quality, public education for DOD military and civilian children stationed overseas. This mission includes appropriate education for children with disabilities and a community college program in Panama.

DODDS is a consistent, servicewide school system run by professional educators. It is one of the nation's largest, with 209 schools spread throughout Belgium, Bermuda, Bahrain, Canada, Cuba, the United Kingdom, Iceland, the Netherlands, Newfoundland, Norway, Panama, the Philippine Islands, Portugal, Germany, Greece, Italy, Spain, Turkey, Japan, Korea, and Okinawa. Policies, textbooks, curricula, graduation requirements, teacher salaries, and credentials are the same everywhere; an Army first-grader in Germany reads the same books as one in Korea does, and a Navy twelfth-grader in Spain has the same graduation requirements as an Air Force twelfth-grader in England.

DODDS vary greatly in size; some have fifteen students, some have more than 2,000. All are accredited by the North Central Accreditation Association and have the core of classes required for graduation. Classes above and beyond that are determined by student body size, interest, and staff preparation. Programs include host nation and intercultural, honors, talented and gifted and compensatory education, U.S. Senate Youth, physical fitness, and computers.

Competitive sports—football, basketball, track, volleyball, golf, wrestling, gymnastics, tennis, soccer, and swimming—are provided if the facilities, money, and student interest are there and if there are enough schools to compete. Logistics play a big part in the facilities DODDS operate in; getting land to build on in foreign countries is not easy; consequently classes are held in everything from sparkling new buildings to pre-World War II barracks and basements.

DODDS students compare favorably with and often exceed the national norm for standardized tests, including the SAT and ACT. They also show a greater interest in foreign languages than do their Stateside counterparts. DODDS rank above the national average in expenditure per pupil, pupil-teacher ratios, and teacher salaries.

To register, a student needs the sponsor's travel orders, a birth certificate, student Social Security number, previous school records, and an immunization record. When the tour is over, the student should get a full record of his overseas work, and as he gets older, should keep a cumulative folder of his national achievement aptitude test scores, placement papers, and report cards. Schools don't always send complete records to the next place, and such a file is particularly necessary for special needs and gifted students. Permanent copies of high school transcripts are retained at DODDS schools for four years after graduation or withdrawal. Then they are forwarded to the regional office. At the end of the fifth year, transcripts (except those from Panama) are stored at the Educational Testing Service. You may request them by writing to ETS, P.O. Box 6605, Princeton, NJ 08541-6605, (800) 257-9484 or (609) 951-6058. Students from

Panama should write DODDS—Panama Region, Unit 0925, APO AA 34002.

Courses interrupted by transfer may be continued if, in the principal's opinion, the time lost in transfer will not have a nega-

> Many military children have a tendency to let their schoolwork slide when learning of a move. Try to impress upon them the importance of doing their work for themselves, not for the school.

tive impact on the student's successful completion of the subject. DODDS accepts all the official grades and courses of transfer students. Students enrolling in DODDS during their senior year may be allowed to fulfill the requirements of their previous schools in order to graduate if, through no fault of their own, they cannot meet DODDS graduation requirements. If a senior is transferred to a Stateside high school and doesn't meet its graduation requirements, he may graduate with his Stateside senior class and receive a diploma from the DODDS high school in which he was last enrolled, assuming he meets the DODDS graduation requirements.

DODDS runs a boarding school in High Wycombe, London, for high school students who don't live near a DODDS school. Other options are to send them to a host nation or an international school. International schools' biggest customers are children of diplomats and businesspeople, but thousands of military families use them, too. Approval to enroll your child in one of these schools is not required, but it is needed before the government will pay the tuition. If you want to enroll your child in such a school even if a DODDS school is nearby, the government may refuse to pay the tuition. Some countries will educate American children free in their public schools; others require payment. Contact the host nation embassy for information on international and host nation schools.

For more information, write to DODDS, 4040 North Fairfax Dr., Arlington, VA 22203-1635, (703) 696-3068.

You may wonder how all this transferring from school to school affects children. Studies have been done on the subject, but one DODDS counselor summed it up this way: "It depends on the kid, the kid, and the kid." Here are a few other comments:

"Looking back on my life as an Army brat, my friends on post were more mature than my civilian friends of the same age. I guess when you change schools, towns, and friends every three years, you mature faster out of necessity. We also are able to figure exchange rates between three different currencies, can speak at least one word in ten different languages, and have friends all over the world."

—COLLEGE STUDENT, TWENTY

"I've seen children who adapt wonderfully to transferring around and others who are traumatized by it. Most seem to fall somewhere in between. I believe you can shape your children's attitudes. Naturally, it's harder for them to move when they are teens than when they're toddlers, but if you make the place sound exciting enough, they'll go. When raising children in the military, it's important that you impress upon them from the very start that they'll be moving. If you have a good attitude toward moving, this isn't so hard. If you manage to make moves fun and exciting, create a loving, stable home wherever you go, and maximize the positives and minimize the negatives, moving children frequently isn't overly traumatic. All three of my children are practicing professionals. I'm very happy about the way they turned out."

—RETIRED NAVY WIFE AND MOTHER OF THREE

"The first week of school, I can tell which are military children and which are civilians without even looking at their records. The military children are more gregarious; they make friends easier. Of course, not all of them are this way, but enough are to make this generalization."

—CIVILIAN MIDDLE SCHOOL TEACHER IN MASSACHUSETTS

≡ Don't Worry

It's understandable if you're a bit nervous about your overseas move by now. There are a lot of unknowns. But with the right attitude and proper preparation, everything will be fine. Talk to people who have just come back from where you're going for ideas on what you should and shouldn't bring in the way of household goods, furniture, appliances, and clothing.

Ask your sponsor about the availability of 110V electricity. Some duty stations have new housing with it, but at others you'll use the host country's 220V system. If you'll be using 220V, don't bring extreme heat–generating appliances like coffeemakers, microwaves, or hair dryers, because the cost of the transformer needed to operate them will exceed the cost of the items.

Don't let worries spoil your mood. This is your chance of a lifetime. Lucky you!

≡ Further Reading

Fodor's Guides. New York: David McKay, Co. (Available for many overseas and stateside locations. Revised annually.)

Keats, John. *See Europe the Next Time You Go There.* Boston: Little, Brown, 1968.

Overseasmanship and Tag-Along to Europe. Booklets available from the Navy Wifeline Association, Washington Navy Yard, Building 172, Washington, DC 20374.

Savage, Barbara. *Miles from Nowhere.* Seattle: The Mountaineers, 1984.

10

≡ On Your Own

We all know that military service is a unique job. One of the things that makes it so is the aspect of separations. Since artillery maneuvers cannot be practiced behind a desk and naval maneuvers cannot be practiced on a chalkboard, temporary duty assignments, unaccompanied tours, sea deployments, and alerts are essential parts of military training. Regular working days are often twelve or thirteen hours long—"no overtime" refers to pay, not hours. The nation's defense simply does not operate on a forty-hour workweek with weekends, anniversaries, and holidays at home guaranteed.

Field problems, ship deployments, and flight time are the operational experience of classroom military training. It's the job. You don't have to like it, but it's critical that you understand it.

While the specific job a servicemember holds has a great deal of influence over how often he's away,* sooner or later everyone must go. With the total force getting smaller each year, each person will deploy longer and more frequently than in the past. Time away can be a week, a month, or even a year. There is also the ever-present possibility of sudden deployment, in which case you won't even be told your husband has left the area until that information is deemed safe to release.

But why are some of those field exercises so long? Why can't we always contact our husbands while they're away. And why are unaccompanied tours necessary?

Let's look at exactly what a field problem is. It's a multitude of tasks done in a simulated war atmosphere. The commanding officer determines how much money he has for the exercise and what facilities

---

*Generally, people in the Air Force have the least time away; those in the Navy have the most. Navy personnel who go to sea have longer separations, but Army and Marine Corps personnel have the most one-year unaccompanied tours. Air Force TDYs are short, but they are irregular, repeated, and frequently unscheduled.

are available. Then he draws on experience to determine how much time the tasks should take. He must be sure his people know what they're doing and are ready to do it. If things don't go properly they must be redone. This might involve staying away extra days or coming home for the weekend just to go out again on Monday.

> To reduce stress, don't sweat the small stuff. And when managed well, everything is small stuff!

> Never give out deployment information to anyone, except for that which has been cleared by the command. You know the saying, "Loose lips sink ships."

Training facilities are often limited, and many units must share them. While the people in your husband's unit are waiting their turn, they might find themselves with a free evening. To you, this might seem like needless time away from the family, but it's a part of training.

Just as you would not be able to easily contact your husband if there really were a war, so it must be with many field problems. Consider this our own basic training. We must be self-reliant enough to care for the children, pay the bills, and handle whatever comes up.

Some wives resent the fact that their husbands go to the field alongside women soldiers, or that women sailors ship out, too. Women who join the service do so for the same reasons as men. They want to serve their country; they want to learn a skill; they want the GI bill for college. Perhaps they're paying off an Academy or ROTC commitment. To insinuate that "something is going on" during field exercises is demeaning to them—and you—and insulting to their professionalism. Here are a few comments from active-duty women:

"I work fourteen-hour days out there executing the orders of the first sergeant and seeing to it that fifteen vehicles are in perfect running order. With all that, plus trying to get my own platoon squared away, I'm too busy even to look at your husband. I have my own at home. My job is tough enough. Don't make it tougher."

—Army Platoon Sergeant

"How can problems between men and women arise more easily on a ship, where privacy is practically nonexistent?"

—Navy Corpsman

"Don't suspect everyone because of the immature behavior of a few."

—Army Field Artillery Officer

Would you like a taste of your husband's operational experience? Sometimes units invite spouses out for a "field day." On such days, Army and Marine Corps wives get to wear the "steel pots" on their own heads, run an obstacle course, and climb into a tank. Navy wives can sail on "dependents' cruises." If you're interested in such a firsthand look at military life, bring it up at the next coffee. It's an event easily arranged. One day spent on a submarine or among camouflage tents may give you a new appreciation of your husband's job.

≡ Unaccompanied Tours

Tours a servicemember does without his family are called unaccompanied, hardship, arduous, or separation tours.

There are areas around the globe that, because of their strategic locations or special facilities, need to be maintained. While many have family support facilities, such as exchanges, commissaries, schools, and hospitals, many don't. Or they're not safe places for family members. But since all servicemembers must share in the responsibility of maintaining them, unaccompanied tours are part of service life. They're shorter than accompanied ones for the precise reason that they *are* unaccompanied, thus considered a hardship. In these cases, the service will typically pay to move you back to your family, to a job, or to school.

Sometimes a servicemember will be sent to an area where adequate support facilities exist, but authorization for his family to accompany him is still denied. This is because the number of families that are allowed to be

Q: What is the Sullivan Act?

A: The Sullivan Act deals with the issue of "sole surviving son" combat exemptions. It was named for five brothers from Waterloo, Iowa, who died during World War II aboard the cruiser *Juneau;* their deaths prompted a move to instigate legislation that would protect the last male heir in a family from combat. Although Congress never passed the Sullivan Act, the military implemented a regulation (DOD 1315.4) that prevents two members of an immediate family from being involuntarily assigned to the same unit or ship. They are not excluded from service in a combat zone, however; they are promised only to be dispersed among units.

If an immediate family member is killed as a result of military service or is captured or missing, other family members on active duty can be granted an administrative discharge.

As a senior NCO, I'll say that the most successful soldiers are the ones who use a year unaccompanied tour to focus on becoming better soldiers. They live in the library and the gym; they use the senior NCOs to guide them in their professional development.

Think hard before deciding to accompany your husband on a non-command-sponsored tour. Your financial concerns will be greater, and the lack of official support can make a big difference in your standard of living.

command-sponsored is limited by law. Budgetary constraints lie behind this: It costs a lot of money to command-sponsor each service-member's family. Sometimes the money just isn't there.

At times like this it may seem the service is coming before the family. It is. It has to. It won't work any other way. A servicemember would not be doing his job by giving anyone or anything else first priority. Take pride in his commitment to country. Such commitment by anyone to anything is rare these days. You can send him away complaining or send him away with a kiss. Either way, he has to go.

Prepare for Separations Now

The time to prepare for separations is *before* they occur. Some separations occur quickly, leaving little time to prepare. If your husband is currently the one who handles all your household and financial affairs, start helping. Find out if a financial management course is offered on base, and take it. Also attend a predeployment briefing. As one Navy wife put it, "When that big gray thing leaves the pier, you need to know where to go for help."

It makes the most sense to have the military paycheck directly deposited to a bank account. This applies to Reservists' monthly drill pay as well. Most of the people who experienced paycheck problems during Desert Storm had hastily arranged direct deposit during the flurry of other activities.

Q: My husband has an allotment that will need to be stopped while he is deployed. How should I handle that?

A: It is easiest to handle if he completes the paperwork before he leaves, with the appropriate stop date. It can be handled during his deployment, but to do so is harder.

Q: How do I receive my husband's Leave and Earnings Statements while he is away?

A: Contact his unit. Typically, you can pick them up, or someone can bring them to you.

It is particularly important for Reservists to have contingency plans based on a possible deployment. Savings reserves for lost income and child-care plans are major items that need to be addressed before a deployment actually happens. Even if a Reservist is not sent to a distant place, he can be suddenly called to fill in for active-duty personnel sent away.

≡ A Home Filing System

One of the first things to do is to set up a home filing system to keep important documents organized and in one place. A large, expensive metal filing cabinet isn't necessary; actually, it isn't even desirable since it always seems to get banged up in moves. Hanging file folders, arranged in a square plastic milk carton, work nicely. They fit neatly into corners, don't take up much space, and travel well. Manila folders inside a large, expandable envelope work well, too. See what your local office-supply store has to set up a home filing system.

Two documents every military spouse should have are a *power of attorney* and a *will*.

═ Powers of Attorney

A power of attorney is a legal document that allows one person to do things in another person's name. There are two types: *general* and *limited*. With a general power of attorney, you can cash your husband's paycheck, ship household goods, sign damage claim forms, move into and clear quarters, open a deferred payment plan account at the exchange, and buy and sell a home. You can withdraw money from an account that is in his name only, sell a car registered in both your names, and apply for emergency relief funds. You can do just about anything!

A limited, or special, power of attorney allows you to do just one or two specific things. This is something you might give a trusted friend if, for instance, you had to leave in a hurry and didn't have time to sell your car, or if you wanted her to rent a place for you or ship your household goods. A medical power of attorney would authorize your child's care-giver to obtain treatment in case of injury.

Obviously, a power of attorney is something you'd give only to someone you trust. Even then, it's a good idea to make it for a limited time. Otherwise, it remains in effect until you either revoke it or die.

═ Wills

A will is a legal document that describes what you want done with your property after you die. Having a will ensures that survivors get what the deceased intended them to get, with a minimum of hassle. Though each state has laws for the division of property, if a person dies intestate (without a will), it takes longer, more paperwork is involved, and it can be a long time before affairs are finally resolved. A will spells out exact intentions for property distribution and names the legal guardian for your underage children. In intestate deaths, property is distributed in accordance with state law.

Periodically review your will to ensure it's accurate. Marriages, divorces, or changes in legal residence prompt people to draft new wills or add amendments to existing ones.

You'll also need an *executor* (or *executrix*) to administer and settle your estate, so make appropriate arrangements.

Powers of attorney and wills can be drawn up at your base legal office. If you don't have these important documents, make an appointment now.

═══ Other Documents

Other documents you should have, in their own folders, are the following:

Marriage license. Also keep any divorce decrees, certificates of other marriages, and court orders about support and custody of children.

Immunization records. Many day-care centers require children's immunization records. If you have a pet, you need to keep its immunization records, too.

Birth certificates, adoption records, citizenship papers. Applying for a passport is just one instance when you would need these documents. If you don't have them, call your state's Office of Vital Statistics under the Department of Health.

Passports. These are needed if you'll be accompanying your husband overseas. Since passports take at least sixty days to process, it's a good idea to get one even if you do not need it immediately.

Credit card numbers and their issuers' phone numbers and addresses and similar information for anything else in your wallet that would leave you vulnerable if it were lost or stolen.

List of serial numbers and photographs of electronic equipment and appliances. Keep one set at home and one in a safe-deposit box. While the chances of recovering stolen items are never great, they evaporate to nothing if you can't supply such information. A videotape of your possessions is also a good idea.

Copies of TDY, TAD, or PCS orders are always needed, especially when arranging a move or filing a claim for damaged household goods.

Documentation of your work history. This includes résumés, SF-171s, certificates of training, professional registration, volunteer work, and anything else you've acquired.

Set up folders for your insurance policies, automobile titles, telephone bill receipts, bank statements and canceled checks, credit card statements, family Social Security numbers, furniture receipts, appliance receipts, warranties and guarantees, LES statements, receipts for donations and other tax-related items, papers from club memberships, an inventory of safe-deposit box contents, a list of savings bond numbers, deeds and mortgage documents, storage and warehouse receipts, copies of letters you've sent to businesses or banks, and anything else you need to hold on to. Valuable documents such as stock and bond certificates are better kept in a safe-deposit box, with copies in your files. A system like this will always be there for you when a problem arises and you need backup information to support your position.

Your Husband's Military File

Once your home file is in order, make sure your husband's military file is, too. Out-of-date personnel records can cause problems for "geographical widows." They're kept at the base personnel or administrative office and describe the servicemember's marital status, number of family members, past and present assignments, special skills and training, civilian and military education, awards, disciplinary measures taken, photographs, security clearances, and efficiency reports. They also contain data such as next of kin and whom to notify in case of emergency. It's the servicemember's responsibility to keep this file up-to-date, not the office's.

Other Preparations

Check that your family's ID cards are current. If they will be expiring soon, get them renewed. If you lose your ID card while your husband is away, call the ID card facility for instructions on getting a new one. The process will be considerably faster if you have a power of attorney. Also check the expiration dates of your insurance policies, subscriptions, lease or rental agreements, and credit cards.

Even if your husband's deployment is fairly lengthy and he cannot take his car, it should remain insured. Ask your insurance company if the premiums can be adjusted since he won't be driving it.

Q: What is "proceed time"?
A: It is time off (up to four days) for people completing or beginning an unaccompanied tour of duty to attend to personal details.

Arrange with the finance office for your husband's paycheck to be sent directly to a bank, if it isn't already. Otherwise it will follow him wherever he goes. If he was suddenly deployed, where would that leave you? If he's going away for a year, arrange for the paycheck to be sent to him and a steady allotment to you, or vice versa. Emergency aid office personnel will vouch for the fact that something always goes wrong with the "just send me a check each month" system. For long separations, individual checking accounts are best. They'll eliminate inadvertent overdrafts and make your phone conversations more pleasant. ("You put $82.50 into checking? Wait . . . let me get a pen.")

Know how your income will be affected by the separation. Most separations involve extra allowances given and others (such as BAS) taken away. Will the sum total be a gain or a loss? What additional expenses (such as baby-sitting) will be incurred? Any savings?

Make sure the house or apartment is in good repair; have the furnace, hot water heater, refrigerator, range, washer, dryer, TV, and other appliances checked. But since things always break down the day after the ship sails and the battalions march off, if you're not the handy type, try to make arrangements with someone who is. Barter services; for example, baby-sit in return for small repairs. Prepare lists of plumbers, mechanics, and other people to call for "fix-its." Tape a list of emergency numbers to the phone. Know where the fuse box or circuit breaker is, how to change fuses or flip switches, and which switches control what.

Know details about your automobile, such as where and when to send the loan and insurance payments. How much are they? What is the phone number of your insurance agent? Has the car been serviced recently? What type of oil does it use, and when should it be changed? Where do you take it for repairs? Does it have good tires? Are the inspection and base stickers and license plates current?

≡ Personal Security

Here are some tips for protecting yourself and your home with extra security measures.

- Many crimes are crimes of opportunity; criminals look for an easy mark. So "case" your home for weaknesses. A burglar's three worst enemies are time, visibility, and noise; a delay of four or five minutes may deter him entirely.
- Keep shrubs trimmed low, and install bright exterior lights.
- Buy deadbolts for exterior doors and locks for the storm and screen windows and doors. Some people also install locks on their bedroom doors. Keep the door locked even when you are home. If you live in a rental unit, you might feel better if you have your own locks installed; previous tenants may have been careless with their keys.

Get extra sets of house and car keys made in case you lose a set.

- Buy timers for your TV, radio, and lights; keeping a house lighted all night announces that it is an empty house.
- Keep the drapes, blinds, or shades drawn; don't advertise your possessions. Install peepholes in the doors.
- Don't wear flashy, expensive jewelry to large public places, such as malls, especially at night.
- You might want to change your phone number to an unlisted one to avoid obscene calls. Report any such calls to the phone company. Local phone companies may temporarily change your phone number at no cost if you're receiving such calls.
- Don't tell telephone solicitors or any other unknown callers who ask for your husband that he is away. Say he can't come to the phone right now, but that you'll give him the message. Don't change the answering machine message to one that greets him or otherwise indicates that he's away.
- Don't share lists of phone numbers of people in the unit with people outside it. Shred them before throwing them away.
- Don't advertise that your husband is going away; people who don't need to know shouldn't be told. Yellow ribbons and other such things advertise that the man of the house is gone.
- Don't let repairmen or solicitors in before verifying their identification by telephone. Report and describe loitering strangers to the police.
- Organize a neighborhood crime watch; if one exists, actively participate in it.
- Some people are comforted by a weapon in the house. If you buy one, take classes on how to use it, and practice occasionally.
- Finally, don't allow yourself to become housebound out of fear. Keep things in perspective!

≡ Base Agencies

The following is a list of base agencies and the problems they handle. Keep the phone number of the Red Cross handy so that you can get in touch with your husband quickly if there's an emergency and he's unavailable by phone.

Finance and Accounting Office: Basic pay, allotments, U.S. savings bonds, federal income tax, life insurance and health benefits deductions, leave balances, living quarters allowances, base differentials.

Housing Office: Assignment of family quarters, certificates of non-availability of quarters, clearing of quarters, complaints about housing, furniture, local economy housing referrals.

Q: My husband is a Reservist. What community services are available for me?

A: The DOD has directed all Reserve units to have a family support system that includes family briefings, orientations, referrals, and local help if problems arise resulting from the military service. Individual units are responsible for the execution, which is spotty. Also, if you're far from a base, such help may be impractical. So know about federal, state, county, and local human service agencies. They include the following:

Armed Services YMCAs
Departments of Social Services
Legal Aid centers
Local churches
Local hotlines
Public health departments
Red Cross
Salvation Army
USO (United Services Organization)
United Way agencies
Department of Veterans Affairs

Military Police: Criminal complaints, customs clearance, disturbances, driver's licenses, firearm registration, installation passes, pet registration, traffic tickets, vehicle registration.

Legal Office: Income tax law, leases and rental contracts, notarizing of legal documents, legal problems.

Red Cross: Notification of next of kin, emergency communication to family, emergency leave verification, emergency financial aid, counseling.

Family Services: Baby-sitters, child care, household lending items, counseling.

Inspector General: Community dissatisfaction, host nation problems, military-oriented complaints, unsatisfied complaints. You can remain anonymous.

Chaplain's Office: Marital counseling, personal counseling, religious retreats and services. You don't have to be religious or of the chaplain's faith to use this resource.

Transportation Office: Unaccompanied baggage, household goods, shipment of privately owned vehicles on orders, temporary storage of household goods.

Facilities Engineers: Quarters repairs.

First Sergeant or Chief Petty Officer: A good source of information, and willing to help with problems.

Ombudsman: (For Navy and Coast Guard wives; called Key Wife in the Marine Corps.) Usually the spouse of a high-ranking enlisted servicemember, the ombudsman is an official, command-recognized position. She is a volunteer who has been nominated by the command and undergoes training for the position. An ombudsman passes along official news of the ship, usually via a telephone tree staffed by other unit wives. She also passes along complaints and suggestions by command family members and helps settle grievances. During deployment, the ombudsman helps families get their needs taken care of. If you don't know who your ombudsman is, ask the command.

If you're not sure who handles the type of problem you have, call Family Services' referral office.

≡ Doing Things on Your Own

Along with knowing which office handles what type of problem, it's necessary to know what *you* should do. When you have a question, call the appropriate office. Don't ask your neighbor or the woman down the street who had a similar problem last year. Something always gets lost in the translation. When you ask someone about something instead of seeking the answer from the proper authority, not only do you run an excellent chance of getting an incorrect answer, but also the answer you do get will be colored by that person's own experience or by what they've heard from other people.

A vital skill called *assertiveness* comes into play here. Assertiveness is defined as "the ability to express oneself forcefully or boldly." It is the skill that leads to gaining information and independence, that enables you to walk away with the glow of "mission accomplished" instead of resentment at having been "treated like a dependent." It is what you need to get your questions answered and the service you want.

Although many of the people who staff office phones and desks are sharp and helpful, others aren't. Don't assume that just because a person works in an office they know what they're doing. If you are not satisfied with an answer (it doesn't sound right, it isn't clear, it isn't complete), push for more. Speak to the boss. If it still doesn't sound right, speak to *his* boss. You can also enlist the aid of your first sergeant, chief petty officer, unit commander, chaplain, or ombudsman. You can write a letter to the inspector general, the base commander, your congressman. There are a lot of links in the chain of command. Just be sure to use the chain in the order in which it is arranged; don't skip any links. If you do that, your problem will take longer to be resolved because it will be passed back down to the people who should have been asked to resolve it in the first place.

> I used to think that because of their rank, officers and senior enlisted got better service than junior enlisted and family members. Now I think it is because the assertion skills they develop in the course of their jobs work just as well outside their offices as they do inside. To help reduce anxiety, imagine a successful assertion and its rewards. You are a customer and have every right to be waited on courteously and efficiently. Don't get caught up in irrational fears and beliefs.

The ability to explain yourself clearly and coherently is critical; a successful assertion can't be accomplished without it. The clerk you're explaining your problem to has seen a lot of people with problems that day, and the better you can explain yours, the better your chances of getting it resolved.

Always call before visiting the office to learn what supporting documents you'll need. If you visit the finance office to resolve paycheck problems, take your LES; if you go to the bank to inquire about your account, take your account number; and if you visit the housing and legal offices to borrow furniture, clear quarters, or file claims, take a power of attorney or a copy of your husband's orders.

If you remain dissatisfied with the answers you're getting from both the clerk and the supervisor, you can always read the regulations pertaining to the subject. Everything the military does is governed by a regulation; these detail everything from how to type a disposition form and what color ink to use to how to procure a multibillion-dollar weapons contract. There are Department of Defense regulations; Army, Air Force, Navy, Marine, and Coast Guard regulations; and more regulations at the individual levels of command. Every base has a complete set of regulations somewhere, usually in the MOS, AFSC, or rating library, or at the legal office, and every office should have a set that pertains to its own operations.

≡ While He's Away

Here's your chance! You can now get those chronically postponed chores done, take those classes and self-enrichment programs, do that big craft project, and participate in the things you've been wanting to do. It's a big world out there with lots to do and see. With a positive attitude, a sense of adventure, and a determination to cope, separations don't have to be so bad.

Here are some tips from people who have been there:

"Tuck homemade cookies, sandwiches, popcorn, a small Thermos of hot coffee, and love notes into his field gear before he goes. Discovering them will be a pleasant surprise."

"My husband was in Operation Just Cause in Panama. My faith in God sustained me; I knew he would never give me anything I couldn't handle."

"Pamper yourself. Give yourself that facial you've been wanting for the past six months. Get a manicure and pedicure. Go to the gym, lose ten pounds. Frost your hair, get a makeover, buy contact lenses. Surprise him with a sharp-looking wife when he gets back."

"*Get your craft projects done. Take classes in sponge and tole painting. Every true Navy wife cross-stitches! When Tim was away for six months, I made an entire queen-size quilt. We broke it in when he got back!*"

"*The last time my husband went away, I weeded the garden, fixed the dripping sink, cleaned the gutters, made my daughter two outfits, and organized the spare room. If he'd go more often, I'd get more done!*"

"*It's not the days that drag by, because during the day he's not home anyhow. It's the nights. So I invite the other women whose husbands are away, and their kids, over for dinner. We go to movies, come back, gab all night. The kids fall asleep on the floor.*"

"*Before Mike goes I think of all the things I want to do that I don't, or wouldn't, do when he's here—things like eating hot dogs and chili with the kids in the middle of the living room floor instead of at the table, and doing jigsaw puzzles afterward. Or pitching a tent in the backyard and sleeping in it. Doing different, special things that we don't do when he's here helps the children adjust better to his absence instead of viewing separations as something to dread. And we really do have a lot of fun. I feel special bonding with my children during these times.*"

"*Fellow submariners' wives: If your husband will be away for his birthday, give the commanding officer a shoebox full of gifts to be given on the appropriate day. Don't send gifts bigger than what will fit in a shoebox, though, or you'll create storage problems. All Navy wives should send every Familygram they're permitted. But know that they're not private; the squadron radioman and who knows who else will see it.*"

"*Keep a notebook of all the chit-chat you'd tell him if he were home, your children's cute remarks, things you forget quickly. Then write them down at the end of the week in a letter or record them on a cassette tape. Or just send him the actual notes! One time when Paul was gone for a month, I sent postcards every day.*"

"*Send lots of letters. They're the number one morale booster. Even if your guy isn't writing back much—most men don't like to write—he still loves to get them. When mail call comes and he's the only one without a letter, how do you think he'll feel? I make up a package every Sunday night and put in any three or four of the following items: Sunday papers, clippings from other papers, favorite catalogs, professional "glamour shots," photos, hand-held video games, gum, tapes of his favorite TV shows, pictures the kids drew, "coupons" for breakfast in bed and backrubs, crossword puzzles, books, cocoa packets, drink mixes, hard candy, simple snacks unavailable to him, Chap Stick, and aloe vera—useful little things he can carry around. It's amazing what you can find in those travel-size bins and dollar stores for this purpose. Such items make my long-distance love travel to him each day. Once I put some confetti hearts in a letter, and they spilled out when he opened it. He said he was picking them up for days, and every time he saw one he thought of me."*

"Send your husband's favorite baked goodies—cakes, fudge brownies, chocolate chip cookies. Use express or airmail so that they'll arrive fresh, and pack them well. One time my husband called, upset because the cake I sent arrived as tiny crumbs. He was practically in tears!"

"If you own a computer and modem, consider subscribing to an on-line service such as America Online. Among its diverse offerings are "chat rooms," where you talk to people all over the country simply by typing on your keyboard. It's endlessly entertaining and helps fight loneliness."

"Get your marriage in the best shape possible before the actual separation. Talk out any problems and lingering concerns, and settle them before he goes. A strong marriage has very little trouble surviving a separation."

"If there's something you had planned to do together, such as play tennis or see a movie, do so regardless of your husband's unit schedule. Unexpected interruptions like alerts may ruin his plans, but they don't have to ruin yours. Don't cancel, sulk, and make your husband feel bad for disappointing you. I'd rather see a few movies without him than never go to them at all."

"Keep at least one week's supply of food in the house in case of illness, bad weather, lack of money, transportation problems, or drop-in visitors who need to share your company. Don't let your tank get less than one-quarter full."

"When Dan got orders for Korea for a year, I thought about going with him; he'd have to live in the BOQ, but I'd find an apartment and we'd be together on the weekends. But then I thought, 'Are you nuts?' Instead, I went to business college and got a degree as a medical secretary."

"I went home once when Jon went away. That works well for some women, especially those who need help with their small kids. But it didn't suit me to make a regular practice of it. My husband was off learning new things, and I felt like I had reverted back to my childhood with my parents taking care of me. If I'm old enough to be married and have a baby, I'm old enough not to

have to run home each time my husband is deployed. Besides, you don't get the support in the civilian community you do in the military one. The military has 'TAD widow' clubs and support groups. But in the civilian community, people ask why you're living at home. They think something is wrong with your marriage; they can't believe the Marines would send your husband away for a year. They keep saying, 'Oh, I could never do that. I could never live like that. You poor thing.' After a while it gets on your nerves."

"At Christmastime send a few ornaments along with your presents so that he can hang them in his room or on the ship's tree. Homemade ones are the best. I make bread dough rings and put family pictures inside."

"Separations are good. They give you a break from each other. And when you realize how many little things he does around the house—coaxing a bad TV or VCR to work, changing light bulbs in high places, starting the grill— you appreciate him all the more when he gets back. It really strengthens a marriage. Furthermore, if you successfully make it through a long separation, it makes anything that follows easy."

"I maintain Pete as the house authority figure even when he's away. If the children are pressing me for something and I'm not sure what to do, if the decision doesn't have to be made immediately, I'll say, 'Wait until Dad calls. We'll see what he says.' If the decision has to be made right away, I'll make it and say, 'I think Dad would agree with this.'"

"Don't change your eating habits. Keep things as normal as possible. You've got to preserve your home and sense of normalcy. A separation needs to be viewed as a time to miss your husband, not a time to completely disrupt your life."

"One time when my husband went away, I opened a savings account for his birthday present. Was he surprised! Now every time he goes away I scrimp and add to it. I love showing him a bigger balance when he gets back. It's our reward for the separation."

"Keep your letters upbeat. When he's away it's easy to blow things out of proportion. Things that wouldn't ordinarily bother us suddenly get honored with three tearful pages. If you write a letter while you're depressed, don't mail it right away. Read it again after a good night's sleep and reevaluate sending it. Remember, he's under stress from the separation too, but he is still trying to do his job. Separations are just as hard and stressful for the servicemember, and I don't want to distract my guy from his job with trivia.

"I tend to not mention problems in letters or phone calls until I have a solution. I don't bug him with small stuff. And if nobody's dead or hospitalized, it's small stuff!"

"Keep a notebook by the phone and jot down all the things you want to tell him so that when he calls, your mind won't go blank."

"Get a job. Join a church group. Volunteer. Helping someone else is a real upper and the best way to shake depression. Take a class in auto repair, because the car always breaks down when your husband goes away!"

"Drugs, booze, and junk food don't cure loneliness. When you are feeling down, call a good friend or work on a hobby."

"When I was on a WESPAC cruise, the spouses and significant others got together and sent us the complete fixings for a Christmas party, down to monogrammed stockings."

"After spending fourteen years among military wives, I've noticed a direct correlation between wives' and children's behavior during absences. If a separation is 'mommy goes bonkers' time, the kids go bonkers, too. But if mommy remains cool, the kids remain cool. So I remain cool!"

"Rent or borrow a camcorder and make a movie of you, your kids, and a bunch of friends all laughing, joking, and gossiping. It will make his day."

"Learn new recipes and surprise him with them when he gets back."

"The sooner you learn to get along on your own the better, because the higher up the ladder your husband goes, the more he'll be working. My husband's a first sergeant and works late all the time, often picking up the slack for subordinates who have to go home to attend to their families' problems. I always thought it was the first sergeants and company commanders who got out of going to the field and went home early every day. Why, they're the ones who work the most!"

"When I know he's at home, I have a pizza sent to him. You have to find a restaurant that will take credit-card orders over the phone to do this."

"Every day he's away I do one thing to improve myself, such as flip through a dictionary to learn a new word, flip through a history book to learn an important date, or study a map to see what countries border Rwanda. Once I started a self-education program where I chose a subject a month and read everything the library had on it."

"There are definite benefits to training exercises. For two whole weeks there's no green laundry and I can watch something on TV besides sports. And because the kids and I eat more macaroni and cheese, turkey franks, and burgers and fries when he's gone, I save money on the food bill and get fewer 'yuks' at the dinner table!"

"I'm so proud to be a soldier's wife that I don't mind the separations. He's out there in the rain, snow, sleet, or hot sun training to protect what we all treasure: freedom. What can I complain about, sitting in my snug quarters? As the soldiers are told to behave in a responsible, professional manner, so should the wives."

"Answer all his questions in your letters. Write with his picture or letter in front of you as though you're talking directly to him. Let him know how much you appreciate his letters. Express your thoughts clearly so that he won't wonder what you meant."

"I dislike writing, so Marty and I bought tape recorders and send 'talking letters' to each other. I always tape somewhere with background noise. He loves to hear cars going by, dogs barking, and other sounds of home. I also let the tape run while our toddler plays so that he can hear her talking to her stuffed animals. Tapes allow you to hear intonations and the voice you miss in a letter, and they're inexpensive to buy and mail. Just wrap brown paper over the tape case."

"During a six-month deployment, my husband's ship docked in Charleston for a week. I flew out with my AAA tourbook (those books are terrific!) and we had a minivacation."

"I've seen divorces occur over long deployments because of one reason: partying. Don't go out dancing with other men even just as friends. Too many times it leads to a broken marriage."

"My kids and I posed for a picture at a place that puts computer pictures on calendars, mugs, sheets, and pillowcases. We bought a pillowcase, and my husband loves sleeping on it."

"I send Corey homemade puzzles. I'll cut paper into little blocks, put one letter on each, and make him unscramble them to read a short note. Or I'll write a letter that he has to use a mirror to read. Anything to keep him laughing."

"Our birds send letters. I give them a sheet of paper to chew up, then write letters over the holes."

"Get involved with your unit's spouse group. You'll get more accurate information—rumors start so easily—and only another wife in the unit can really understand what you're going through. When our husbands were gone over Valentine's Day, we wives got dressed up and went to a fancy restaurant. Other times we've gotten together, baked brownies, and watched rented movies. It sure beats staying home alone."

"I hate separations, but I would no sooner ask my husband to give up a career he loves (and that he had before we met) than I would give up my own career as a mother. My mission is to support him, and he's worth it! Face it: Someone is going to have to sacrifice something."

"Have a nice dinner ready when he gets home, but don't be surprised if he just goes to sleep instead of eating. Don't have any activities planned for the day he comes home, or the day after."

"Before my husband leaves, I write some cards to him. I pack them in his gear with the envelopes labeled 'Save This for a Bad Day,' 'Save This for When You Need a Laugh,' and so forth."

"I'm a submariner's wife. When my husband is out to sea, we both keep a journal, recording the good and the bad of our days. When he returns, we read each other's. It gives each of us a perspective of what the other goes through."

"All the separations Navy life requires has had the effect of keeping our marriage a very romantic one, even after ten years."

"I hire a sitter three times a week so that I can go to aerobics or the library, just have time to myself."

"I mention safety a lot in my letters and warn him to do his job carefully. My daughter draws safety pictures and encloses them."

"My husband is a battery commander, and I organized a phone tree and chain of concern when his unit was deployed for one month. I want wives

to know that although support systems are in place for families, some wives expect too much. You have to ask for and seek help; it isn't automatically given. Don't get upset if you don't get a call from a person working a phone tree; often the callers are unable to reach someone."

"If you're separated during a birthday or holiday, don't celebrate it on that day; just postpone it. Take your honeymoons when you can get them."

"I rent comedy tapes when I feel lonely. I also spray my husband's cologne around the room."

"John does routine things such as lowering the shades and checking the locks before we go to bed. Before he leaves for a long separation, I start doing them instead."

"I love planning our reunions. I make hotel reservations and buy fancy lingerie."

"When you've handled something especially challenging, reward yourself with something you've been wanting to buy. Put it on layaway."

"When I accepted my husband's proposal thirteen years ago, I gave him a hand-carved 'yes.' It hangs in the kitchen to remind me that I agreed to separations and other challenges of this way of life."

"I never liked separations until my husband had recruiting duty. Separations are cake next to that!"

"Refer to the books 1001 Ways to Be Romantic and 1001 Ways to Be More Romantic for ideas."

"Think about the good times you've had and plan for more."

≡ Helping Children Deal with Separations

Here are some tips on helping your child through a separation.

- Talk everything out with your kids. If they seem unusually quiet, preoccupied, rowdy, or feisty, ask what's bothering them. Encourage questions, and pinpoint areas of concern. Try rephrasing their questions to see how they respond. Be honest, and explain things in a way they can understand.

- Keep them on the schedule they were on before the separation.
- Assure them that you are here even though their father may be away, and that you're not going anywhere.
- Show them a map of where Daddy is; use the separation as an opportunity for them to learn some geography and facts about the place.
- Have your husband record some bedtime stories before he leaves, and play them after he goes.
- Stick pictures of your husband on the refrigerator so that young children don't forget who he is. Take a family photo right before he goes so that the picture is recent. Also stick up any postcards he sends, and explain the pictures to the children.
- Balance exciting events and trips for the children between when your husband's away and when he's home, so that they don't have to anticipate special things only one way or the other.
- Put a framed photograph of your husband in the child's room.
- One military spouse shares the following tactic: "When my wife left for a year, I found this trick helpful in keeping the kids aware of when she'd return: I glued a deck of cards to a posterboard with rubber cement. Each Thursday (the day she left) we took one card down, and what was left was how many more weeks we had to go."

≡ Managing Stress

Some deployments are more stressful than others. Rwanda, Haiti, and Desert Storm are examples. But any deployment can be stressful if you are not accustomed to being by yourself or experiencing a lot of problems.

Life is largely a process of adapting to the positive and the negative changes around us. Whether it's moving, waiting out a traffic jam, saying good-bye to a friend, or coping with the demands of single parenthood, we need to adapt. How happy and healthy we are depends, in large part, on how successful we are in this adaptation. Different things are stressful to different people. Be aware that stress is something we ourselves create, and it depends on how we interpret situations and relate to the world around us. Many people think that other people and situations around us are responsible for our stress. Actually, no one can make us feel sad, angry, jealous, foolish, or incompetent—or stressed—except ourselves.

No one can avoid stress; such a thing isn't even desirable. Positive stresses are beneficial. But we can learn how to minimize stress's damaging side effects, or "distress."

Differentiate between a *worry* and a *concern*. A worry is something you can't do anything about—and if you can't do anything, why make yourself miserable? Worrying is counterproductive. It makes you think you're accomplishing something when you're not. It makes you avoid doing unpleasant tasks; it's easier to worry about them than to actually do them.

When you find yourself worrying about your husband, try to turn your worry into a concern. Do something around the house that he'll appreciate upon his return. Ask yourself what's the worst thing that could happen, and what you would do if it did. Then make plans just in case. This will transform your worry into a concern.

If you absolutely *can't* not worry, try setting aside a specific amount of time to spend worrying, and set an alarm clock to ring when the time is up.

People who cope with stress best have certain things in common: a sense of being in control of their life, a reliable network of friends or family, flexibility, and optimism.

── Managing Anger

Bottling up anger creates health problems; venting anger can have disastrous results on those around you. Studies on anger show that people who brood have the highest blood pressure, people who blow up have the second highest, and people who take steps to resolve their anger have the lowest of anyone. Here are some tips that may help if you're prone to brooding or blowing up.

- Make a list of the things you're angry about. This might help you clarify the problem so that you can take steps to solve it.
- Rethink the situation. Instead of brooding or blowing up when someone says something rude, cuts you off in traffic, or whatever, rethink things. Tell yourself that the person is probably having a bad day (we all have them). Empathize instead of judging.
- How do you feel? When you're hot, hungry, tired, or headachy, you're more likely to become angry than when you're not. Try not to say anything to anyone until you've had something to eat, gotten some sleep, or taken a shower or aspirin.
- Beware of "shoulds." We often get angry because people don't act like they "should" or because things don't happen the way they "should." It helps dissipate anger when we realize there is no reason why other people should live up to our standards or why things should happen the way we want or think they should happen.
- Discuss. This is a calm and constructive way to solve problems. Your energy will be focused on problem solving instead of on venting anger.
- Take a parenting skills class at the local YMCA or your Family Services center.

Proven Stress Reducers

- Get up fifteen minutes earlier in the morning. Morning delays will then be less stressful.
- Practice preventive maintenance. Your car and appliances will be less likely to break down at critical times.
- Restrict the amount of caffeine in your diet.
- Procrastination is stressful. If you have an unpleasant task ahead, get it over with early. Then the rest of the day will be anxiety free.
- Plan ahead. Keep your cupboards and gas tank filled.
- Don't tolerate something that doesn't work right. If your windshield wipers, toaster, or cabinet door hinge is a constant aggravation, get it fixed or buy a new one.
- Have contingency plans for everything.
- Relax your standards. So what if your house doesn't get cleaned one weekend.

> God grant me the courage to change what I can, the serenity to accept what I can't, and the wisdom to know the difference.

- Give yourself time every day for privacy and quiet or for doing something you really enjoy, such as reading or working out. Hire a babysitter.
- Do something for someone else.
- "Inoculate" yourself against a dreaded event. Just as a vaccine containing a virus can protect you from illness, if you expose yourself to one or more of the dreaded aspects of an experience beforehand, you often can mitigate your fears.
- When you're feeling stressed, your muscles are knotted and your breathing is shallow. Relax all your muscles and take several deep, slow breaths. Check out library books on meditation and relaxation techniques.
- Get enough sleep.
- Take a hot bath, or a cool one in summer, to relieve tension.
- Exercise is a terrific stress reducer. Thirty minutes on an exercise bike, a swim, or an aerobic walk around the block can refresh and relax you and make your problems seem more manageable.
- Count your blessings! For everything that goes wrong, there is something that is right.
- Finally, if you remain overwhelmed, seek professional help. Visit your Family Services center or chaplain, or make an appointment at the hospital's mental health facility.

☰ Emergencies

In the unhappy event of a death, serious illness, or injury, a servicemember can be called back to the family. But before you initiate such action, make sure the situation is grave indeed. Attempting to call your husband out of the field, out of school, or from deployment for anything but the most serious of problems is a distraction to his training, an irritant to his superiors, and a burden on his peers. It also cheats him of what might someday be critical knowledge and reflects poorly on you and your ability to cope on your own.

Depending on where he is, calling him can be as simple as calling the unit and having your message relayed. Other times you'll have to contact the Red Cross, which will send an emergency message. The Red Cross will also verify the emergency, something that must be done before leave can be granted. If you're unsure what to do, contact the wife of your husband's supervisor or commander first. She's been a part of service life longer than you have and will know what to do.

☰ Homecoming

Q: What is MARS?

A: MARS is the Navy and Marine Corps MARS Military Affiliate Radio System. It consists of ham radio enthusiasts (MARS members) across the country who voluntarily assist with thirty-four-word-maximum messages sent via radio. The service is free, and is available to family and friends. MARS volunteers also offer phone patches. These are one-way communications via radio with the MARS volunteer as the intermediary. Not too convenient, but it's a way to talk to your husband when he's away and otherwise unavailable. If the MARS call is collect, the charge is only from where the MARS operator is located Stateside; there are no overseas or satellite charges.

Contact HQ MARS, Radio Station Building 13, NAVCOMMDET, Cheltenham, Washington, DC, (301) 238-2266 or –2268, for more information and to find a MARS operator near you.

Q: What is a USOgram?

A: A USOgram is a way to send electronic messages overnight to those aboard Navy ships. To send a message from shore, you buy a specially formatted computer disk from the USOgram center, type a message up to one and a half pages long, then return the disk to the USO staff. The USO sends the messages by computer modem to the ship. To return the message, the sailor buys another disk on board, types his letter on any available personal computer, then returns the disk to the USOgram center aboard ship for a return trip.

Homecomings are great! But if the separation has been a long one, the reunion can be hard. People change during long separations.

There can be problems with a homecoming. You've assumed responsibilities that your husband may want back, but you may not be willing to give them up. The children may need to feel him out and get readjusted. Your own relationship with him may have to be rebuilt a little. Or you may have had this glorious fantasy of what he looks like, and when he steps off the plane, ship, or five-ton truck, he's tired, dirty, and unshaven, has lost or gained weight, and just wants to go home and sleep. Or it may be the opposite. One woman recalled a homecoming where she was in the hospital recovering from a difficult childbirth and her husband walked in tanned, smiling, and wearing a new leather jacket. And even though for the past seven months she'd looked forward to the homecoming, she fixated on that jacket and became furious.

But overall, homecomings are wonderful. Some women make reservations in a luxury hotel for a night or weekend to reconnect with their emotions and marriage before dealing with other things in their lives. Others warn of the need to reestablish the family and get the service-member reacquainted with young children before whisking him away on an adults-only vacation. Everyone finds what works best for them.

Here are some tips from wives who have lived through home-comings:

"In anticipation of my husband's homecoming from Bahrain, I spent a week making plans of ways to spoil him! One was saving money so that I could treat him to a shopping spree at his favorite sporting goods store."

"Money is often a major issue during our homecomings. I offer to show my husband the checkbook and bank statements before he asks, and we discuss how I spent our money. Huge bills run up during a separation can cause problems."

"Don't play an 'I had it harder than you' game when he returns. Both of you had stresses during the separation."

"Wear an outfit your husband especially likes instead of a new one for the homecoming. There will be enough that's new about both of you, and that familiar one will make you look especially dear."

"Although I maintain a normal schedule when Dewayne's at sea, I'm flexible the week he comes home. I treat it as a honeymoon time; it takes a while to settle back into routines. And although I may have a list of repairs and projects I want him to do, I don't ask him that first week."

"Keep your husband informed of your activities during a separation. Being surprised with a major purchase, or even a change in hairstyle, can put a damper on a homecoming."

"Treat each other courteously. Jared doesn't come home and throw his field gear all over; he puts it away. Then he usually takes the kids to the park while I finish cooking dinner. I don't ask him to help with the housework afterward."

"The day Leon comes home, I try to have 'his space' in the family room just as he left it: the ottoman in front of his chair, the remote control handy, and his magazines in the basket next to the chair."

Make a separation something to *grow* through, not something to *go* through. The rewards of being able to shop, buy a house, sell a car, discipline the children, move, resolve problems, and cope on your own are the warm feelings of independence, assurance, and self-confidence, and they're known only to those who have done it.

It almost makes the separation worth it.

≡ Further Reading

Brewer, Kristine C. *The Stress Management Handbook*. Overland Park, KS: National Press Publications, 1991.

Cox, Wesley. *Crime Stoppers: Low-Cost, No-Cost Ways to Protect Yourself, Your Family, Your Home, and Your Car for $10*. New York: Crown Publishers, 1983.

Daddy's Days Away. Deployment activity book for parents and children, available from the Commandant of the Marine Corps (MHF), HDQS USMC, Washington, DC 20380-0001.

Flannery, Raymond B. *Becoming Stress-Resistant through the Project SMART Program*. Del Mar, CA: Continuum, 1990.

Motley, James B. *Protect Yourself, Your Family, Your Home*. McClean, VA: Brassey's, 1994.

Ordered to Active Duty: What Now? A Guide to Reserve Component Families. DOD publication, available at Reserve Centers and units.

Powell, Barbara. *Alone, Alive, and Well: How to Fight Loneliness and Win*. Emmaus, PA: Rodale Press, 1985.

So Your Mom's Going to a Ship. Coloring book available from the Navy Family Service Center, NSB King's Bay, GA 31547.

11

≡ Sponsoring a Family

Throughout this book I've talked about making friends through the various outlets military life offers. There's a program that enables you to make friends immediately upon arrival at each new duty station: the Sponsorship Program.

The Sponsorship Program was created to help ease the strain of moving. It provides you, the newcomer, with someone to greet you, tell you about the place, possibly invite you to dinner, and show you around. For the program to work properly, however, both the sponsor and sponsored have certain obligations they must fulfill.

≡ Importance of Being a Sponsor

Being a sponsor is an important responsibility. Sponsors represent the unit and are a newcomer's first contact with it. These first impressions can be long-lasting. Just as being well treated makes a newcomer and his family feel an important and integral part of the unit, a poor reception creates negative feelings that are often hard to shake. These feelings spread to the children, and the result can be a whole family with a bad attitude toward the place.

≡ When You're Asked to Be a Sponsor

When a servicemember receives a new assignment, he is asked to complete a "Request for Sponsor" form, which is forwarded to the new duty station. The receiving commander assigns a sponsor, usually matching job, rank, and marital status—the last in hopes that you, the family member, will assist the new family member while your spouse assists the new servicemember.

Upon receiving a sponsorship assignment, a servicemember should send a letter and welcome packet to the newcomer immediately. It doesn't matter whether the newcomer isn't due for another ten months; the sooner communication starts, the better. Welcome packets are available at Family Services, and sample letters might be available at the unit. Typical letters contain

When you sponsor someone, it helps to view any relocation videos, information packets, and brochures about your duty station in the reference library of the Family Services office, as well as any computer services, such as SITES. This will refresh your memory about what your town offers and give you ideas for the newcomers.

information on the housing situation, availability of quartermaster furniture, length of time for car shipment if overseas, duty uniform and patches worn, anticipated temporary duties, mission of the unit, and so on. One soldier ended her letter with the friendly advice, "By the way, our caserne is on a hilltop. Therefore our physical training runs *always* take us up steep inclines, through vineyards and small towns. We run a minimum of two miles. I advise you to stay in good shape. Keep smiling!" Such efforts give a form letter a nice personal touch.

If the newcomer is married, a gesture that is sure to be appreciated is to enclose a letter to the new spouse. Here is a letter one wife wrote to the wife of an infantryman her husband was sponsoring:

Dear Nichelle,

I understand you and your husband will be joining us at Fort Benning. I think you'll like it here! We sure do. Columbus is a good-sized town with nice shops, job opportunities, and lots of recreational facilities. We love the Destin Recreation Center, located right on the Gulf Coast and operated by Fort Benning. They have trailer pads and campers available on a first-come, first-served basis. And Atlanta is only an hour and a half drive away—some great shopping there!

Do you have children? The schools on post are K–8, and there's a nursery school, too. We've got an excellent hospital; I've never had a problem getting an appointment.

It gets extremely hot in the summer, so I hope you have lots of light clothes. Winter temperatures are mild, too.

Do you plan to live on post or in town? Let me know. We live in quarters, so I'm not familiar with the economy housing situation, but I can ask around for good apartments or a reputable Realtor.

Looking forward to hearing from you.

Sincerely,
Gayle

Nothing fancy, nothing that took any research or more than twenty minutes to write, just a short description of what Gayle found enjoyable. But this simple effort certainly brightened Nichelle's day!

Notice how upbeat Gayle was. If you have any negative opinions about the place, keep them to yourself. There's no need to add to the apprehensions the newcomers are sure to have, and your worst tour may turn out to be their best ever.

The first letter should be addressed to their home. If you don't get a response within a month, send another, this time to the unit. People with orders are people on the move. They visit relatives, take vacations, attend schools, and tie up all the loose ends a move creates. If the newcomer isn't there anymore, the unit will forward your letter. If you still don't receive an answer, your husband should let his commander know; he can then phone the newcomer's unit to investigate. You've both done your jobs.

When you receive a letter with the family's exact date of arrival, acknowledge it. It makes people nervous when they get no response to important information like that. A phone call at this point is a nice touch.

≡ The First Week

"Do unto others as you would have others do unto you" never applies more than when discussing what you can do for an arriving family. There are no rules here; common sense and courtesy govern. Think about what your sponsor could have done to make life easier for you when you were moving in.

> Offer practical advice, such as how to register a car, where the nicest housing is, and good places to buy furniture and housewares.

Here are some suggestions:

- When the family arrives, have a nice dinner ready, either at your house or in their hotel room. They've had a long drive and probably feel too tired to go to the commissary and too scruffy to go to a restaurant. A hot meal would be wonderful—they've probably had their fill of cold cuts and fast food.

- While the new servicemember gets in-processed and introduced to his chain of command, the spouse often sits neglected in the hotel room. Give her a call. Better yet, take a few hours to show her around base. Show her where the PX, commissary, hospital, dental clinic, Family Services building, library, school, and child-care center are. Take her into town and point out your favorite shops. Give her a list of beauty salons, repair shops, baby-sitters, base numbers, and school addresses. If she's looking for work, take her to the civilian personnel office. Show her the nice parts of town to live in.
- In the event the family is able to move into quarters immediately, take her to the commissary while the guys are at work.
- If the family has special needs, find out what accommodating programs are available or gather some phone numbers to give them.
- Accompany the new wife to the next coffee.
- Let her know she can call you with questions.
- If you want to do a really super job, do something for the children. See if the Family Services center has a youth sponsorship program. All Marine Corps Family Services centers do. If your own children are roughly the same age, have them write letters.

≡ Overseas

There's a special need to be helpful when you're sponsoring a family overseas. The adjustments can be overwhelming. All the above, plus a few more considerations, will do wonders to help ease the frustrations a new arrival is likely to encounter her first week or two in an overseas environment.

- Assume the family has a lot of luggage with them, since vacationing and visiting prior to overseas moves is common. Pick them up in the largest car available to you.
- Have available some extra money in the local currency that they can buy from you. The banks might be closed, and they might need to purchase food or other essentials on the local economy.
- Explain how the phone system works. It's very frustrating not to be able to place calls because of ignorance of the local signals, recordings, and prefixes.

This is all a lot of work. But difficult as it may be for you to accomplish these tasks, imagine what it would be like for her with no help at all. The efforts involved will take only a few hours on your part, and they won't go unappreciated. You'll have helped the military in its mission of giving a warm welcome to newcomers, and you will probably also have laid the groundwork for a fast friendship.

If you can't help the new spouse, see whether your husband or someone else can. If you're having car problems, arrange with someone else in the unit to pitch in. If you had planned to go on leave during the time they'll be arriving, make arrangements to have someone else sponsor them. Always have a backup plan.

≡ When You're Being Sponsored

When you, the incoming family, receive your welcome packet, write back expressing thanks for the letter and asking any questions you might have. It's essential that you keep your sponsor and his chain of command aware of any changes to your plans, such as orders to a different unit, an earlier date of arrival, or attendance at a school first. All it takes is a letter. If the sponsor hears of such plans, he needs to keep you informed. Don't count on the units to do it for you. Granted, both units *should* have up-to-date information about your present and future whereabouts and be in constant communication with each other, but the Department of Defense is big business and wires often get crossed. The problem of arriving and having no sponsor is rarely the fault of an uncaring unit; it's often just the result of the unit's being unaware of the latest plans. This is why early and constant communication between newcomer and sponsor is critical. If you haven't heard anything from your new unit—no letter from the commander, no letter from the sponsor—chances are they don't know you're coming. So it's up to you to inform them. Of course, we're assuming here that your husband receives his orders well ahead of the time he's told to report. A not infrequent occurrence in service life is being issued orders and told to report almost immediately. When this happens, just make phone contact. If you've made several efforts to contact your sponsor and have received no response, contact his supervisor.

Let your sponsor know how many children you have, how many pets, and what your special needs are. The very day you know your exact date of arrival, let your sponsor know, to better your chances of getting reservations at the base guest house. A phone call at this point is a good idea; government lines are usually authorized for this purpose. Phone contact can turn the business relationship of sponsor and newcomer to that of friends.

≣ Sponsorship Success Stories

Here are comments from some of the people who have made the sponsorship program a success:

"I was full of worries about what Altus Air Base would be like. After four years at Wichita, we'd put down roots. I wasn't sure I could ever like a place as much as I liked Wichita. Getting a letter from our sponsor's wife made me feel much better. It made me feel that there was someone there who cared, someone who would welcome me when I got there."

"The couple we sponsored stayed in a hotel for three weeks before they found an apartment. I bought two bags of groceries for them when they arrived and lent them a small refrigerator to use while they were in the hotel."

"Our sponsor's wife baked chocolate chip cookies and presented them to us at the airport, tied up in a red ribbon."

"We took the family we sponsored around town and invited them for dinner, and I bought her a welcoming gift. We're very good friends now; we exchange baby-sitting hours, and she even made me a dress for a Christmas formal. I often hear people say that commanders should enforce the sponsorship program. I don't understand why commanders should be expected to enforce a program that simply asks people to be nice to each other."

"When we moved to Mystic, Connecticut, our sponsor gave us a cutting from one of her plants. That was two moves ago, and I still have it; it's big and bushy and looks lovely on my windowsill. Every time I see it, it brings back good memories."

"The family we sponsored had a big dog, and none of the hotels would accept it, so we kept it for them until they got quarters. It was fun having a dog for a few weeks."

"Our sponsor knew I was looking for work as a paralegal, so he copied some pages from the phone book of all the law firms in the area and sent them to me. That way, I could start making calls right away."

"Our sponsors treated us so well that when they PCSd, we returned the favor and sponsored them! We drove them around their last week here (they were going overseas and had sold their car) so they could out-process and do other errands, and after they cleared quarters we had them stay with us so that they wouldn't have to pay for a hotel."

Clearly, the Sponsorship Program can benefit both the sponsors and the sponsored family. It takes some effort, but the rewards are well worth it.

12

≡ Dealing with the Drawdown

Welcome to the smaller force! The U.S. military is in the process of downsizing. Brigades are deactivating, missions are changing, and everything from gas stations to entire bases are closing. Manpower is being cut accordingly. By the end of 1997 the Pentagon plans to have 1.4 million members on active duty (there were about 1.6 million in 1994). Hardest hit is the Army, being the most manpower intensive. Reserve strength is also being cut.

Some servicemembers are leaving voluntarily; others are not. If your husband will be separating from the military before a twenty-year retirement, this chapter is for you.

≡ Preparing Emotionally

Being a member of the military community makes one feel part of a large, worldwide family. Some have a hard time coping with the idea that they will no longer be part of this family. Here are some comments from recently separated people on easing the emotional transition.

Personnel who remain in the military after the drawdown can expect increased opportunities open to them.

"We knew we would have to leave the military in fifteen months. We started making the emotional transition early. When we PCSd to another base, we deliberately didn't move into quarters even though they were available; we wanted to adjust to living on the civilian economy before we actually had to. Since we knew we'd buy a house wherever we ended up, we moved into a rental house. It was an ideal transition to our own home. We were able to sample living

in a house and learned about such things as maintenance, qualities we liked and didn't like in a neighborhood, and so on, without having the accompanying financial responsibilities."

"Before the separation, my family became less involved with military groups and facilities and more with civilian ones. We started going to the local church instead of the post chapel. We also joined the YMCA for its gym and other offerings (such as craft classes) and lessened our use of the post facilities. I stopped volunteering on post and started working as a volunteer for the local United Way."

"We began researching different parts of the country for places to live. We considered not only the job market, but also climate, cost of living, nearby recreational facilities, and educational opportunities. It was fun knowing that we were going where we wanted to go, not where we were ordered."

"I investigated the job market when we learned Tim was leaving the Air Force. I hadn't worked in three years, and learning that there were employment options for myself made my worries about a drop in his income more manageable."

"I visited civilian supermarkets to ease 'sticker shock' and was pleased to learn that warehouse clubs and stores where you bag your own groceries have favorable prices."

"Leaving the Army turned out to be positive. It forced our family to sit down, clarify our goals, and decide what we wanted out of life. In the military we were always told what to do, which made us complacent. I suggest that you evaluate your interests, values, and abilities. It's critical in creating a life you'll be happy with."

"I had a good, secure job when my husband got PCS orders. I chose to stay behind because we were doubtful about his upcoming promotion and I didn't want us both to be unemployed."

"When my husband had to leave the Army, we initially thought it was the end of the world. But we both found good jobs, bought a lovely house, and are enjoying our new civilian life. So don't worry; with hard work and perseverance you'll end up just fine. It's a big world out there, with lots of opportunities. When life gives you lemons, make lemonade!"

≡ Preparing Financially

Start your financial preparations as soon as you even suspect you will be leaving the service. You can never start too soon to prepare for such a life-changing event. Begin saving money. There might be a period of unemployment, a temporary reduction in income, or unexpected expenses. Visit the finance office to determine what, if any, deductions will be made from the final paycheck. You may have some moving expenses, and you'll need money for suits or other civilian work clothes and for traveling to interviews, printing résumés, and other job hunt expenses. You don't want financial worries compounding other stresses the separation will generate.

> The Reserves are a way to preserve your investment in the military. You'll get extra money, benefits, and a pension. Look up Reserve recruiter numbers in the blue pages under "U.S. Government." Some Reserve components take members from other services. If you're unsure what your counterpart in another service is called, check the DOD Occupational Conversion Manual, which lists each service's specialties and matches them to similar jobs.

Decide whether it would be better to sell any unused leave or to take terminal leave, which is granted after the last day of work until the drop from the rolls. During terminal leave, your husband will continue to draw his full pay and allowances and you may keep your ID cards, giving you access to base facilities. The ID cards must be returned or mailed back when the leave is over.

If you are making installment payments via allotment from the military paycheck, arrange a different method.

Take advantage of any needed services the military provides free. If you don't yet have a will or power of attorney, get one. Get routine checkups and have prescriptions filled.

Check into life and health insurance. You may convert your Serviceman's Group Life Insurance (SGLI) into the VA-administered Veterans Group Life Insurance (VGLI) within 120 days following separation. VGLI is a five-year nonrenewable term policy. After five years it is discontinued, but it may be automatically converted to an individual whole life policy with any participating insurance company without a physical. There is also a CHAMPUS-like health plan, called the Continued Health Care Benefit Program (CHCBP), designed to tide families over until the next job. It covers preexisting conditions and can be used for up to thirty-six months after separation. Write CHCBP Administrator, P.O. Box 1870, Rockville, MD 20849, or telephone (800) 809-6119. Finally, investigate private insurance policies while still on active duty. Some, especially those offered by military-affiliated organizations, are very competitive.

Separated servicemembers are eligible for unemployment benefits. They may draw them four weeks after leaving the military, for up to thirteen weeks.

≡ Separation Benefits

Involuntarily separated servicemembers are eligible for special benefits and programs, as long as the separation is due to the drawdown and not to poor performance, misconduct, or anything other than an honorable discharge. New ID cards stamped "TA," for "transition assistance," are issued to the family after separation. They're good for two years and are nonrenewable. They access the following:

≡ Medical Care

Military hospitals and CHAMPUS may be used for between 60 and 120 days after separation, depending on length of time in service. There are additional provisions for hardship cases. Preexisting conditions, including pregnancy, are covered for one year after separation if Uniformed Services Voluntary Insurance Program insurance is purchased before the medical benefits expire.

≡ Commissary, Exchange, and Recreational Facilities

These may be used for two years after separation. Local limitations may be imposed on the recreation facilities, such as no night access or limited or no access to ones heavily used by the active-duty component.

≡ Relocation

A servicemember is entitled to one move to the place of his choice. If he doesn't yet know where that place is, the government will store his household goods for up to one year free of charge. And if his commander permits, he may be granted up to forty days permissive and excess leave for house or job hunting. This move is handled similarly to any other PCS move. A per diem allowance is given; however, advance pay, dislocation, move-in, and temporary lodging allowances are not. A damage claim may be filed at the transportation office of the nearest military base.

> Be cautious about buying a house immediately upon acceptance of a new job. You might wait a year to see how the job works out.

Base Housing

If you live in quarters, you may stay there for up to 180 days after separation. You will need to pay rent equal to your BAQ and VHA. This may be waived in hardship cases. This benefit may be denied if there is a long list of active-duty families waiting for housing.

Education

Separating servicemembers with a fully honorable discharge may enroll in the New Montgomery GI Bill if they have no other veterans' education benefits. A $1,200 contribution must be made before separation; this makes up to $10,800 in education benefits available.

Schools

If your children have completed their junior year at a DOD school, they may complete their senior year there, too.

Excess Leave

Commander permitting, a servicemember may take up to thirty days' unpaid leave to job hunt. He will not be required to use accrued leave first.

Separation Counseling

Centers on base provide details on all the above, plus information on joining the National Guard and Reserves and job hunting. This assistance is provided to family members, too.

The Transition Assistance Program (TAP) offers a three-day seminar that covers résumé writing, interviewing, career counseling, and converting descriptions of military duties into language civilian employers can understand. Fit this seminar into your schedule early; it's infrequently offered and fills up fast.

Separation Pay

This takes the form of the Special Separation Benefit, the Voluntary Separation Incentive, exit bonuses, and early retirement pay. Moneywise, there are tremendous differences among them. They have different formulas for computation, conditions of award, and stipulations such as time in service. Exit bonuses are not given if the servicemember accepts a DOD job within 180 days of separation.

All of the options are generous and provide a comfortable cushion for reentry into civilian life. Participation for a certain length of time in either the Selected Reserves or Individual Ready Reserves is required. Be aware that if a military pension is earned via the Reserves, the separation money must be paid back before complete pension benefits are awarded (no interest is charged). Know that all separation moneys are taxable, and in case of a Reserve pension, the government will recoup its before-tax sum, not what was actually received after taxes. Discuss with an out-placement counselor which you're eligible for and which are the best for your circumstances.

Separation Pay for Reservists

The Reserve Transition Assistance Program helps Selected Reservists whose units or billets are relocated, eliminated, or inactivated and gives them priority placement in another unit or billet within a reasonable commuting distance (as defined by each commander). Local conditions such as traffic routes and congestion help determine this.

Priority placement does not guarantee a new job in the same specialty, however. If the unit moves to another place within reasonable commuting distance or if it closes and offers a new job within reasonable commuting distance, the position must be accepted or the separation is considered voluntary and the servicemember will not be eligible for separation transition benefits.

Guardsmen involuntarily separated between October 1, 1991, and September 30, 1995, may be eligible for separation pay, early retired pay qualification after fifteen years, the Montgomery GI Bill, and commissary, exchange, and recreational privileges. To be able to retire after fifteen years, the Reservist must be offered the option; he cannot simply choose to do so. Reservists who are offered early retirement are typically those whose billets are eliminated or relocated out of the commuting distance or who are in overstaffed jobs. Reduced benefits accompany this retirement because not as many creditable points have been built up.

The Job Search

Once he's learned of the separation, the servicemember will need to begin looking for a civilian job. Here are some tips on the job search:

- It's never too early to start the job hunt! Starting early will help the separating servicemember prepare for a job he'll be happy with. He cannot start a month before separation and expect something great to materialize. Furthermore, starting late will not give either of you the time to obtain any needed professional certifications or schooling.
- The servicemember should obtain professional certificates for his field, if such exist. There are programs through which formal recognition of skills and training is bestowed by unions and professional groups.

- If the servicemember has a military skill of limited use in the private sector, investigate DOD civil service jobs that use that skill. Contact civilian firms that have contracts on base. Apply with defense contractors. Read the *Federal Jobs Digest*, a bimonthly newspaper available at your library.
- This is a stressful time for the whole family. Form a support group of families in the same situation; swapping tips helps boost morale. Ask others for help. The job hunt has no room for false pride. Hundreds of books have been written on the subject; read some.
- Ask outplacement assistants about the following:

The Defense Outplacement Referral System is a computer network that matches job applicants' qualifications with openings posted by employers and faxes the résumés to the employers. Jobs with federal agencies are in this system.

The Transition Bulletin Board is a computer network through which employers place job ads, military and veterans' associations advertise job fairs, and state employment offices send updates on the job situations in their states.

SMOCTA (the Service Members Occupational Conversion and Training Act) is run by the Department of Labor and offers companies an incentive to hire newly separated veterans.

Troops to Teachers is a program that offers financial assistance and a streamlined path to becoming a teacher. For more information, contact the Defense Activity for Nontraditional Educational Support, 6490 Saufley Field Rd., Pensacola, FL 32509-5243, telephone (800) 452-6616.

≡ Veteran Preferences in the Job Hunt

The government gives veterans some edges in the hunt for a federal job. All involuntarily separated servicemembers have a one-time preference in non-appropriated-fund DOD jobs and

Q: How do I obtain copies of my evaluations years after having left active duty?

A: Fill out a Standard Form 180, available at any base, armory, or VA office or by telephoning the national VA office, (800) 827-1000. Send the completed form to the National Personnel Records Center, 9700 Page Blvd., St. Louis, MO 63132.

priority for existing or projected vacancies in Guard and Reserve units. Additionally, all honorably discharged veterans have the following advantages:

The DOD occasionally hosts job fairs that link potential employer and separating servicemembers. They're held both stateside and overseas. Here are some tips for getting the most out of a job fair:

- Ask for a list of which companies are participating, and research them before you go.
- Develop a résumé targeted to the positions you desire.
- Wear a business suit or full military uniform.
- Don't bring family and friends. This isn't a social event.
- Arrive early and stay late. Most fairs run from six to eight hours, and there are often long lines at each booth. Allow yourself time to visit as many as possible. Visit booths you're not interested in for interviewing practice.
- When you approach the booth, smile, extend your hand, and have your résumé handy.
- Get the recruiter's business card, and follow up your meeting with a thank-you note that expresses your interest in the position.

Include your military experience on your résumé, but don't use military jargon. The thirty-five-year-old MBA who reads it may throw it out simply because he doesn't understand it.

- A five-point preference for all federal jobs; ten points if disabled. Seventy points are typically needed to qualify for a federal job. Persian Gulf veterans have particular preference. The Southwest Asia Service Medal is needed as proof of participation.
- Eligibility for a Veterans Readjustment Appointment. This enables a veteran to get a federal job without taking employment exams or competing with nonveterans.
- Postal Service preference, such as being able to take the postal service exam at times other than when it's officially offered and, if passing, being put immediately on the hiring list.
- Former active-duty personnel who don't qualify for retired pay may, in the federal civil service, have their active-duty time count the same as their federal civilian time for protection from cutbacks and determining how much leave they may accumulate per pay period.

Further Reading

Budahn, P. J. *Drawdown Survival Guide.* Annapolis, MD: Naval Institute Press, 1993.

The Entrepreneur's Business Success Resource Guide. Mail-order catalog of books for those starting their own businesses. Available from Aegis Publishing Group, 796-W Aquidneck Ave., Newport, RI 02842.

Federal Benefits for Veterans and Dependents. Stock #051-000-00-200-8. Booklet published by the Department of Veterans Affairs. Send $3 to Superintendent of Documents, U.S. Government Printing Office, Washington, DC 20402-9325.

Fitzpatrick, William G. *Does Your Resume Wear Combat Boots?* Berkeley, CA: Ten Speed Press, 1991.

Henderson, David G. *Job Search: Marketing Your Military Experience, 2nd edition.* Mechanicsburg, PA: Stackpole Books, 1995.

Leaving the Military. Booklet available from USAA, telephone (800) 531-0283 (or 498-7700 in San Antonio, TX).

Lee, W. Dean. *Beyond the Uniform: A Career Transition Guide for Veterans and Federal Employees.* New York: John Wiley and Sons, 1994.

McDonald, Scott A. *The Complete Job Finders Guide for the '90s.* Oak Park, MI: Impact Press, 1994.

13
≡ Wrapping It Up

Finances and Family Services, coffees and child care, schools and sponsors, moving and medicine—it's a start.

You pick up the ball from here. Military life is what you make it. It's a fact that the person who brings to it enthusiasm, a joy in living, and a willingness to grow, change, and be flexible will find it a good life. Certainly there are trade-offs. Your attitude toward accepting those trade-offs will determine how well you adjust to them.

Attitude is everything. A positive attitude will give you the flexibility, humor, and patience that are needed to make military life fun no matter where you're stationed, what benefits you have access to, and what your husband's rank is.

What is a positive attitude? It's a state of mind that booms, "Now I'm going to get something done!" instead of, "Today is a drag like every other day." It affects how you look, how you feel, what you do, and what you say. It determines your success in achieving your life goals. It's the most important characteristic you have.

Your willingness to help make your world a better place will indeed make it a better place. Work with the system to obtain the things you want; make your suggestions known. Most installations have suggestion programs that solicit advice on how to make things work better. Suggestions are welcomed from all quarters, not just from military or civilian employees. Monetary awards sometimes reward suggestions that save money.

Discover what's offered at your base or post. Learn the structure of what surrounds you and the reasons behind the rules and regulations that affect your life. There are a lot of people who feel that the military is their spouse's job, not theirs. They feel they have nothing to do with it, that the military doesn't affect them. They must be asked the following:

Do you shop at the commissary? Do you eat at the club? Are your baby's checkups performed by an Army doctor, a Navy nurse, an Air

Force physician's assistant? Does your child attend a DODDS school? Is your blouse from the exchange? Do you live in quarters? Did you obtain your federal job with an edge from the Military Spouse Employment Act? Do you survive separations? Did you quit a good job to move with your spouse—*did* you move with your spouse? Does your morale boosting make him the Wing's Wonderful Wizard or does your negativity make him the Company's Chronic Complainer? Is your spouse's paycheck the main or the sole source of income in your family?

Do you still say you have nothing to do with the military?

The person who marries a servicemember but expects to have nothing to do with the system is quite mistaken. If your spouse is an E-1, in for the minimum two years, this might be true. Otherwise, the higher up the ladder he goes, the more will be expected of him—and of you. Hardly anyone can give 100 percent, but 15 percent, 10 percent, even 2 percent will certainly be observed and appreciated. Things aren't as rigid as they once were, but some guidelines do remain. Learn what they are, what protocol exists, what is and isn't expected, what can and can't be done. This can make your life easier. Those who aren't willing to make such an effort might want to reevaluate whether military life is for them, because with each increase in rank, a lack of understanding and concern is sure to bring friction.

Keep abreast of current issues. Scrutinize congressional voting records. It's in your best interest. The combined strength of the 5 million active-duty servicemembers, Reservists, retirees, and family members could be a powerful voting force indeed. You might wish to support the National Military Family Association, a private, nonprofit organization that monitors issues of interest to military families, such as spouse employment, housing, and child-care policies. It also monitors legislation that affects us and lobbies on our behalf. Write to the organization at 6000 Stevenson Ave., Suite 304, Alexandria, VA 22304-3526, or telephone (703) 823-6632.

Here are some final thoughts from military spouses:

"To help make your world a better place, start with your unit. Many wives' groups have a 'chain of concern,' a voluntary telephone tree through which information is disseminated, activities are coordinated, and help is available. Some groups even have a 'wife-on-call' system: A wife responsible for a certain day or hour takes another, perhaps a young mother lacking transportation, on a diaper run or to a doctor appointment. This shows that people in the community care, and it cuts down on calling servicemembers away from their jobs. If your wives' group has neither a chain of concern nor a wife-on-call system, start one. If it has one, participate in it."

"If there's an organization that has helped you in the past—crisis line, thrift shop, the hospital—turn around and help it."

"If you've been treated well by a sponsor, pass it on. If you've learned something helpful, some tip, hint, or way to make life easier, pass that on, too."

"If the youth activities aren't all you would like them to be, offer to be a team mom or coach. Help DODDS instructors do paperwork so that they can spend more time teaching your children. When you're invited to a planning session for a morale-boosting activity, go! If there's no Girl Scout troop around, start one. If you would like to see something done, there must be others who feel the same way."

"No marriage is easy, but a military marriage is especially challenging. Here are some tips for a happy one: Never assume anything—discuss everything with your husband. Both of you should act as individuals; both of you should participate in decisions. One shouldn't be completely dependent upon the other. Maintain other adult friends and contacts; at some time you are going to need them."

"Be flexible in everything. Military life has no room for rigidity. Make the best of whatever you're given"

"Don't overlook the single servicemembers. Invite them over on holidays and other occasions for a home-cooked meal. They'll love it. Meatloaf in a family setting beats steak in the mess hall any day. Bake cookies at Christmas and send them to the barracks. At planning sessions for unit parties, include activities and gifts for them."

"Anyone can be a spouse, but it takes a special person to be a military spouse. I love the travel, having friends of all races and creeds, and how handsome my husband looks in his uniform. Live life to its fullest—it's too short to spend fretting over careless movers, unfamiliar surroundings, and deployments."

"As a Marine wife of twenty-two years, I can say that you're in for the time of your life! It's a challenging life, but one that will make both you and your spouse better people. We've lived in fourteen homes and have visited some of the most interesting places on earth. How I envy you, just starting out. Hang on for a great ride!"

Military service isn't a job. It's a lifestyle.

At retirement ceremonies you will often observe the moving sight of servicemember spouses shedding tears, evidence of the ties that have formed after years of this lifestyle. A large number of the military's volunteers are retired servicemembers and spouses who desire to keep in touch with the military and its young, active-duty members. Can any civilian company boast of this?

If you have a spark of adventure in your soul, you will love military life. The opportunities it affords to see the world, to meet different people, and to instill patriotism and pride are endless.

As the women of the Navy Wifeline Association are so fond of saying, "Good luck and HAVE FUN!"

≡ Appendix A

The Metric System

When you go overseas you'll find things measured in meters, liters, and grams, and temperatures quoted on the Celsius scale. Here's a household conversion chart.

Volume

Multiply	by	To Get
teaspoons (tsp.)	5	milliliters (ml)
tablespoons (tbsp.)	15	milliliters (ml)
fluid ounces (fl. oz.)	30	milliliters (ml)
cups (c.)	0.24	liters (1)
pints (pt.)	0.47	liters (1)
quarts (qt.)	0.95	liters (1)
gallons (gal.)	3.8	liters (1)
cubic feet (ft.³)	0.03	cubic meters (m³)
cubic yards (yd.³)	0.76	cubic meters (m³)

Length

Multiply	by	To Get
inches (in.)	2.5	centimeters (cm)
feet (ft.)	30	centimeters (cm)
yards (yd.)	0.9	meters (m)
miles (mi.)	1.6	kilometers (km)

Area

Multiply	by	To Get
square inches (in.²)	6.5	square centimeters (cm²)
square feet (ft.²)	0.09	square meters (m²)

square yards (yd.^{2})	0.8	square meters (m^2)
square miles (mi.^{2})	2.6	square kilometers (km^2)
acres	0.4	hectares (ha)

Temperature

$32°$ F $=$ $0°$ C
$41°$ F $=$ $5°$ C
$50°$ F $= 10°$ C
$68°$ F $= 20°$ C
$86°$ F $= 30°$ C
$104°$ F $= 40°$ C

Weight

½ oz.	=	15 gm
1 oz.	=	30 gm
1 lb.	= 455 gm
1 lb., ½ oz.	= 500 gm
2 lbs., 3 ozs.	=	1 kg

Appendix B

VA Offices

ALABAMA
Montgomery (RO) 36104
474 S. Court St.

Birmingham (MC) 35233
700 S. 19th St.

Montgomery (MC) 36193
215 Perry Hill Rd.

Tuscaloosa (MC) 35404
3401 Loop Rd.

Tuskegee (MC) 36083

ALASKA
Anchorage (RO) 99501
235 E. 8th Ave.

ARIZONA
Phoenix (RO) 85012
3225 N. Central Ave.

Phoenix (MC&D) 85012
Seventh St. and Indian School Rd.

Prescott (MC) 86301

Tucson (MC) 85723

ARKANSAS
Little Rock (RO) 72114
Building 65, Fort Roots
Mailing: P.O. Box 1280·
North Little Rock 72215

Fayetteville (MC) 72701

Little Rock (MC)
72205-5484
4300 W. Seventh St.

CALIFORNIA (Northern)
San Francisco (RO) 94105
211 Main St.

Fresno (MC) 93703
2615 E. Clinton Ave.

Livermore (MC) 94550
4951 Arroyo Rd.

Martinez (MC) 94553
150 Muir Rd.

Palo Alto (MC) 94304
3801 Miranda Ave.

Key: VAO—VA Office; MC—Medical Center; D—Domiciliary; RO—Regional Office; IC—Insurance Center
Source: VA pamphlet 27-82-2, *A Summary of VA Benefits*

CALIFORNIA (Northern) (cont'd.)
San Francisco (MC) 94121
4150 Clement St.

CALIFORNIA (Southern)
Los Angeles (RO) 90024
Federal Bldg., 11000 Wilshire Blvd.

San Diego (RO) 92108
2022 Camino Del Rio North

Loma Linda (MC) 92357
11201 Benton St.

Long Beach (MC) 90822
5901 E. Seventh St.

Los Angeles (MC) 90073
(Brentwood)

Los Angeles (MC&D) 90073
(Wadsworth)

San Diego (MC) 92161
3350 La Jolla Village Dr.

Sepulveda (MC) 91343
16111 Plummer St.

COLORADO
Denver (RO) 80225
44 Union Blvd., P.O. Box 25126

Denver (MC) 80220
1055 Clermont St.

Fort Lyon (MC) 81038

Grand Junction (MC) 81501

CONNECTICUT
Hartford (RO) 06103
450 Main St.

Newington (MC) 06111
555 Willard Ave.

West Haven (MC) 06516
950 Campbell Ave.

DELAWARE
Wilmington (RO&MC) 19805
1601 Kirkwood Highway

DISTRICT OF COLUMBIA
Washington (RO) 20421
941 North Capitol St., NE
(Benefits to veterans residing in foreign
    countries not specifically listed herein
    are under the jurisdiction of VARO,
    Washington, DC)

Washington (MC) 20422
50 Irving St., NW
(Medical benefits to veterans residing in
    foreign countries not specifically listed
    herein are under the jurisdiction of VAMC,
    Washington, DC)

FLORIDA
St. Petersburg (RO) 33731
P.O. Box 1437, 144 First Ave., South

Bay Pines (MC&D) 33504

Gainesville (MC) 32602
1601 S.W. Archer Rd.

Jacksonville (VAO) 32206
1833 Boulevard, Rm. 3105

Lake City (MC) 32055

Miami (MC) 33125
1201 N.W. 16th St.

Miami (VAO) 33130
Federal Bldg., Room 120
51 S.W. First Ave.

Pensacola (VAO) 32503
312 Kenmore Rd., Room 1G250

Key: VAO—VA Office; MC—Medical Center; D—Domiciliary; RO—Regional Office;
IC—Insurance Center
Source: VA pamphlet 27-82-2, *A Summary of VA Benefits*

FLORIDA (cont'd.)
Tampa (MC) 33612
13000 Bruce B. Downs Blvd.

GEORGIA
Atlanta (RO) 30365
730 Peachtree St., NE

Atlanta (MC) 30033
1670 Clairmont Rd.

Augusta (MC) 30910
2460 Wrightsboro Rd.

Dublin (MC&D) 31021

HAWAII
(Including American Samoa, Wake, Midway,
    and the Trust Territory of the Pacific Islands)
Honolulu (RO) 96813
P.O. Box 50188, 96850
PJKK Federal Bldg.
300 Ala Moana Blvd.

IDAHO
Boise (RO) 83724
Federal Bldg. and U.S. Courthouse
550 W. Fort St., Box 044

Boise (MC) 83702
500 W. Fort St.

ILLINOIS
Chicago (RO) 60680
P.O. Box 8136
536 S. Clark St.

Chicago (MC) 60611
(Lakeside)

Chicago (MC) 60680
820 S. Damen Ave. (West Side)

Danville (MC) 61832

Hines (MC) 60141

ILLINOIS (cont'd.)
Marion (MC) 62959
2401 W. Main St.

North Chicago (MC) 60064
3001 Greenbay Rd.

INDIANA
Indianpolis (RO) 46204
575 N. Pennsylvania St.

Fort Wayne (MC) 46805
2121 Lake Ave.

Indianapolis (MC) 46204
1481 W. 10th St.

Marion (MC) 46952

IOWA
Des Moines (RO) 50309
210 Walnut St.

Des Moines (MC) 50310
30th and Euclid Ave.

Iowa City (MC) 52240
Highway 6 West

Knoxville (MC) 50138

KANSAS
Wichita (RO&MC) 67218
5500 E. Kellogg

Leavenworth (MC&D) 66048

Topeka (MC) 66622
2200 Gage Blvd.

KENTUCKY
Louisville (RO) 40202
600 Martin Luther King Jr. Pl.

Lexington (MC&D) 40511

Louisville (MC) 40202
800 Zorn Ave.

Key: VAO—VA Office; MC—Medical Center; D—Domiciliary; RO—Regional Office;
IC—Insurance Center
Source: VA pamphlet 27-82-2, *A Summary of VA Benefits*

LOUISIANA
New Orleans (RO) 70113
701 Loyola Ave.

Alexandria (MC) 71301

New Orleans (MC) 70146
1601 Perdido St.

Shreveport (MC&VAO) 71130
510 E. Stoner Ave.

MAINE
Togus (RO&MC) 04330

Portland (VAO) 04101
236 Oxford St.

MARYLAND
Baltimore (RO) 21201
Federal Bldg., 31 Hopkins Plaza

Baltimore (MC) 21218
3900 Loch Raven Blvd.

Fort Howard (MC) 21052

Perry Point (MC) 21902

MASSACHUSETTS
Boston (RO) 02203
John F. Kennedy Bldg., Government Center

Bedford (MC) 01730
200 Spring Rd.

Boston (MC) 02130
150 South Huntington Ave.

Brockton (MC) 02401

Northampton (MC) 01060

Springfield (VAO) 01103
1200 Main St.

West Roxbury (MC) 02132
1400 Veterans of Foreign Wars Parkway

MEXICO
(Benefits to veterans residing in Mexico are
under jurisdiction of VARO, Houston, TX)

MICHIGAN
Detroit (RO) 48226
Patrick V. McNamara Federal Bldg.,
477 Michigan Ave.

Allen Park (MC) 48101

Ann Arbor (MC) 48105
2215 Fuller Rd.

Battle Creek (MC) 49016

Iron Mountain (MC) 49801

Saginaw (MC) 48602
1500 Weiss St.

MINNESOTA
St. Paul (RO&IC) 56111
Federal Bldg., Fort Snelling

Minneapolis (MC) 55417
One Veterans Dr.

St. Cloud (MC) 56301

MISSISSIPPI
Jackson (RO) 39269
100 W. Capitol St.

Jackson (MC&D) 39216
1500 E. Woodrow Wilson Dr.

Biloxi (MC&D) 39531
400 Veterans Dr.

MISSOURI
St. Louis (RO) 63103
Federal Bldg., 1520 Market St.

Key: VAO—VA Office; MC—Medical Center; D—Domiciliary; RO—Regional Office;
IC—Insurance Center
Source: VA pamphlet 27-82-2, *A Summary of VA Benefits*

MISSOURI (cont'd.)
Columbia (MC) 65201
800 Hospital Dr.

Kansas City (MC) 64128
4801 Linwood Blvd.

Kansas City (VAO) 64106
Federal Bldg., 601 E. 12th St.

Poplar Bluff (MC) 63901

St. Louis (MC) 63125

MONTANA
Fort Harrison (RO&MC) 59636

Miles City (MC) 59301

NEBRASKA
Lincoln (RO) 68516
5631 S. 48th St.

Grand Island (MC) 68801

Lincoln (MC) 68510
600 S. 70th St.

Omaha (MC) 68105
4101 Woolworth Ave.

NEVADA
Reno (RO) 89520
1201 Terminal Way

Reno (MC) 89520
1000 Locust St.

NEW HAMPSHIRE
Manchester (RO) 03101
Norris Cotton Federal Bldg.,
275 Chestnut St.

Manchester (MC) 03104
718 Smyth Rd.

NEW JERSEY
Newark (RO) 07102
20 Washington Place

East Orange (MC) 07019
Tremont and S. Center St.

Lyons (MC) 07939
Knollcroft Rd.

NEW MEXICO
Albuquerque (RO) 87102
Dennis Chavez Federal Bldg.
U.S. Courthouse
500 Gold Ave., S.W.

Albuquerque (MC) 87108
2100 Ridgecrest Dr., S.E.

NEW YORK (Eastern)
New York (RO) 10001
252 Seventh Ave., at 24th St.

Albany (MC) 12208

Albany (VAO) 12207
Leo W. O'Brien Fed. Bldg.
Clinton Ave. and N. Pearl St.

Bronx (MC) 10468
130 W. Kingsbridge Rd.

Brooklyn (MC) 11209
800 Poly Place

Castle Point (MC) 12511

Montrose (MC) 10548

New York (MC) 10010
First Ave. at E. 24th St.

Northport (MC) 11768

NEW YORK (Western)
Buffalo (RO) 14202
Federal Building, 111 W. Huron St.

Key: VAO—VA Office; MC—Medical Center; D—Domiciliary; RO—Regional Office; IC—Insurance Center
Source: VA pamphlet 27-82-2, *A Summary of VA Benefits*

NEW YORK (Western) (cont'd)
Batavia (MC) 14020

Bath (MC) 14810

Buffalo (MC) 14215
3495 Bailey Ave.

Canandaigua (MC) 14424

Rochester (VAO) 14614
Federal Bldg. and Courthouse
100 State St.

Syracuse (VAO) 13202
344 W. Genesee St.

Syracuse (MC) 13210
Irving Ave. and University Pl.

NORTH CAROLINA
Winston-Salem (RO) 27155
Federal Bldg., 251 N. Main St.

Asheville (MC) 28805
1100 Tunnel Rd.

Durham (MC) 27705
508 Fulton St.

Fayetteville (MC) 28301
2300 Ramsey St.

Salisbury (MC) 28144
1601 Brenner Ave.

NEW DAKOTA
Fargo (RO&MC) 58102
655 First Ave. North

Fargo (MC) 58102
2101 Elm St.

OHIO
Cleveland (RO) 44199
Anthony J. Celebrezze
Federal Bldg.
1240 E. Ninth St.

Chillicothe (MC) 45601

Cincinnati (MC) 45202
3200 Vine St.

Cincinnati (VAO) 45202
The Society, Suite 210, 36 E. 7th St.

Cleveland (MC) 44106
10701 East Boulevard

Columbus (VAO) 43215
Federal Bldg., Room 309
200 N. High St.

Dayton (MC&D) 45428

OKLAHOMA
Muskogee (RO) 74401
Federal Bldg., 125 S. Main St.

Muskogee (MC) 74401

Oklahoma City (MC) 73014
921 N.E. 13th St.

Oklahoma City (VAO) 73102
Federal Bldg., 200 N.W. Fourth St.

OREGON
Portland (RO) 97204
Federal Bldg., 1220 S.W. Third Ave.

Portland (MC) 97207
3710 S.W. U.S. Veterans Hospital Road

Roseburg (MC) 97470

White City (D) 97501

PENNSYLVANIA (Eastern)
Philadelphia (RO&IC) 19101
P.O. Box 8079, 5000 Wissahickon Ave.

Coatsville (MC) 19320

Lebanon (MC) 17042
1700 S. Lincoln Ave.

Key: VAO—VA Office; MC—Medical Center; D—Domiciliary; RO—Regional Office; IC—Insurance Center
Source: VA pamphlet 27-82-2, *A Summary of VA Benefits*

PENNSYLVANIA (Eastern) (cont'd.)
Philadelphia (MC) 19104
Univ. and Woodland Aves.

Wilkes-Barre (VAO) 18701
19–17 N. Main St.

Wilkes-Barre (MC) 18711
1111 East End Blvd.

PENNSYLVANIA (Western)
Pittsburgh (RO) 15222
1000 Liberty Ave.

Altoona (MC) 16602
2907 Pleasant Valley Blvd.

Butler (MC) 16001

Erie (MC) 16504
135 E. 38th St.

Pittsburgh (MC) 15206
Highland Dr.

Pittsburgh (MC) 15240
University Drive C

PHILIPPINES
Manila (RO) 96528
1131 Roxas Blvd., APO San Francisco

PUERTO RICO, COMMONWEALTH OF
(including the Virgin Islands)
San Juan (RO) 00918
Federico Degetau Fed. Bldg. and Courthouse
Carlos E. Chardon Ave.
Gregg St., Hato Rey

San Juan (MC) 00921
Barrio Monacillos
Rio Piedras

RHODE ISLAND
Providence (RO) 02903
380 Westminster Mall

Providence (MC) 02908
Davis Park

SOUTH CAROLINA
Columbia (RO) 29201
1801 Assembly St.

Charleston (MC) 29403
109 Bee St.

Columbia (MC) 29201

SOUTH DAKOTA
Sioux Falls (RO&MC) 57117
P.O. Box 5046, 2501 W. 22nd St.

Fort Meade (MC) 57741

Hot Springs (MC&D) 57747

TENNESSEE
Nashville (RO) 37203
110 Ninth Ave., South

Memphis (MC) 38104
1030 Jefferson Ave.

Mountain Home (MC&D) 37601

Murfreesboro (MC) 37130
3400 Lebanon Rd.

Nashville (MC) 37203
1310 24th Ave., South

TEXAS (Northern)
Waco (RO) 76799
1400 North Valley Mills Drive

Amarillo (MC) 79106
6010 Amarillo Blvd., W.

Big Spring (MC) 79720
2400 S. Gregg St.

Bonham (MC&D) 75418
9th & Lipscomb

Key: VAO—VA Office; MC—Medical Center; D—Domiciliary; RO—Regional Office;
IC—Insurance Center
Source: VA pamphlet 27-82-2, *A Summary of VA Benefits*

TEXAS (Northern) (cont'd.)
Dallas (VAO) 75242
U.S. Courthouse and Federal Bldg.
1100 Commerce St.

Dallas (MC) 75216
4500 S. Lancaster Rd.

Fort Worth (VAO) 76102
819 Taylor St.

Lubbock (VAO) 79410
U.S. Courthouse and Federal Bldg.
1205 Texas Ave.

Marlin (MC) 76661
1016 Ward St.

Temple (MC&D) 76501
1901 S. 1st St.

Waco (MC) 76711
4800 Memorial Drive

TEXAS (Southern)
Houston (RO) 77054
2515 Murworth Dr.

Houston (MC) 77211
2002 Holcombe Blvd.

Kerrville (MC) 78028

San Antonio (VAO) 78229-2041
3601 Bluemel Rd.

San Antonio (MC) 78284
7400 Merton Minter Blvd.

UTAH
Salt Lake City (RO) 84147
Federal Bldg., 125 S. State St.

Salt Lake City (MC) 84148
500 Foothill Blvd.

VERMONT
White River Junction (RO&MC) 05009

VIRGINIA
Roanoke (RO) 24011
210 Franklin Rd., SW

Hampton (MC&D) 23667
100 Emancipation Rd.

Richmond (MC) 23249
1201 Broad Rock Rd.

Salem (MC) 24153
1970 Blvd. & Roanoke

WASHINGTON
Seattle (RO) 98174
Federal Bldg., 915 Second Ave.

Tacoma (MC) 98493
American Lake

Seattle (MC) 98108
1660 S. Columbian Way

Spokane (MC) 99208
N. 4815 Assembly St.

Walla Walla (MC) 99362
77 Wainwright Drive

WEST VIRGINIA
Huntington (RO) 25701
640 Fourth Ave.

Beckley (MC) 25801
200 Veterans Ave.

Clarksburg (MC) 26301

Huntington (MC) 25704
1540 Spring Valley Dr.

Key: VAO—VA Office; MC—Medical Center; D—Domiciliary; RO—Regional Office; IC—Insurance Center

Source: VA pamphlet 27-82-2, *A Summary of VA Benefits*

WEST VIRGINIA (cont'd.)
Martinsburg (MC&D) 25401

WISCONSIN
Milwaukee (RO) 53295
5000 W. National Ave., Bldg. 6

Madison (MC) 53705
2500 Overlook Terrace

Tomah (MC) 54660

Milwaukee (MC&D) 53295
5000 W. National Ave.

WYOMING
Cheyenne (RO&MC) 82001
2360 E. Pershing Blvd.

Sheridan (MC) 82801

Key: VAO—VA Office; MC—Medical Center; D—Domiciliary; RO—Regional Office; IC—Insurance Center

Source: VA pamphlet 27-82-2, *A Summary of VA Benefits*

≡ Glossary

Accepts CHAMPUS assignment. Health-care provider that accepts the amount CHAMPUS will pay for specific services. Also known as a *participating provider.*

Accompanied tour. Tour of duty on which a servicemember is accompanied by his family.

Active duty. Full-time duty in the active military services of the United States.

ADT. Active duty for training. Full-time duty that Reservists and Guardsmen do. Includes annual training, military school attendance, and training exercises.

Aeromedical evacuation. Transporting medical patients to treatment facilities by plane.

AFSC. Air Force Specialty Code. Air Force term for a servicemember's military job.

Airborne troops. Ground units whose primary mission is to make assault landings from the air.

Air group. A military unit consisting of a headquarters, support squadrons, and two or more flying squadrons.

Alert. The period of time during which servicemembers stand by in readiness for action.

Allotment. A portion of military pay automatically sent to another person or institution.

AMC. Air Mobility Command. Air Force operation that flies servicemembers and their families to overseas duty stations.

Appropriated funds. Money specifically designated by Congress to support base activities.

AWOL. Absent without leave. Being away from the duty station without proper authorization.

BAQ. Basic allowance for quarters. Money for housing expenses.

BAS. Basic allowance for subsistence. Money for food given to married personnel, personnel living off base, and all officers.

Base. Place from which operations are conducted or supported. Also called *garrison* or *post.*

Battalion. A military unit with a headquarters and three or more companies or batteries.

Battery. *See* Company.

CACO. Casualty assistance calls officer. Navy and Marine Corps term for person assigned to help families in case of servicemember death.

Cadet. Army and Air Force term for a student at a service academy.

Camouflage. The use of concealment and disguise to minimize detection or identification.

Certificate of deposit. Financial instrument bought to obtain a higher interest rate than that available from regular passbook savings accounts.

Chain of command. Organization of superiors and subordinates.

CHAMPUS. Civilian Health and Medical Program of the Uniformed Services. A program for family members that supplements on-base medical care.

CHAP. Children Have a Potential. Air Force term for a Family Services program that assists children with special physical or mental needs.

Clothing allowance. Money given to enlisted servicemembers to maintain and replace uniforms.

CO. Commanding officer. Officer in charge of a specific group or unit of personnel.

Coffee. Monthly social meeting for spouses.

COLA. Cost of living allowance. Money to help pay living expenses at overseas duty stations.

Combat service support. Administrative and logistical support provided to combat forces.

Combat support. General support provided to combat forces.

Command. 1. Authority that a commander lawfully exercises over subordinates by virtue of rank or assignment. 2. Order given by a commander. 3. A unit, organization, or area under the authority of one individual.

Command post exercise. Exercise in which war is simulated. Also called a *maneuver.*

Commissary. On-base grocery store where food and beverages are bought.

Commission. 1. To make ready for service, as to commission an aircraft or ship. 2. A written order giving a person rank and authority as an officer in the armed forces.

Company. Basic administrative and tactical unit. Below a battalion and above a platoon. Also known as a *troop.*

Concurrent travel orders. Orders permitting a servicemember and family to travel together to a new duty station.

Co-payment. *See* Cost share.

Corps. Tactical unit larger than a division and smaller than a field army.

Cost share. The portion of medical care a family member pays under CHAMPUS. Also known as a *co-payment.*

CPO. Civilian personnel office. Office responsible for hiring civilian workers.

DANTES. Defense Activity for Non-Traditional Educational Support. Umbrella activity under which many educational programs operate.

Date of rank. Date a servicemember became full-time active duty.

Debarkation. Unloading of troops, supplies, and equipment from a ship.

Deductible. Uninsured portion of an insurance policy; e.g., the first $200 of damage costs that the insured pays.

DEERS. Defense Eligibility Enrollment Reporting System. List of all people eligible to use military health-care facilities or CHAMPUS.

Dependent. Term for a person who receives all or some financial support from a servicemember. Includes spouses, unremarried widows or widowers, and unmarried children.

Deployment. 1. Extending battalions and smaller units to increase readiness for action. 2. Relocation of forces to desired areas of operation.

Dislocation allowance. Money given to help pay moving expenses.

DITY. Do-it-yourself move. Self-help move in which a servicemember packs and moves himself instead of having a government-hired mover do it for him.

Division. Military unit with a headquarters and four regiments.

DODDS. Department of Defense Dependents Schools. K–12 schools for military children at overseas duty stations.

Drill. Training exercise for Reserve members.

DVA. Department of Veterans Affairs, formerly the Veterans Administration. Agency that handles veterans' benefits and concerns.

EFMP. Exceptional Family Member Program. Army and Marine Corps term for a Family Services program that assists children with special physical or mental needs.

Enlistment. Period of time a servicemember is obliged to serve in the armed forces.

Environmental morale leave. Vacation time granted to personnel in remote, isolated locations.

Exchange (PX/AAFES/NAVRESSO/MCX). Post Exchange/Army and Air Force Exchange Service/Navy Resale and Services Support Office/Marine Corps Exchange. On-base department store where household goods are sold.

Executor/executrix. Person appointed to administer a deceased person's estate.

Expanded Legal Assistance Program. Program under which service-members E-4 and below may have a military lawyer defend them, free of charge, in a civilian court.

Explanation of Benefits (EOB). A form CHAMPUS or a health insurance company sends you after you submit a claim. The EOB describes what action, if any, was taken on the claim.

Family member. A servicemember's authorized benefits recipient.

Family separation allowance. Money given to help pay for expenses caused by family separations.

Fleet. Organization of ships, aircraft, marine forces, and shore-based water activities.

Flight. 1. Group of aircraft engaged in a common mission. 2. The basic tactical unit in the Air Force. Consists of four or more aircraft in two or more elements. 3. A single aircraft airborne on a nonoperational mission.

Functional category. General term for a group of occupationally related jobs. Called *branch* in the Army, *group* in the Navy and Coast Guard, *career field* in the Marine Corps, and *career specialty* in the Air Force.

Garrison. *See* Base.

GI Bill. Program to help servicemembers pay for college tuition.

Group. Military unit with a headquarters, support squadrons, and two or more flying squadrons.

Hop. A MAC flight taken for pleasure, not for transport, to an overseas duty station. Also called Space-A travel.

Host nation. Nation that receives the forces and supplies of allied nations, or their transit through its territory.

Household goods. Personal goods shipped to a new duty station.

Installation. Group of facilities in the same vicinity that support particular functions. Installations may be elements of a base.

IRR. Individual Ready Reserve. Part of the Ready Reserve. These are Reservists who are not in the Selected Reserve but are liable for mobilization.

Joint Chiefs of Staff. Military advisory group to the president. The head of the Joint Chiefs of Staff is the highest link in the military chain of command.

Joint travel regulations. Weight allowances and rules pertaining to accompanied travel.

Key Wife. *See* Ombudsman.

Leave. Vacation time, accrued at the rate of two and a half calendar days for each month of active duty.

LES. Leave and Earnings Statement. A monthly statement of a servicemember's earnings, deductions, leave balance, and other information.

Liberty. Short amount of uncharged vacation time (usually a weekend). Also known as a *pass.*

Lodging plus. Money given to reimburse temporary-duty travel expenses.

Maneuver. *See* Command post exercise.

Medevac. Medical evacuation. Air transport of people to medical facilities at another base.

Midshipman. Navy term for a student at a service academy.

Military training. Instruction to enhance combat readiness.

Mobilization. Assembling and organizing national resources in case of war or national emergency. Includes activating all or part of the Reserve components.

MOS. Military occupational specialty. Army and Marine Corps term for a servicemember's military job.

MP. Military police. Army term for police officers whose jurisdiction is the base.

Mutual fund. Financial instrument usually bought for investment purposes.

NAF. Nonappropriated funds. Money generated by military and civilian personnel and their families. Supplements funds appropriated by Congress to provide morale-building welfare, religious, educational, and recreational programs.

NCO. Noncommissioned officer. Enlisted servicemember above the rank of E-4.

NCOIC. Noncommissioned officer in charge. NCO in charge of a particular unit or activity.

Need to know. Security procedures that require the recipients of classified information to prove they need the information in order to perform their jobs.

NOE. Notice of eligibility. Paper received by Reservists informing them they have completed twenty years of military service. Also known as the "twenty-year letter."

Nonconcurrent travel orders. Orders that do not permit a servicemember and his family to travel together to a new duty station.

OCC. Officer Candidate Class. Marine Corps term for a program that enables enlisted servicemembers to become officers.

OCS. Officer Candidate School. Army and Navy term for a program that enables enlisted servicemembers to become officers.

OHA. Overseas housing allowance. Money given to offset the higher cost of living at some overseas duty stations.

OIC. Officer in charge.

Ombudsman. A volunteer, official liaison between Navy families and the command. Typically a senior enlisted spouse. Also known as *key wife.*

On the economy. Goods and services bought from local civilian vendors rather than at military facilities.

Operating forces. Those forces whose primary mission is to participate in or support combat.

OTS. Officer Training School. Air Force term for a program that enables enlisted servicemembers to become officers.

Participating provider. *See* Accepts CHAMPUS assignment.

Pass. *See* Liberty.

PCS. Permanent change of station. Relocation from one permanent duty station to another.

Per diem. Daily expense allowance.

Port call. Place and date a servicemember reports for transportation to an overseas duty assignment.

Post. *See* Base.

Premium. Monthly insurance payment.

Protocol. Etiquette for military affairs.

Provider. In health-care terminology, a physician, hospital, clinical psychologist, nurse practitioner, clinic, pharmacy, physician's assistant, or other entity that provides health-care services. An *authorized provider* is one whose professional credentials meet CHAMPUS criteria and may receive payment from the government for services provided to CHAMPUS beneficiaries. A *participating provider* is an authorized provider who accepts CHAMPUS payment as payment in full. A *nonparticipating provider* is an authorized provider who does not agree to CHAMPUS payment as payment in full. *Nonauthorized providers* are not entitled to receive claim money from the government.

Public affairs. Information and community relations activities directed by the military to the general public.

Quartermaster furniture. Government-supplied furniture for use in base housing.

Quarters. On-base government housing.

Rate. Navy and Coast Guard term for a person's pay grade.

Rating. Navy and Coast Guard term for a military job.

Ready Reserve. Units and individual members liable for duty in wartime or national emergency. Includes the Selected Reserve and the Individual Ready Reserve.

Regiment. Military unit with a headquarters and three battalions.

Reserve. 1. Portion of a body of troops kept to the rear, or withheld from action at the beginning of an engagement, that are available for a critical moment. 2. Members of the military services who are not in active service but are subject to call to active duty.

Reserve components. Army National Guard of the United States, Army Reserve, Naval Reserve, Air National Guard of the United States, Air Force Reserve, and Coast Guard Reserve. In each component there are three categories: Ready Reserve, Standby Reserve, and Retired Reserve.

Retired Reserve. Reservists who have attained retirement through their Reserve service. Can be ordered to active duty only if the secretary of their branch of service decides there are not enough qualified personnel to meet mobilization requirements.

ROTC. Reserve Officers' Training Corps. Program to teach leadership skills to college students who intend to enter the service as officers.

SAO. Survival assistance officer. Army and Air Force term for person assigned to help families in case of servicemember's death.

Search and rescue. Use of aircraft, surface craft, submarines, specialized rescue teams, and equipment to search for and rescue personnel in distress.

Selected Reserve. Part of the Ready Reserve. Provides trained units and personnel for the "total force" concept.

Service academy. College run by the Defense Department to provide the services with active-duty officers. These colleges are the U.S. Military Academy, the U.S. Naval Academy, the U.S. Air Force Academy, and the U.S. Coast Guard Academy.

SF-171. Standard Form 171. Application for federal employment.

SGLI. Servicemen's Group Life Insurance. Up to $50,000 of coverage that can be purchased by active-duty personnel.

SN. Special Needs. Navy term for a Family Services program that assists children with special physical or emotional needs.

SP. Security police. Air Force term for police whose jurisdiction is the base.

Sponsor. 1. The active-duty servicemember. 2. A servicemember assigned to help a newcomer and family in-process and settle into a new duty station.

Squadron. 1. Organization of two or more divisions of ships, or two or more divisions (Navy) of flights of aircraft. 2. The base administrative aviation unit of the Army, Navy, Air Force, and Marine Corps.

Staff Judge Advocate. Legal office that serves as legal advisor to the installation commander and provides advice and trial defense lawyers for servicemembers charged under the UCMJ.

TAD. Temporary additional duty. Navy and Marine Corps term for time spent away from the permanent duty station.

TDY. Temporary duty. Army and Air Force term for time spent away from the permanent duty station.

Theater. Geographical area outside the continental United States for which a commander is assigned military responsibility.

TLA. Temporary lodging allowance. Helps pay temporary living expenses when making an overseas move.

Tri-Care. A medical health-care program the DOD is in the process of implementing.

Troop. *See* Company.

Troops. Collective term for uniformed military personnel (usually not applied to naval personnel afloat).

UCMJ. Uniform Code of Military Justice. Set of federal laws that defines what actions are crimes in the military.

Unaccompanied baggage. Basic necessities shipped to the new duty station ahead of the rest of the household goods.

Unaccompanied tour. Tour of duty a servicemember does unaccompanied by his family.

VEAP. Veterans Educational Assistance Program. Program to help servicemembers pay for college tuition.

VHA. Variable housing allowance. Money given to servicemembers not living in quarters to help offset the price of housing in high-cost areas.

Welcome packet. Folder of information about a duty station. Includes such items as emergency and convenience telephone numbers; local and military services available; recreational facilities; exchange, commissary and hospital hours; and other useful information.

Wing. A military unit with headquarters, support elements, and two or more groups.

XO. Executive officer. Second in command.

Note: For further reading, see Joint Chiefs of Staff. *Dictionary of Military Terms.* London: Greenhill Books and Presidio Press, Lionel Leventhal, 1990.

☰ Index